THE ROLE OF COMPETITORS IN THE ENFORCEMENT OF STATE AID LAW

This book explores the tools that the European rules on State aid place in the hands of competitors when it comes to fighting subsidies and other State measures of financial assistance to firms. In order to do so, the book scrutinises the means of redress available to competitors before national courts (private enforcement), as well as the opportunities that they have to make their voice heard in the course of the European Commission's enforcement procedures (public enforcement). The insights provided by the book lead to a better understanding of the rights of private parties under the rules and practices that govern the enforcement of State aid law.

Volume 16 in the series Hart Studies in Competition Law

Hart Studies in Competition Law

The Private Enforcement of Competition Law in Ireland
David McFadden

Cross-Border EU Competition Law Actions
Edited by Mihail Danov, Florian Becker and Paul Beaumont

Competition Laws, Globalization and Legal Pluralism: China's Experience
Qianlan Wu

Joint Ventures and EU Competition Law
Luis Silva Morais

Sanctions in EU Competition Law: Principles and Practice
Michael Frese

Fairness in Antitrust: Protecting the Strong from the Weak
Adi Ayal

European Merger Remedies: Law and Policy
Dorte Hoeg

Media Ownership and Control: Law, Economics and Policy in an Indian and International Context
Suzanne Rab and Alison Sprague

The Interface between Competition and the Internal Market: Market Separation under Article 102 TFEU
Vasiliki Brisimi

Anti-Cartel Enforcement in a Contemporary Age: Leniency Religion
Edited by Caron Beaton-Wells and Christopher Tran

Public Procurement and the EU Competition Rules
Albert Sánchez Graells

The Concept of Abuse in EU Competition Law: Law and Economic Approaches
Pınar Akman

The Competitive Effects of Minority Shareholdings: Legal and Economic Issues
Panagiotis Fotis and Nikolaos Zevgolis

The More Economic Approach to EU Antitrust Law
Anne C Witt

Private Power, Online Information Flows and EU Law
Angela Daly

The Role of Competitors in the Enforcement of State Aid Law

Fernando Pastor-Merchante

•HART•
PUBLISHING
OXFORD AND PORTLAND, OREGON
2017

Hart Publishing
An imprint of Bloomsbury Publishing Plc

Hart Publishing Ltd
Kemp House
Chawley Park
Cumnor Hill
Oxford OX2 9PH
UK

Bloomsbury Publishing Plc
50 Bedford Square
London
WC1B 3DP
UK

www.hartpub.co.uk
www.bloomsbury.com

Published in North America (US and Canada) by
Hart Publishing
c/o International Specialized Book Services
920 NE 58th Avenue, Suite 300
Portland, OR 97213-3786
USA

www.isbs.com

First published 2017

British Library Cataloguing-in-Publication Data
A catalogue record for this book is available from the British Library.

ISBN: HB: 978-1-50990-659-8
ePDF: 978-1-50990-658-1
ePub: 978-1-50990-660-4

Library of Congress Cataloging-in-Publication Data

Names: Pastor-Merchante, Fernando, author.

Title: The role of competitors in the enforcement of state aid law / Fernando Pastor-Merchante.

Description: Oxford ; Portland : Hart Publishing, An imprint of Bloomsbury Publishing Plc, 2017. | Series: Hart studies in competition law ; volume 16 | Based on author's thesis (doctoral - European University Institute, 2014) | Includes bibliographical references and index.

Identifiers: LCCN 2016053053 (print) | LCCN 2016055153 (ebook) | ISBN 9781509906598 (hardback : alk. paper) | ISBN 9781509906604 (Epub)

Subjects: LCSH: Subsidies—Law and legislation—European Union countries. | Antitrust law—European Union countries.

Classification: LCC KJE6437 .P383 2017 (print) | LCC KJE6437 (ebook) | DDC 343.2407/42—dc23

LC record available at https://lccn.loc.gov/2016053053

Typeset by Compuscript Ltd, Shannon
Printed and bound in Great Britain by Lightning Source UK Ltd

ACKNOWLEDGEMENTS

This book is a revised and updated version of the doctoral thesis that I wrote at the European University Institute in Florence, with the financial support of the Spanish Government (*Salvador de Madariaga* fellowship program). My gratitude goes to all those who helped me complete this project.

I am particularly grateful to my supervisor, Giorgio Monti, for his invaluable guidance and support, and to Marise Cremona, Leigh Hancher and José María Rodríguez de Santiago, who generously accepted to be on my examining board. I am also grateful to Heike Schweitzer, who guided me through the first stages of my research, and to Christophe Giolito and Jorge Piernas, who shared with me, on many occasions, their State aid expertise. I thank Advocate General Cruz Villalón, who gave me the opportunity to do a *stage* in his cabinet. Special thanks also go to Anu Bradford, under whose supervision I worked during my *LL.M.* studies at Columbia.

I thank Francisco Velasco Caballero, who allowed me to form part of his team at the *Universidad Autónoma de Madrid* and to broaden my horizons beyond the topic of this doctoral dissertation. Everyone at the *Área de Derecho Administrativo* has my appreciation, but Silvia Díez Sastre and Sofia Simou deserve special recognition. At the *Universidad Autónoma de Madrid* I also thank Javier Díez-Hochleitner and Carmen Martínez Capdevila, who initiated me into EU law, and Juan Arrieta, without whose encouragement I would never have undertaken this project in the first place.

I have been fortunate to share the joys and tribulations of the doctorate with a lot of people, but I want to single out my closest friends in New York (Manfredo and Pablo) and at the EUI (Gonçalo, Mislav, Jorge, Emilie, Dorothy, Chiara, Neja, Tamara, Lisa, Marina and Teimur; Spyros, Tiago, Katerina and Danai; Juana, Germán, Jeni and the family formed around our apartment in San Marco; and, of course, Mateja). I am thankful to all of them.

Back in Spain, I thank César, Javi and Dámaso—no need to tell them why, or how much—and all of my friends in Madrid, El Escorial and elsewhere. I also thank my beloved grandma, Pepa, and the rest of my family—I am lucky to have too many uncles, aunts and cousins to list here, but my gratitude goes to all of them for their unfailing support. Finally, I dedicate this book to my parents, Fernando and Concha, to my brothers, Alfonso and Juan, and to my nephew, Carlos.

CONTENTS

TABLE OF CASES

Judgments and Orders of the Court of Justice of the European Union

Judgments and Orders of the General Court

Opinions

Commission Decisions

TABLE OF LEGISLATION

Regulations

Directives

Soft Law

Introduction

I. Background

The starting point of this book is the narrative built by political scientist Mitchell Smith to explain the way in which the Commission has tightened its own power in the control of State aid, despite the ambiguity of the treaties with regard to both 'the precise scope of [its] authority' and 'the enforcement mechanisms' available in this field.[1] Smith makes the point that

> the Commission faces a dilemma in wielding the discretion at its disposal in the state aid area: while the subjective nature of state aid regulation gives the Commission sufficient flexibility to accommodate special circumstances, only the development of a rules-based regime can insulate the Commission from the sometimes intense political pressures brought to bear on state aid cases by Member State governments.[2]

This 'dilemma of discretion'[3] explains the policy followed by the Commission in the field of State aids, where it has incrementally developed a superstructure of rules that have come to limit its own discretion in the application of current Article 107 TFEU. By fostering this process of juridification, the Commission has thus achieved a certain trade-off: it has relinquished some leeway, but it has also insulated itself against the intense pressure coming from Member States in a politically sensitive area. It has thus carved out a space of 'autonomy by the rules'. The main puzzle that Smith addresses in his work is the failure by Member States to control this process more closely. In so doing, however, he provides important insights into the role played by private actors (in general) and competitors (in particular) within this context.

Smith shows that one of the effects of the process of juridification has been the mobilisation of private actors and competitors. 'By articulating a growing web of state aid rules, [the Commission] has fostered increased activism at the European level by firms and industrial associations interested in a regime of rigorous scrutiny'.[4] This has had, in turn, two effects. On a first level, the mobilisation of private actors has increased the effectiveness of the system of State aid control, by bringing to the attention of the Commission aids that would otherwise

[1] Mitchell P Smith, 'Autonomy by the Rules: The European Commission and the Development of State Aid Policy' (1998) 36 *Journal of Common Market Studies* 55, 57.

[2] ibid.

[3] ibid, 59.

[4] ibid, 73.

go unnoticed, either directly (through complaints) or indirectly (via national courts). On a second level, their mobilisation has contributed to the strategy of the Commission to appear as the neutral administrator of a superior set of rules, rather than as a political actor engaged in the deployment of its own policy.[5] From this double perspective, then, private actors have essentially acted as the Commission's allies.

Smith's work also shows, however, that the mobilisation of private actors has had a sort of boomerang effect, as 'this involvement increasingly has threatened to impose constraints on [the Commission] itself'.[6] This is because, besides lodging an ever-growing number of complaints, private actors have had increased recourse to the European Courts in order to challenge the decisions of the Commission that did not live up to their expectations in terms of rigorous enforcement. It is the receptivity of the courts to some of their demands that has threatened the control of the Commission over its own resources and agenda. This is the phenomenon that this book analyses.

II. Aim of the Book

Indeed, the book seeks to test the proposition that private actors (in general) and competitors (in particular) have become a constraint for the Commission in the enforcement of State aid law. This question calls for an examination of the extent to which competitors may rely on the rules on State aid to protect themselves against the potentially harmful effects of subsidies and other forms of state financial assistance to firms. This endeavour raises two challenges. The first challenge is to identify the channels through which competitors may voice their interest in the context of a system of governance to which they are in principle alien. This is the *issue of access*. The second challenge is to assess the likelihood that the Commission will pay heed to the concerns voiced by competitors. In other words, the challenge is to gauge the power of influence that competitors may exert through each of these channels. This is the issue of *leverage*. Framed in those terms, the question that runs through this book calls for (at least) three clarifications.

Competitors

The first clarification concerns the notion of *competitors*. State aids may of course have an impact on a broad range of private actors, who may therefore have a stake

[5] ibid, 63.

[6] ibid, 73. For similar argument, albeit referring to the general infringement procedure, see Richard Rawlings, 'Engaged Elites: Citizen Action and Institutional Attitudes in Commission Enforcement' (2000) 6 *European Law Journal* 4, 5: 'Biting the hand that feeds it is a facet of this form of private policing'.

in the way in which State aid rules are enforced. Although it is not easy to map out the whole range of actors concerned, it is possible to think of them as falling within two broad categories.

The first category comprises *State aid beneficiaries* and any other actor sharing their interest in a *lenient enforcement* of the rules on State aid, be it their suppliers, their customers or their employees. These are likely to be the stakeholders that are most strongly affected by the enforcement of State aid law, since it may foreclose access to revenues that are critical to their development.[7] They may (and actually do) demand to have a say in State aid procedures.[8] There is therefore no reason to exclude, a priori, the possibility that they too may operate as a constraint for the Commission. It should be noted, however, that the interest of State aid beneficiaries is often—yet not always[9]—in alignment with that of the granting Member State, whose participation in the enforcement of State aid rules is firmly secured in primary and secondary law, in the practice of the Commission and in the case law of the European Courts. This is the reason why the book focuses on the second category.[10]

The second category is made up of the *competitors* of State aid beneficiaries and of all the other actors that share their interest in a *strict enforcement* of the rules on State aid. Because State aids represent by definition a financial advantage, the recipients' competitors may rightly fear that the advantage might be used to outcompete them in their common product market. They may be moved, more simply, by the objective of extending the scope of the regulatory benefit granted to another company[11]—but *more* State aid is never a remedy for State aid—or to get that benefit in lieu of another company, in a zero-sum game that is typical of situations in which excluded bidders challenge the regulatory benefits granted through competitive tendering procedures.[12] It should be noted, however, that undertakings operating in other markets may have similar concerns. For example, undertakings operating in adjacent markets may fear that the aid could be used by its recipient as a lever to secure entry into their own market, or to outbid them in their competition for a scarce input in an upstream market.[13]

[7] Eric Morgan de Rivery, Sabine Thibault-Liger and Jacques Derenne, 'Procedure' in Jacques Derenne and Massimo Merola (eds), *Economic Analysis of State Aid Rules. Contributions and Limits* (Berlin: GCLC-Lexxion, 2007) 17.

[8] See, eg, Case T-198/01 *Technische Glaswerke Ilmenau v Commission* [2004] ECR II-2717; Joined Cases C-74 and 75/00 *Falck SpA and Acciaierie di Bolzano SpA v Commission* [2002] ECT I-7862; and Case C-276/03 P *Scott SA v Commission* [2005] ECR I-8437.

[9] See Case T-103/14 *Frucona Kosice v Commission*, ECLI:EU:T:2016:152, para 54, acknowledging that the Member State and the beneficiary 'may have diverging interests' in the context of the State aid procedure.

[10] On the procedural status of State aid beneficiaries see Hans P Nehl, 'The Imperfect Procedural Status of Beneficiaries of Aid in EC State Aid Proceedings. Note on Case C-276/03 P, Scott SA v. Commission' (2005) 4 *European State Aid Law Quarterly* 57.

[11] See, eg, Case C-518/13 *Eventech Ltd v Parking Adjudicator*, ECLI:EU:C:2015:9.

[12] See, eg, Case T-182/10 *AISCAT v Commission*, ECLI:EU:T:2013:9.

[13] See, eg, Case C-83/09 P *Commission v Kronoply and Kronotex* [2011] ECR I-4441.

As it is used throughout the book, the term 'competitor' is meant to capture all these possible relationships. The book is therefore concerned with the constraints imposed on the Commission by 'competitors', meaning all those firms whose position on the market may be negatively affected by the concession of State aid and who will therefore normally demand a strict enforcement of the prohibition laid down by Article 107(1) TFEU.

Enforcement

The second clarification concerns the notion of *enforcement* of the rules on State aid. Article 17(1) TEU entrusts the Commission with the task of ensuring the application of the Treaties. In the field of State aid, this task basically entails two functions. The first function is to ensure that the State aid plans put into place by Member States do not distort competition and trade (control of new aids). The second function is to control the implementation of previously approved State aid programmes (control of existing aid). Competitors may have an important role to play in the control of existing aid, but it is mainly through the control of new aids that the Commission defines what constitutes 'good' and 'bad' State aid.[14] This is the reason why this book focuses on the role played by competitors in the *control of new aids*.

The supervisory task of the Commission in relation to new aids is to be accomplished through the special procedure sketched out in Article 108(2) and (3) TFEU. This is an ex ante control procedure that relies on the obligation of Member States to notify their State aid plans to the Commission before putting them into place—and on the exclusive competence of the Commission to authorise new State aids. It follows that the control of new aids raises three different challenges for the Commission. The first one is to protect its own prerogative, ensuring that new State aid plans actually go through the authorisation procedure (*detection*); the second one is to assess State aid plans and to determine which ones shall be blocked or authorised (*assessment*); the last one is to ensure that Member States comply with its determinations (*follow-on enforcement*). Competitors may have a role to play in the fulfilment of all these tasks, yet—again—it is mainly at the detection and assessment stages that the Commission defines what is good and bad State aid. This is the reason why this book is *not* concerned with the role of competitors in the enforcement of State aid decisions (and with important issues such as follow-on recovery actions brought before national courts), but rather with the way in which competitors may shape the content of those decisions in the first place.

This book is not concerned either with the adoption of rules in the field of State aid. Hard- and soft-law rules play a major role in the definition of the State aid

[14] I borrow the wording of this distinction from Michael Blauberger, 'Of "Good" and "Bad" Subsidies: European State Aid Control through Soft and Hard Law' (2009) 32 *West European Politics* 719.

policy of the Commission. The Enabling Regulation[15] empowers the Commission to exempt certain categories of aid from the notification obligation through the adoption of *de minimis* and block exemption regulations.[16] Furthermore, the Commission has made increased use of guidelines and other soft-law instruments to define its position on the interpretation of State aid rules.[17] The consultation of interested parties in the adoption of these rules (which is imposed by secondary law, in the case of the *de minimis* and block exemption regulations,[18] and a matter of administrative practice in the case of the Commission's soft law)[19] creates new opportunities for competitors and other private actors to influence the views of the Commission on the rules on State aid. These developments raise some problems of their own, analysed by the literature on the participation of individuals in rulemaking, a topical issue in EU administrative law.[20] Thus, the focus of this book is on the input of competitors to *individual State aid decisions* rather than to the definition of the Commission's State aid policy through general measures—that is to say, on adjudication rather than rulemaking.

Constraint

The last clarification concerns the very idea that competitors may represent a *constraint* for the Commission. Albeit framed by the political science narrative outlined above, this book adopts a purely legal approach,[21] in that it seeks to identify and estimate the efficacy of the legal tools that competitors have at their disposal

[15] Council Regulation (EC) No 994/98 of 7 May 1998 on the application of Articles 107 and 108 of the Treaty on the Functioning of the European Union to certain categories of horizontal State aid (OJ L142, 14.05.1998, p 1), as amended by Council Regulation No 733/2013 of 22 July 2013 amending Regulation (EC) No 994/98 on the application of Articles 92 and 93 of the Treaty establishing the European Community to certain categories of horizontal State aid (OJ L204, 31.07.2013, p 11).

[16] See Commission Regulation (EU) No 1407/2013 of 18 December 2013 on the application of Articles 107 and 108 of the Treaty on the Functioning of the European Union to *de minimis* aid (OJ L352, 14.12.2013, p 1) (*De minimis* Regulation) and Commission Regulation (EU) No 651/2014 of 17 June 2014 declaring certain categories of aid compatible with the internal market in application of Articles 107 and 108 of the Treaty (OJ L187, 26.6.2014, p 1) (General Block Exemption Regulation).

[17] See, eg, Francis Rawlinson, 'The Role of Policy Frameworks, Codes, and Guidelines in the Control of State Aid' in Ian Harden (ed), *State Aid: Community Law and Policy* (Cologne: Bundesanzeiger Verlagsgesellschaft, 1993) 53–55; Michelle Cini, 'The Soft Law Approach: Commission Rule-Making in the EU's State Aid Regime' (2001) 8 *Journal of European Public Policy* 192, 198–201; and Blauberger (n 14) 726–29.

[18] Article 6 of the Enabling Regulation.

[19] See Herwig CH Hofmann, 'Administrative Governance in State Aid Policy' in Herwig CH Hofmann and Alexander H Türk (eds), *EU Administrative Governance* (Cheltenham: Edward Elgar, 2006) 203, who argues that 'one of the most problematic aspects in the area of State aid control is the lack of participation of interested and affected private parties in the Commission's administrative rulemaking'.

[20] See, eg, Joana Mendes, *Participation in EU Rule-Making. A Rights-Based Approach* (Oxford: Oxford University Press, 2011).

[21] See Karen Yeung, *Securing Compliance* (Oxford: Hart Publishing, 2004) 81, who defines her approach as a 'public law approach' whose aim is to identify, examine and critique the nature and scope of legal constraints that inform and shape the activities of regulatory agencies.

to affect the administration of the rules on State aid. Thus, it looks at the mechanisms created by primary and secondary legislation, by the administrative practice of the Commission and, especially, by the case law of the European Courts—and overlooks other possible mechanisms of influence, namely formal and informal mechanisms to influence the political and the administrative process. This excludes from the scope of the inquiry, for instance, the issue of lobbying.[22]

As noted earlier, the main problem addressed in this book can be broken down into two separate issues: the issue of access and the issue of leverage. With regard to the former, this book adopts a holistic approach that considers 'private' as well as 'public enforcement' channels. In other words, the book considers both the opportunities for the enforcement of State aid law available to competitors before national courts (Chapter 3) and the opportunities to make their voice heard in the context of the enforcement procedures controlled by the Commission. This includes the possibility to bring complaints (Chapter 4) and to participate in the course of the administrative procedure (Chapter 5), but also the possibility to seek judicial review of State aid decisions before the European Courts (Chapter 6).

As far as the issue of leverage is concerned, this book is informed by the idea that access to decision-making procedures—in the form of information and participation rights, including rights of access to the judiciary—can be a 'placebo'[23] if it is not attached to any device intended to ensure 'the right to be taken seriously'.[24] Sherry Arnstein made this point in her seminal article on the 'ladder of participation', where she developed the idea 'There is a critical difference between going through the empty ritual of participation and having the real power needed to affect the outcome of the process'.[25] This is the reason why, besides identifying the different channels through which competitors may express their preferences with regard to the way in which State aid rules are applied, this book seeks to assess the power of influence that they may exert through each of these channels.

III. Literature Review

This book is born out of the observation of a certain mismatch between the influential narrative built by Mitchell Smith and the discourse that is dominant in the *legal* literature, which tends to stress the weakness of the procedural status

[22] On the latter, Raj S Chari and Francesco Cavotorta, 'Economic Actors' Political Activity in "Overlap Issues": Privatisation and EU State Aid Control' (2002) 25 *West European Politics* 119.

[23] Carol Harlow, 'Citizen Access to Political Power in the European Union' (1999) *EUI—Robert Schuman Centre for Advanced Studies Working Paper*, 19.

[24] Jonathan Weinberg, 'The Right to Be Taken Seriously' (2012) 67 *University of Miami Law Review* 149.

[25] Sherry R Arnstein, 'A Ladder of Citizen Participation' (1969) 35 *Journal of American Institute of Planners* 216, 216.

assigned to private actors within the system of State aid control.[26] It is indeed common amongst legal scholars and commentators to highlight the 'bilateral' design of State aid procedures,[27] a phrase that captures the idea that these procedures are meant to unfold as an exclusive dialogue between the Commission and the concerned Member State, with hardly any information or participation rights for any other party, including State aid beneficiaries and their competitors.[28]

Except for a handful of early articles,[29] State aid procedures and the position occupied therein by individuals did not attract the attention of legal scholarship until the early 1990s. This is hardly surprising given the evolution of the policy of the Commission in this field, which was characterised by a very cautious and incremental approach to the enforcement of the Treaty provisions on State aids.[30] It was only after the discipline acquired some bite in the late 1980s[31] that the position of private actors became an issue, as shown by cases like *Cook*, where the Court was called to define the rights of interested parties in the face of a Commission decision to clear a State aid without going through the consultation phase of current Article 108(2) TFEU.[32] The judgment of the Court in this case, which was adopted in 1990, was certainly amongst the factors that triggered the first

[26] See, eg, Andreas Bartosch, 'The Procedural Regulation in State Aid Matters. A Case for Profound Reform' (2007) 6 *European State Aid Law Quarterly* 474, 476; Henrik Peytz and Thomas Mygind, 'Direct Action in State Aid Cases—Tightropes and Legal Protection? A Review of Recent Jurisprudence on Direct and Individual Concern and Reviewable Acts. Part Two' (2010) 9 *European State Aid Law Quarterly* 617, 626.

[27] See, eg, Jacques Derenne and Cédric Kaczmarek, 'La récupération des Aides illégales: le rôle du juge national dans le "private enforcement" du droit des aides d'état' (2009) 10 *ERA Forum* 251, 253.

[28] Adinda Sinnaeve, 'Procedures before the Commission, Council Regulation 659/1999' in Martin Heidenhain (ed), *European State Aid Law* (Munich: Verlag CH Beck, 2010) 575: 'a basic principle of State aid law is that only the Commission and the Member State concerned are parties to the procedures'. See also: Claus-Dieter Ehlermann, 'State Aids under European Community Competition Law' (1994) 18 *Fordham International Law Journal* 410, 430; Michael Niejahr and Tibor Scharf, 'Third Parties in State Aid Control: More Than Just a Source of Information?' in *EC State Aid Law/Le droit des aides d'État dans la CE. Liber Amicorum Francisco Santaolalla Gadea* (The Hague: Kluwer Law International, 2008) 348–49.

[29] Alan Dashwood, 'Control of State Aids in the EEC: Prevention and Cure under Article 93' (1975) 12 *Common Market Law Review* 43; Erik H Pijnacker Hordijk, 'Judicial Protection of Private Interests under the EEC Competition Rules Relating to State Aids' (1985) 12 *Legal Issues of European Integration* 67; Malcom Ross, 'Challenging State Aids: The Effect of Recent Developments' (1986) 23 *Common Market Law Review* 867; David R Gilmour, 'The Enforcement of Community Law by the Commission in the Context of State Aids: The Relationship between Article 93 and 169 and the Choice of Remedies' (1981) 18 *Common Market Law Review* 63.

[30] For an overview of its evolution, see Wolfgang Mederer, 'Evolution of State Aid Control' in Wolfgang Mederer, Nicola Pesaresi, Marc van Hoof and Brice Allibert (eds), *EU Competition Law*, IV (Leuven: Claeys & Casteels, 2008) 19–63. See also Mitchell P Smith, 'Integration in Small Steps: The European Commission and Member State Aid to Industry' (1996) 19 *West European Politics* 563; and J Jorge Piernas López, *The Concept of State Aid under EU Law: From Internal Market to Competition and Beyond* (Oxford: Oxford University Press, 2015) 45–65.

[31] Michelle Cini and Lee McGowan, *Competition Policy in the European Union* (Basingstoke: Macmillan, 2008) 144–46.

[32] Case C-198/91 *William Cook plc v Commission* [1993] ECR I-2487.

significant wave of legal scholarship on the position of private actors within State aid procedures.[33]

One of the recurring themes that ran through this first generation of articles was precisely the weakness of the procedural position occupied by private parties within State aid procedures. Their procedural position had been strengthened as a result of *Cook*, which empowered interested parties to enforce their right to be consulted in the second phase of the procedure. However, the general perception was that their position remained fragile given the opacity of State aid procedures[34] and given certain 'procedural anomalies'—such as the totally secondary role assigned to State aid beneficiaries[35] or the paradoxical rule according to which the consultation phase foreseen in Article 108(2) TFEU is a precondition to applying the default rule in this field (ie, to block State aids) rather than to depart from it (ie, to clear State aids).[36]

Some of these concerns were addressed by the judgment of the Court of First Instance (CFI) in *Sytraval*, where the Court adopted an expansive interpretation of the rights of complainants in State aid cases, which included the right to a reasoned response to the arguments raised in the complaint but also to those that would have been raised had the complainant been given full access to the file.[37] This judgment gave new impetus to the literature on the position of private parties in State aid procedures, for it seemed to mark a shift towards a more complainant- and individuals-friendly stance in the case law.[38] However, the ruling of the CFI in *Sytraval* would eventually be reversed (for the most part) by the Court of Justice, which imposed a much more restrictive reading of the rights of complainants.[39] More importantly perhaps, the CFI ruling prompted the EU legislator to adopt for the first time a Procedural Regulation in the field of State aid and to codify the 'cartelistic relationship' between the Commission and Member States on which State aid procedures had traditionally rested.[40]

The judgment of the European Court of Justice (ECJ) in *Sytraval* and the adoption of the Procedural Regulation were a sort of anti-climax after the upheaval

[33] Philip Bentley, 'State Aid, Subsidies and Complainants' (1990) 1 *European Business Law Review* 91; Johannes A Winter, 'Supervision of State Aid: Article 93 in the Court of Justice' (1993) 30 *Common Market Law Review* 311; Michel L Struys, 'Questions choisies de procédure en matière d'aides d'état' (1993) 29 *Revue Trimestrielle de Droit Européen* 17; Luc Gyselen, 'La transparence en matière d'aides d'État: Les droits des tiers' (1993) 3–4 *Cahiers de Droit Européen*, 417; Evanna Fruithof, 'Procedural Anomalies in State Aid Cases' (1994) 10 *European Business Law Review* 227; Leigh Hancher, 'State Aids and Judicial Control in the European Community' (1994) 15 *European Competition Law Review* 134.

[34] Ehlermann (n 28) 431; Gyselen (n 33) 430–31.

[35] Fruithof (n 33).

[36] Gyselen (n 33) 419–20; Hancher (n 33) 134.

[37] Case T-95/94 *Sytraval and Brink's France SARL v Commission* [1995] ECR-II 2651, para 66.

[38] Ignace Maselis and Hans M Gilliams, 'Rights of Complainants in Community Law' (1997) 22 *European Law Review* 103; Christian Nordberg, 'Judicial Remedies for Private Parties under the State Aid Procedure' (1997) 24 *Legal Issues of Economic Integration* 35. See also the different contributions to Association Europénne Des Avocats (ed), *Un rôle pour la défense dans les procédures communautaires de concurrence: Congrès organisé les 25 et 26 novembre 1996* (Brussels: Bruylant, 1997).

[39] Case C-367/95 P *Commission v Sytraval and Brink's France SARL* [1998] ECR I-1719, paras 73–78.

[40] Smith (n 1) 232.

caused by the lower Court's ruling. In a way, these developments cooled down the interest of the legal literature in the status of private parties in State aid governance—at least insofar as the Commission's procedures were concerned. The focus shifted somewhat to the opportunities for the enforcement of State aid law available to private parties before national courts.[41] The ECJ had long declared the direct effect of the standstill clause laid down by current Article 108(3) TFEU, which empowered interested parties to fight unlawful State aids before national jurisdictions. However, it was only in the mid-1990s that the Commission started to actively promote this course of action, with a series of communications in which it spelled out the powers and responsibilities of national courts in the enforcement of State aid law.[42] The decentralisation dimension of the modernisation projects launched in the fields of antitrust (in the early 2000s)[43] and State aid law (in the mid-2000s)[44] further contributed to placing 'private enforcement' at the centre of the academic agenda.[45]

This succinct review cannot end without a reference to the State Aid Modernisation plan adopted by the Commission in 2012 (SAM).[46] The ultimate goal of this plan was to foster growth, in line with the Europe 2020 strategy of the Commission.[47] Yet, in order to achieve that goal, the plan proposed a series of specific institutional reforms designed to allow the Commission to focus its attention

[41] Phedon Nicolaides, 'Decentralised State Aid Control in an Enlarged European Union: Feasible, Necessary or Both?' (2003) 26 *World Competition* 263; James Flynn, 'The Role of National Courts' in Andrea Biondi, Piet Eeckhout, and James Flynn (eds), *The Law of State Aid in the European Union* (Oxford: Oxford University Press, 2004); Malcom Ross, 'Decentralization, Effectiveness and Modernization: Contradictions in Terms?' in ibid; Adinda Sinnaeve, 'Editorial: What to Expect from National Courts in the Fight against Unlawful State Aid?' (2005) 4 *European State Aid Law Quarterly* 1; Ingeborg Simonsson, 'On the Emerging Obligation for Member State Authorities to Supervise and Enforce EC State Aid Law, and the Resulting Need to Consider Decentralisation' in Nils Wahl and Per Cramér (eds), *Swedish Studies in European Law* (Oxford: Hart Publishing, 2006).

[42] Notice on cooperation between national courts and the Commission in the State aid field (OJ C312, 23.11.1995, p 8), later replaced by the Notice on the enforcement of State aid law by national courts (OJ C85, 9.4.2009, p 1).

[43] 'White paper on the modernisation of the rules implementing Articles 85 and 86 of the EC Treaty' COM (1999) 101 final, and Council Regulation (EC) No 1/2003 of 16 December 2002 on the implementation of the rules on competition laid down in Articles 81 and 82 of the Treaty (OJ L1, 04.01.2003, p 1).

[44] 'State Aid Action Plan. Less and better targeted state aid: a roadmap for state aid reform 2005–2009' COM (2005) 107 final.

[45] Simonsson (n 41); Barbara Brandtner, Thierry Beranger and Christof Lessenich, 'Private State Aid Enforcement' (2010) 9 *European State Aid Law Quarterly* 23; Alena Zemplinerova, 'The Community State Aid Action Plan and the Challenge of Developing an Optimal Enforcement System' in Ioannis Lianos and Ioannis Kokkoris (eds), *The Reform of EC Competition Law: New Challenges* (New York: Wolters Kluwer, 2010); Martin Köhler, 'Private Enforcement of State Aid Law—Problems of Guaranteeing EU Rights by Means of National (Procedural) Law' (2012) 11 *European State Aid Law Quarterly Journal* 369.

[46] 'Communication from the Commission to the European Parliament, the Council, the European Economic and Social Committee and the Committee of the Regions on EU State Aid Modernisation (SAM)' COM (2012) 0209 final).

[47] SAM, paras 10–18.

on the most significant or dangerous measures of government support to firms, without compromising the overall effectiveness of the system of State aid control. The SAM has thus resulted in the reform of the *de minimis*[48] and block exemption regulations[49]—both of which affect the room left for *private enforcement* in this area—and of the Procedural Regulation—with the insertion of an express reference to complainants,[50] which has revived the academic debate on the role of private parties within the *public enforcement* side of the system of State aid governance.[51]

IV. Structure of the Book

The book is divided in two parts, each of which is made up of three chapters. The first part of the book is more theoretical, in that it reflects on the role that the substantive and the institutional rules on State aid assign to competitors, as a preliminary step to the empirical (read, case law-based) analysis carried out in the second part.

Part I

Chapter 1 analyses the position occupied by competitors within the theory of harm that informs the rules on State aid. It reviews the main theories produced by the literature on international trade and on the EU to explain the normative rationale of the system of State aid control, reflecting on the relevance that each

[48] *De minimis* Regulation (n 16).

[49] General Block Exemption Regulation (n 16).

[50] Council Regulation (EU) No 734/2013 of 22 July 2013 amending Regulation (EC) No 659/1999 laying down detailed rules for the application of Article 93 of the EC Treaty (OJ L204, 31.7.2013, p 15. See codified version: Council Regulation (EU) 2015/1589 of 13 July 2015 laying down detailed rules for the application of Article 108 of the Treaty on the Functioning of the European Union (OJ L248, 24.9.2015, p 9).

[51] Thomas Jaeger, 'The Inquisition Retakes Brussels' (2013) 12 *European State Aid Law Quarterly* 1; Conor Quigley, 'The European Commission's Programme for State Aid Modernization' (2013) 20 *Maastricht Journal of European and Comparative Law* 35; Massimo Merola and Leonardo Armati, 'Complainants' Rights in State Aid Matters. Lost in Modernisation?' in Inge Govaere and Dominik Hanf (eds), *Scrutinizing Internal and External Dimensions of European Law. Liber Amicorum Paul Demaret* (Brussels: Peter Lang, 2013) 569; Hans P Nehl, '2013 Reform of EU State Aid Procedures: How to Exacerbate the Imbalance between Efficiency and Individual Protection' (2014) 13 *European State Aid Law Quarterly* 235; François-Charles Laprévote, 'A Missed Opportunity?: State Aid Modernization and Effective Third Parties Rights in State Aid Proceedings' (2014) 12 *European State Aid Law Quarterly* 426; María J Segura Catalán and Marianne Clayton, 'State Aid Modernisation: Another Reform?' (2013) 14 *ERA Forum* 21; Albert Sánchez-Graells, 'Digging Itself Out of the Hole? A Critical Assessment of the European Commission's Attempt to Revitalize State Aid Enforcement After the Crisis' (2016) 2 *Journal of Antitrust Enforcement* 157.

of these theories assigns to the potentially negative effects that State aids may have on competitors. It then extends the same analysis to the way in which the rules on State aid are applied in practice. The main claim made in this chapter is that the interest of competitors in shielding their market position against the distortionary effects of State aids is not the only concern that drives the system of State aid control.

The implications of this finding for the inquiry of the book are explored in Chapter 2, the main one being that the involvement of competitors in the enforcement of State aid law cannot be grounded on a straightforward 'scope of protection' type of theory. A more elaborate theory is needed, and it can be one of two sorts: an 'instrumental theory' (that grounds their involvement on the added value that they bring to the Commission's supervisory task) and a 'legal protection theory' (that grounds their involvement on their entitlement to some form of legal protection against the injury caused by otherwise irregular State aid). The second part of the chapter shows that, in its inception at least, the institutional design of the system of State aid control seems to be informed by an instrumental conception of the role of individuals (in general) and competitors (in particular) within that system. The corollary of this conception is that competitors are likely to have some voice (access) but little chance of influence (leverage) in the enforcement of the rules on State aid. This proposition is then revisited and tested in the rest of the book.

Chapter 3 wraps up the first part of the book with an investigation of the opportunities for access and leverage afforded to competitors before national courts, ie, by the 'private enforcement' of State aid. The chapter shows that the EU institutions (the Commission, the EU legislator and the European Courts themselves) have pinned high hopes on the development of an effective system of private enforcement in the field of State aid. The chapter also shows, however, that this system suffers from certain structural limitations that restrict the possibilities of redress that competitors may achieve through the national route. This is the reason why the second part of the book focuses in its entirety on the participatory opportunities offered to competitors in the course of the Commission's 'public enforcement' procedures.

Part II

The second part of the book scrutinises the opportunities for voice offered to competitors within the 'public enforcement' side of the system of State aid control, which are basically three: the possibility to lodge complaints as a prelude to the preliminary phase, the possibility to submit comments in the course of the formal investigation phase, and the possibility to seek judicial review of State aid decisions. Each of these opportunities is analysed in a separate chapter.

Yet the approach followed in all of them is roughly the same. The analysis always starts with a general discussion that seeks to identify the appropriate benchmark to assess the value in terms of access and leverage of the participatory opportunity discussed in each case. The analysis then moves on to look more closely at the evolution of the case law and, where relevant, secondary legislation, to assess the extent to which they have departed from the purely instrumental role associated with the original design of the system of State aid control. The findings of the different chapters are drawn together in the Conclusion.

PART I

1

The Substantive Rules on State Aid

Introduction

State aids represent by definition a financial advantage granted to certain undertakings. Economic theory posits that such an advantage is harmless for competitors in two types of markets: in monopolistic markets (where there are no competitors) and in perfectly competitive markets (where the financial advantage is likely to result in an increase of benefits, without any impact on output).[1] In practice, however, most markets are imperfectly competitive, and it is in this scenario where State aids are most likely to affect the beneficiaries' output (be it quantity, quality or price-wise) and hence to have a potentially negative impact on the market position of their competitors. This chapter considers the relevance that this risk has from the perspective of the theory of harm that informs the discipline on State aid. In other words, it inquires into the position that the substantive rules on State aid assign to the interest of competitors.

The chapter begins with a brief review of the reasons why governments grant subsidies and other forms of State aid. This review sets the background for the inquiry carried out in the second part, which maps out the main theories produced to explain the rationale for the establishment of the system of State aid control and reflects on the relevance that they assign to the interest of competitors. The last part of this chapter carries the inquiry one step further by looking at the relevance that the interest of competitors has in the actual operation of the rules on State aid. This includes the application of the general prohibition set forth by Article 107(1) TFEU and the administration of the exemptions foreseen in Article 107(3) TFEU.

I. The Political Economy of Subsidies and Other Forms of State Aid

Article 107(1) TFEU defines the concept of State aid on the basis of four criteria. In order to be caught by the definition (and hence by the prohibition) of State

[1] Timothy Besley and Paul Seabright, 'The Effects and Policy Implications of State Aids to Industry' (1999) 14 *Economic Policy* 13, 21.

aid, a measure needs to (i) involve the transfer of state resources, (ii) favour certain undertakings or the production of certain goods, (iii) distort or threaten to distort competition and (iv) affect trade between Member States. Public subsidies granted to private firms are the paradigmatic example of the notion of aid, but the definition is broad enough to encompass many other forms of financial assistance to firms: regulatory benefits in the form of exemptions from taxes or social security contributions, overpriced purchases, under-priced sales, preferential loans or guarantees, etc.[2]

The reasons why governments may decide to resort to this type of instruments are very varied. State aids are, indeed, a form of public intervention in the market, and their goals may be as diverse as those of any other regulatory policy whereby the power of government is leveraged to affect the outcomes produced by the market. In its report on 'Competition Policy in Subsidies and State Aid', the Organisation for Economic Co-operation and Development OECD) listed some of these goals. State aids are usually granted in order to:

— encourage economic activity in a region, or to encourage firms to locate within a specific region;
— obtain services that the market would not otherwise provide (as might be the case in, say, the support for broadcasting or for transport or communication services in remote areas);
— slow the rate of decline of an industry (as may be the case for subsidies for coal and steel);
— offset fluctuations due to natural phenomena (as may be the case in agriculture);
— maintain the incomes of producers;
— correct other market failures (such as support for R&D or support for environmental improvements);
— enhance employment (including employment of specific groups such as the young, women or handicapped); or to
— expand market share of subsidised firms at the expense of firms in other jurisdictions.[3]

Economists generally consider that all this myriad of objectives can be synthesised into two: the use of subsidies to correct market failures (efficiency objectives) and the use of subsidies to redistribute wealth (equity objectives).[4] On the first front, the objective sought by the grant of a subsidy may be, for example, to correct a negative externality (eg, subsidies to encourage the use of environmentally friendly technologies); to correct the free-rider problem associated to positive externalities (eg, subsidy to encourage research and development by firms); or to address

[2] On 'the forms of governmental action covered by EC state aid rules', see, eg, Luca Rubini, *The Definition of State Aid: WTO and EC Law in Comparative Perspective* (Oxford: Oxford University Press, 2010) 151–80.

[3] OECD, 'Competition Policy in Subsidies and State Aid' (DAFFE/CLP(2001)24) 7.

[4] See, eg, Hans W Friederiszick, Lars-Hendrik Röller and Vincent Verouden, 'EC State Aid Control: An Economic Perspective' in Michael Sánchez Rydelski (ed), *The EC State Aid Regime—Distortive Effects of State Aid on Competition and Trade* (London: Cameron May, 2006) 153–57, which is where most of the following examples are taken from.

information asymmetries (eg, in the financial market for SMEs). On the equity front, subsidies are often used to ensure a fair distribution of wealth throughout the territory (eg, subsidies to promote investments in underdeveloped regions); to promote the employment of certain social groups (eg, subsidies to promote the employment of youth or disabled people) or to achieve cultural objectives (eg, subsidies to ensure media plurality).

This is only meant to be an illustration of the broad range of goals that governments may pursue when they grant subsidies and other forms of financial assistance to firms. The point to note is that some of these objectives appear (at first sight at least) as legitimate and desirable policy goals, which begs the question of the rationale behind the establishment of a supranational system of control that proscribes as a general rule the use of this type of instruments within the EU. The following section summarises the main ideas produced by the general literature on international trade and by the more specific literature on the EU State aid regime to answer this question.

II. The Political Economy of State Aid Control

This section maps out the main theories produced to explain the rationale of the system of State aid control. There are, broadly, three groups of theories. The first group focuses on the incapability of national governments to design or implement their State aid programmes in a way that actually achieves their goals. This is what I call the 'institutional rationale'. The second group justifies the need to control State aids on the basis that they may be used as a protectionist tool. In the context of the EU, this is obviously linked to the internal market paradigm, which is why I refer to them as 'internal market rationale'. The last group sees State aid law as a mechanism designed to prevent the potentially welfare-impairing effects of subsidies and other forms of financial assistance to firms, hence the label 'efficiency rationale'.

1. The Institutional Rationale

The institutional rationale assumes that subsidies are in theory an appropriate instrument to further certain legitimate, regulatory goals, but casts doubt on the capacity of governments to design their subsidies in a way that actually achieves these goals.

The most extreme version of this theory calls into question the capacity of governments to target the right industry players and hence to design their industrial policy in a way that effectively achieves its goals.[5] The problem with this

[5] Brander assigns this idea to Krugman in James A. Brander, 'Rationales for Strategic Trade and Industrial Policy', in Paul K. Krugman (ed), *Strategic Trade Policy and the New International Economics* (Boston, MA: MIT Press, 1986) 45.

government-failure argument is that it does not really justify the establishment of supranational mechanisms of control, because there is no reason to assume that supranational institutions are immune to the same type of cognitive limitations that affect infra-national and national governments.[6] If anything, this theory calls for a policy choice between the error bias of two extreme options: an over-inclusive, absolute ban on subsidies (that will necessarily generate many false positives) or no regulation at all (an approach that necessarily tolerates many false negatives).[7]

A less extreme version of this theory accepts the capacity of governments to define a good policy of subsidies and State aids (ie, to target the right players and to define the optimum level of financial assistance granted to them) but casts doubt on their capacity to stick to that policy. Several factors may cause this problem. There is, first of all, the risk of capture arising from the exposure of governments to the pressure stemming from powerful sectors of their constituencies. From this perspective, the rationale of setting up supranational mechanisms of control is to shift the decision-making process 'far away from national political pressures' in order to counterbalance the influence of private interest groups over their governments.[8] Again, the assumption that supranational institutions are not vulnerable to capture seems implausible, but the involvement of an additional, more remote institution may mitigate the problem.

There is, secondly, the 'domestic commitment problem'[9] generally raised by regulatory policies whose benefits are more immediate and concentrated than their costs.[10] Democratically accountable authorities have a strong incentive to disregard costs and to over-subsidise in order to win elections. This generates, in turn, a 'soft-budget constraint' type of problem[11]—it can lead to subsidies becoming part of the ordinary regulatory environment and to firms systematically counting on them when making their investment decisions. From this perspective, the establishment of a supranational discipline on subsidies and State aids may provide the same type of independent control that national banks exercise over monetary policy.[12] The independent source of control that this theory demands need not be supranational, but supranational mechanisms of control are certainly a possible solution to the problem.[13]

6 David Spector, 'L'économie politique des aides d'État et le choix du critère d'appréciation' (2006) 2 *Concurrences* 34, 34–35.

7 See Alan O Sykes, 'The Questionable Case for Subsidies Regulation: A Comparative Perspective' (2010) 2 *Journal of Legal Analysis* 473, 501, who questions the capacity of the supranational disciplines on subsidies (WTO and EU) 'to identify subsidization at all, much less to distinguish undesirable from desirable subsidies'.

8 Spector (n 6) 36 (translation mine). See also Pietro Crocioni, 'Can State Aid Policy Become More Economic Friendly?' (2006) 29 *World Competition* 89, 93.

9 Friederiszick, Röller and Verouden (n 4) 163.

10 Spector (n 6) 36.

11 The term was coined by János Kornai, 'The Soft Budget Constraint' (1986) 39 *Kyklos* 3.

12 Spector (n 6) 36.

13 Mathias Dewatripont and Paul Seabright, '"Wasteful" Public Spending and State Aid Control' (2006) 4 *Journal of the European Economic Association* 513, 521.

The institutional concerns that underpin these theories are present in the academic literature on the rationale of the European system of State aid control, but they are rarely if ever invoked as a stand-alone justification for the creation of that system. This is because they point to some of the reasons why State aids may fail to achieve their (a priori) legitimate objectives, but they do not identify the cross-border or EU-wide concerns that explained the insertion of this system into the Treaty of Rome and, later, into its progeny. This is the reason why the discussion has chiefly focalised around the two alternative rationales, which are considered next.

2. The Internal Market Rationale

The internal market rationale builds on the insights of the general literature on international trade, which has described the capacity of subsidies to neutralise the effects of market access and free trade agreements.[14] The premise of this theory is that subsidies may be used as a protectionist tool in order to bypass the reciprocal commitments embodied in market access agreements over tariffs and quotas. The idea is that, in the absence of international disciplines on subsidies, national governments would use their financial resources to favour their own producers, which would in turn grant them an advantage on both the domestic and foreign markets that goes beyond what the tariff and quota concessions allow.

Within the EU, this theory is linked to the objective of 'establishing or ensuring the functioning of the internal market',[15] a concept that the Treaty defines as comprising 'an area without internal frontiers in which the free movement of goods, persons, services and capital is ensured in accordance with the provisions of the Treaties'.[16] This objective entails a greater degree of market integration than the one sought in the context of the World Trade Organization, because it rests on a customs union that is inimical to all tariffs and quotas between Member States[17] and on a set of fundamental freedoms that seeks to ensure the free movement of all the factors of production and not only of products themselves.[18] If the need to ensure that subsidies are not used to achieve protectionist effects justifies their control from the perspective of international trade, there is therefore an even stronger reason to control them within the EU.

Thus, the internal market rationale propounds that the main purpose of the system of State aid control is to prevent Member States from using their financial resources to circumvent the rules that govern the internal market. This theory is

[14] Sykes (n 7) 495–99.

[15] Article 26(1) TFEU.

[16] Article 26(2) TFEU.

[17] Article 30 TFEU (prohibition of customs duties on exports and imports) and Article 34 TFEU (prohibition of quantitative restrictions).

[18] Articles 28 ff TFEU (free movement of goods) and Articles 45 ff TFEU (free movement of persons, services and capitals).

based on the premise that State aids can replicate the protectionist effects of the measures proscribed by the provisions on free movement. Rather than imposing customs duties on importers, Member States could decide—for instance—to grant subsidies to their national producers so as to put them in a better position than their foreign counterparts, without imposing any charge on the latter. In the same vein, they could sidestep the prohibition of discriminatory taxation providing national producers with fiscal benefits refused to foreign importers. This is only meant to be an illustration of the concerns that fuel the internal market rationale. The point to note is that it relies on a theory of harm that places free movement at its heart.

3. The Efficiency Rationale

The efficiency rationale is based (partially at least) on the insights of the literature on strategic trade, whose origins can be traced back to a series of papers by Brander and Spencer.[19] Their profit-shifting model shows that under certain circumstances subsidies are welfare enhancing, both from a domestic and from a worldwide perspective. From a domestic perspective, subsidies are welfare enhancing because they allow the beneficiary to increase output and to expand its share in foreign markets. This is the reason why the benefits brought about by subsidies may exceed their cost to the taxpayers and thus enhance total domestic welfare. Despite the strong predatory element that is associated with this strategy, the model also shows that subsidies may enhance global welfare. Their point is that 'The welfare improvement comes about because the subsidy acts to reduce the monopoly distortion in [an] imperfectly competitive industry'.[20]

According to their model, the rationale for controlling subsidies lies in the risk that the deployment of a similar strategy by different governments may result in a race that is 'jointly suboptimal from the point of view of producing nations taken together'.[21] Their work uses game theory to show that the use of export subsidies as a predatory tool is likely to push governments into a prisoner's dilemma, whereby 'unilateral predatory policy is attractive if the other country is passive, but mutual non-intervention would give the highest combined total return'.[22] Under this model, then, the rationale for controlling subsidies is to set up a cooperative structure that forecloses collectively wasteful subsidy wars.

Whereas this theory may explain, in part, the rationale of the EU system of State aid control, it does not capture all the efficiency losses that subsidies and other

[19] James A Brander and Barbara J Spencer, 'Tariff Protection and Imperfect Competition' in Henryk Kierzkowski (ed), *Monopolistic Competition and International Trade* (Oxford: Oxford University Press, 1984); James A Brander and Barbara J Spencer, 'Export Subsidies and International Market Share Rivalry' (1985) 18 *Journal of international Economics* 83.

[20] Brander (n 5) 45.

[21] Brander and Spencer, 'Export Subsidies and International Market Share Rivalry', n 19, 98.

[22] Brander (n 5) 38.

forms of aid may cause within an integrated market. The efficiency rationale of EU State aid control can therefore be grounded on a broader theory of harm than its international counterpart. From this perspective, the most obvious risk that these rules should seek to avert is the use of State aids to keep inefficient producers afloat. Besides facilitating predatory strategies that may result in the exclusion of efficient competitors and in a long-term rise in prices, this course of action would harm dynamic efficiency by reducing the incentives of efficient producers to innovate. There are certainly other ways in which State aids may harm efficiency. The efficiency rationale assigns to State aid control the task of identifying them so as to ensure that the State aid policies of Member States do not reduce the efficiency of the internal market.

4. Competitors and the Rationales of State Aid Control

The preceding analysis has shown that, within the EU, the debate on the rationale behind the establishment of a system of State aid control has crystallised around two theories: the internal market rationale, which sees State aid law as a complement to the provisions on free movement, and the efficiency rationale, which sees it instead as a mechanism designed to prevent the efficiency losses that State aids may generate. Needless to say, the goals set by both theories do not necessarily exclude each other.[23] It is indeed possible to argue that the system of State aid control exists in order to protect the internal market *and* to maximise its efficiency—or, even more generally, that the goal of the internal market itself is to maximise efficiency and welfare across the EU.

Be that as it may, the point to note is that neither of these theories relies exclusively on the potentially harmful effects of State aids on competitors to justify the existence of a system of State aid control. They do not assign to State aid law the goal of protecting the market and its operators against the financial lever of Member States; nor do they rely on the notion of 'competition on the merits'[24] (ie, on the idea that the market alone should reward market actors on the sole basis of their performance) to explain its rationale. Their approach is broader, in that they focus on the need to protect the structure and the efficiency of the internal market as a whole rather than on the narrower concerns of some of its actors.

[23] Rubini (n 2) 62; Andrea Biondi and Piet Eeckhout, 'State Aid and Obstacles to Trade' in Andrea Biondi, Piet Eeckhout and James Flynn (eds), *The Law of State Aid in the European Union* (Oxford: Oxford University Press, 2004) 108.

[24] On the idea of competition on the merits, see generally Eleanor M Fox, 'State Aids Control and the Distortion of Competition—Unbundling "Distortion"', in Barry E. Hawk (ed), *Annual Proceedings of the Fordham Corporate Law Institute. International Antitrust Law and Policy* (Irvington-on-Hudson, NY: Juris Publishing, 2002). See also Eleanor M. Fox, 'What Is Harm to Competition? Antitrust, Exclusionary Practices and the Elusive Notion of Anticompetitive Effect' in Josef Drexl (ed), *The Future of Transnational Antitrust—from Comparative to Common Competition Law* (Berne: Staempfli/Kluwer Law International, 2003) 94.

Of course, this is not to say that the type of State aid control that both theories propound cannot, indirectly, afford protection to private firms against the distortive effects of State aids. After all, the internal market enterprise seeks to ensure that national markets are open to foreign traders, which has an obvious impact on cross-border competitors. In the same vein, the efficiency rationale justifies the sacrifice of the interest of competitors when the distortions of competition generated by State aids contribute to enhance the overall efficiency of the market. This logic also demands, however, that care be taken not to harm efficient competitors. But it seems that protecting competitors is not the main goal that drives the rules on State aid. The next section tests this proposition by looking at the actual operation of the rules. In contrast to the theoretical approach followed so far, the next section will therefore look at the way in which the rules on State aid are applied in practice.

III. The Operation of the Rules on State Aid

1. Overview of the Rules on State Aid

The application of the rules on State aid takes place in two different phases. The first phase of the analysis is governed by Article 107(1) TFEU, which defines the concept of State aid on the basis of four criteria (state resources, selective advantage, distortion of competition, effect on trade). The second phase of the analysis is governed by sections (2) and (3) of the same Article, which empower the Commission to authorise certain State aids in derogation from the general prohibition of section (1).

Article 107(1) TFEU will be considered first. Besides defining the notion of aid, this provision performs two functions. First, it lays down the default rule that State aids are prohibited, which comes down to raising a presumption of irregularity against any measure falling within the definition of aid. Secondly, it triggers the standstill and notification obligations of Article 108(3) TFEU, which provides that Member States shall notify and suspend any plan to grant State aid until authorised by the Commission. Article 107(1) TFEU can therefore be read as a jurisdictional clause that defines the conditions under which the power to decide on the implementation of state measures of financial support to firms shifts from the national to the supranational level.

It is once this shift is operated that Article 107(2) and (3) come into play. The first provision contains a set of three exemptions that leave no margin of discretion to the Commission ('shall'). The situations they contemplate are rare (aid for individual consumers, aid linked to natural disasters, aid linked to the reunification of Germany) and their use is very marginal, which is why they will not be considered in this chapter. The focus will therefore be directed to the exemptions foreseen in Article 107(3) TFEU, which leave a broad margin of discretion to the Commission[25] and which constitute the backbone of its State aid policy.[26]

2. The Definition of State Aid

Article 107(1) TFEU defines the notion of aid. The European Courts have repeatedly held that this notion is objective, in the double sense that it leaves no discretion to the Commission[27] and that its application depends on the effects rather than on the aims of the measures under scrutiny.[28] Their form is also irrelevant according to the text of the provision, and so is the level of government responsible for the decision, according to well-established case law.[29] These are the general principles that govern the interpretation of the four criteria that make up the definition of aid: State resources, selectivity, distortion of competition and effect on trade. For reasons that will become apparent immediately, the analysis will start with the second two criteria.

(a) Distortion of Competition and Effect on Trade

On their face, the conditions that relate to competition and trade seem particularly apt to test the relevance of the interest of competitors in the operation of the rules on State aids. From a methodological perspective, then, it would seem sensible to look at their application in order to verify the extent to which they echo a concern for the potentially harmful effects that State aids may have on competitors. The problem with this approach is that the last two conditions of Article 107(1) TFEU are those to which the Commission and the European Courts have devoted less attention, which makes it difficult to deduce clear principles from their operation.

Indeed, despite its centrality to the language of the provision, the application of Article 107(1) TFEU has never required a fully fledged economic analysis of the distortion of competition caused by the aid. Although the Commission is under an obligation to identify the product market that is likely to be affected by the aid, and its failure to do so may result in the annulment of its decisions,[30] the distortion of competition 'may be easily presumed'.[31] In fact, the analysis of the effects of

[25] Case 78/76 *Steinike & Weinlig v Germany* [1977] ECR 595, para 8; Case 74/76 *Iannelli & Volpi SpA v Ditta Paolo Meroni* [1977] ECR 557, paras 12–13.

[26] Wolfgang Mederer, 'Evolution of State Aid Control' in Wolfgang Mederer et al (eds), EU *Competition Law*, IV (Leuven: Claeys & Casteels, 2008) 21.

[27] Case C-487/06 P *British Aggregates Association v Commission* [2008] ECR I-10515, para 111.

[28] Case 173/73 *Italy v Commission* [1974] ECR 709, para 13.

[29] Case 248/84 *Germany v Commission* [1987] ECR 4013, para 13.

[30] Joined Cases 62 and 72/87 *Exécutif Régional Wallon v Commission* [1988] ECR 1573, para 15; Case T-155/98 *SIDE v Commission* [2002] ECR II-1179, para 71.

[31] Conor Quigley, *European State Aid Law and Policy*, 3rd edn (Oxford: Hart Publishing, 2015) 53.

aids on competition is often conflated with the analysis of their effect on trade,[32] which makes it difficult to offer a precise account of the meaning of this condition. What is certain, however, is that the application of Article 107(1) TFEU misses the type of sophisticated welfare analysis that one finds in modern antitrust.[33]

Similarly, the analysis of the effect on trade requirement has not played a particularly important role in the application of Article 107(1) TFEU by the European institutions. The first wave of cases where the European Court had the occasion to discuss the definition of State aid involved subsidies specifically designed to support exports.[34] The exact meaning of the effect on trade requirement was not discussed, but this was due to the fact that the cross-border dimension of the contested measures was obvious. The aids at stake fell squarely within the typical scenario contemplated by the literature on strategic trade, and it was therefore logical to dispense with a close analysis of their (obvious) cross-border effects.

Later cases suggest, however, that the analysis of the effects on trade need not be very probing either when the cross-border dimension is less obvious. This is the result of the seminal *Philip Morris* case, where the ECJ held that 'When state financial aid strengthens the position of an undertaking compared with other undertakings competing in intra-community trade the latter must be regarded as affected by that aid'.[35] It is certainly the case that the Commission may not completely overlook this condition: in the *Leeuwarder* case, for instance, the Court annulled a decision of the Commission on the ground that it had failed to set out 'the slightest information concerning the situation of the relevant market, the place of [the recipient of the alleged aid] in that market, the pattern of trade between Member States in the products in question or the undertaking's exports'.[36] However, there is no doubt that *Philip Morris* set a very loose standard of proof for the Commission to establish that an aid affects trade, which is why little attention is generally devoted to this condition.

As noted earlier, the cursory treatment generally given to the distortion of competition and effect on trade requirements may come out as a surprise from the viewpoint of the two main theories on the rationale of State aid control. Yet neither of these theories is proven wrong by this approach, which can be read as a choice in favour of an over-inclusive definition of aid that defers to a later stage the individualised analysis of their effects. Indeed, it implies that the definition of

[32] See, eg, Case 234/84 *Belgium v Commission (Meura)* [1986] ECR 2263, para 22, and Case 730/79 *Philip Morris Holland BV v Commission* [1980] ECR 2671, discussed below.

[33] Christian Ahlborn and Claudia Berg, 'Can State Aid Control Learn from Antitrust? The Need for a Greater Role for Competition Analysis under the State Aid Rules' in Andrea Biondi, Piet Eeckhout, and James Flynn (eds), *The Law of State Aid in the European Union* (Oxford: Oxford University Press, 2004) 47–48.

[34] See, eg, Joined Cases 6 and 11/69 *Commission v France* [1969] ECR 523 and Case 47/69 *France v Commission* [1970] ECR 487. See discussion in J Jorge Piernas López, *The Concept of State Aid under EU Law: From Internal Market to Competition and Beyond* (Oxford: Oxford University Press, 2015).

[35] Case 730/79 *Philip Morris Holland BV v Commission* [1980] ECR 2671, para 11.

[36] Joined Cases 296 and 318/82 *Netherlands and Leeuwarder Papierwarenfabriek v Commission* [1985] ECR 809, para 24.

aid casts a wide net on state measures of financial support to firms when it comes to considering their effects on competition and trade, which is actually consistent with both theories. The problem with this approach—for the purposes of this inquiry—is that it reveals very little about the normative concerns that inform the application of the rules on State aid. This is the reason why the rest of the analysis will focus on the only two conditions that operate as an effective filter at definition stage, namely, the state resources and the selectivity criteria.

(b) Transfer of State Resources

The prohibition of State aids laid down by Article 107(1) TFEU only affects 'aid granted by a Member State or through State resources'. On its face, this phrase captures two different conditions, which can be termed as state resources and imputability to the state.[37] Furthermore, both conditions are seemingly alternative, in the sense that it suffices that a measure fulfils one of them to be caught by the definition. In practice, however, the case law of the European Courts sees both conditions as cumulative. After some hesitations with regard to the possibility of finding aid in cases where it was not financed from State resources,[38] the Court held in *PreussenElektra* that 'only advantages granted directly or indirectly through State resources are to be considered aid within the meaning of Article [107(1) TFEU]',[39] which means that the definition of aid only covers measures that are both imputable to the state *and* financed through its resources.

Unlike the distortion of competition and effect on trade conditions, this requirement does work as an effective filter. The European Courts have favoured an extensive interpretation of this requirement, which 'embraces not only positive benefits, such as the subsidies themselves, but also measures which, in various forms, mitigate the normal burdens on the budget of an undertaking'.[40] However, they have shown that the concept is not limitless by refusing to stretch the concept of aid so as to catch regulatory benefits that have an equivalent effect to State aids but no impact on the budget of the state.[41]

Yet, although conceptually and practically important, the state resources condition is not relevant for the inquiry carried out in this chapter. This is because it acts as an outer limit for the concept of aid, but tells very little about the relevance

[37] Kelyn Bacon, *European Community Law of State Aid* (Oxford: Oxford University Press, 2009) 69.

[38] Case 290/83 *Commission v France* [1985] ECR 439, para 18; Joined Cases 67, 68 and 70/85 *Kwekerij Gebroeders van der Kooy and others v Commission* [1988] ECR 219, para 32-9; Case 57/86 *Greece v Commission* [1988] ECR 2855, paras 11–13. See also Opinion of Advocate General Darmon in Joined Cases C-72 and 73/91 *Firma Sloman Neptun Schiffahrts AG v Seebetriebsrat Bodo Ziesemer der Sloman Neptun Schiffahrts AG* [1993] ECR I-887.

[39] Case C-379/98 *PreussenElektra AG v Schhleswag AG* [2001] ECR I-2099, para 58.

[40] Case C-276/02 *Spain v Commission* [2004] ECR I-8091, para 24.

[41] This is also the result of *PreussenElektra* (n 39) where the Court held at paras 59 and 62 that 'the obligation imposed on private electricity supply undertakings to purchase electricity produced from renewable energy sources at fixed minimum prices does not involve any direct or indirect transfer of State resources' and 'cannot be regarded as constituting a means of granting to producers of electricity from renewable energy sources a particular advantage at the expense of the State'.

assigned to competitors by the theory of harm that informs the operation of the rules on State aid, which is why it need not be considered any further.

(c) Selectivity

Amongst the four defining conditions laid down by Article 107(1) TFEU, the notion of selectivity—'the favouring [of] certain undertakings or the production of certain goods'—has clearly become the most decisive one. Provided that the state resources and state imputability requirement is satisfied, it will normally constitute the kernel of the analysis at the definition stage, so much so that the fulfilment of the distortion of competition and effect on trade requirements will normally be presumed whenever a measure is found to be selective.

The notion of selectivity also happens to be one of the most complex aspects of the law on State aids. The question it asks is whether the measure under scrutiny confers a selective advantage on its beneficiary. The fulfilment of this condition raises no problems when the measure at stake takes the form of an individual subsidy, ie, a lump-sum transferred to a particular undertaking.[42] In practice, however, most cases involve more general and heterodox forms of aid. The question is then governed by a thick web of jurisprudential rules that do not lend themselves easily to simplification. In order to overcome this problem, my analysis will build on the work of de Cecco, who draws a distinction between the tests that preside over the application of the concept of aid in three different contexts: where the state acts as 'regulator', where it acts as 'market participant' and where it acts 'in a hybrid context'.[43]

Where national regulatory measures are at stake (eg, tax or social security measures), the application of the notion of selectivity depends on a discrimination test that considers the treatment afforded by the alleged State aid to undertakings which are in a 'comparable legal and factual situation'.[44] This test is based on 'legal criteria' rather than on 'economic considerations'.[45] Its application brings within the notion of State aid measures that discriminate in favour of certain sectors (eg, aid in favour of the textile industry)[46] or certain regions (regional aid).[47]

There are two points to note in relation to the application of this test. The first point is that the benchmark for the comparison is national: the comparison

[42] Quigley (n 31) 13.

[43] Francesco de Cecco, 'The Many Meanings of "Competition" in EC State Aid Law' (2006) 9 *Cambridge Yearbook of European Legal Studies* 111, 113.

[44] Case C-143/99 *Adria-Wien Pipeline GmbH v Finanzlandesdirektion für Kärnten* [2001] ECR I-8365, para 41. Note that *Adria-Wien* is the leading case on the exception that excludes from the notion of State aid selective, regulatory measures that are justified 'by the nature or general scheme of the system of which [they] are part' (para 41). This is one of the rules that adds to the complexity of the notion of aid but that can be overlooked here.

[45] de Cecco (n 43) 122.

[46] See, eg, Case 173/73 *Italy v Commission* [1974] ECR 709, para 15; Case 248/84 *Germany v Commission* [1987] ECR 4013, para 18; Case C-75/97 *Belgium v Commission (Maribel)* [1999] ECR I/3671, para 33.

[47] See, eg, Case 248/84 *Germany v Commission* [1987] ECR 4013.

need not (in fact, should not) be drawn between undertakings operating in different Member States.[48] This is because the notion of selectivity does not seek to bring within the purview of the Commission any regulatory imbalance between Member States, but only those measures that reveal a preferential treatment in favour of certain operators—indeed, State aid law does not limit regulatory competition between Member States provided it is confined to measures of general application.[49] The second point to note is that the discrimination need not be established between undertakings that are in a competitive relationship with each other,[50] as shown by the possibility of finding that a measure is selective on the ground that it favours a whole economic sector.

This is not to say that the effects of State aids on competitors are irrelevant to the notion of selectivity. The notion of selectivity adopts a broader approach, in that the test can be satisfied without pinpointing specific competitive relationships. However, finding that a measure favours certain undertakings in relation to their competitors is one of the ways in which selectivity can be established. Furthermore, even in those cases where this type of relationship is less evident, the discrimination approach embodied by the selectivity test can be seen as a proximate test to identify those measures that are likely to improve the relative position of the beneficiary in relation to the competitors placed in other regions (regional aid) or Member States (sectoral aid). This is the reason why some commentators have claimed that State aid law is more concerned with 'preserving equality among competitors than with harm to competition' and that the approach followed in relation to regulatory measures 'ensures fairness and equality among competitors in relation to regulation' rather than 'efficiency'.[51]

A different test applies where the Member State acts as market participant. In that scenario, the application of the notion of selectivity depends on a test that 'compares the actions of the state with the hypothetical behaviour of a typical private market operator'.[52] This test is reflected in the various 'state aid filters' that the case law has elaborated to consider the different ways in which the state may participate in the market: the 'private investor test', the 'private creditor test', the 'private purchaser test', the 'private vendor test', and the 'market economy operator test'.[53] However, all these filters essentially assess the 'market rationality' of the measure under scrutiny in order 'to ensure that the process of competition

[48] Penelope Papandropoulos, Massimo Merola, Jacques Derenne, Rainer Nitsche, Bernard van de Walle de Ghelcke, Denis Waelbroeck, Frédéric Louis, Pablo Ibáñez Colomo, Julien De Beys and Julie Bousin, 'Selectivity, Economic Advantage, Distortion of Competition and Effect on Trade' in Jacques Derenne and Massimo Merola (eds), *Economic Analysis of State Aid Rules. Contributions and Limits* (Berlin: GCLC-Lexxion, 2007) 129.

[49] See de Cecco (n 43) 126–27.

[50] David Renders (ed), *Les subventions* (Brussels: Larcier, 2011) 139; de Cecco (n 43) 98.

[51] de Cecco (n 43) 122.

[52] ibid, 113.

[53] Erika M Szyszczak, *The Regulation of the State in Competitive Markets in the EU* (Oxford: Hart Publishing, 2007) 185–93.

is not altered in favour of inefficient undertakings'.[54] Thus, the application of the notion of selectivity in the second scenario does not depend on a 'fairness test' but rather on an 'efficiency test', which is not concerned with the effects of aids on competitors.

The same happens in the third scenario, which covers those 'forms of public intervention combining a commercial element with a strong regulatory element', the main example being the assistance granted to providers of services of general economic interest.[55] The concept of selectivity depends, within this 'hybrid context', on the four-prong test coined by the Court in the seminal *Altmark* case.[56] This test basically seeks to ensure transparency and proportionality in the financial arrangements concluded with public services providers, but the fourth condition incorporates into the test an efficiency dimension by providing that:

> [W]here [the recipient] is not chosen pursuant to a public procurement procedure which would allow for the selection of the tenderer capable of providing those services at the least cost to the community, the level of compensation needed must be determined on the basis of an analysis of the costs which a typical undertaking, well run and adequately provided with means ... to be able to meet the necessary public service requirements.[57]

The preceding analysis suggests that the effects of State aids on competitors are central to the operation of the notion of selectivity when applied to regulatory measures. Although it does not look squarely at the effects of aids on competitors, this seems to be one of the main concerns that inform the discrimination test applied in that scenario. It should be noted, however, that this is only part of the picture. First, the test applied to assess the selectivity of measures adopted by the state as market participant or in the 'hybrid context' represented by services of general economic interest relies more heavily on efficiency considerations. As a result, the interest of competitors is completely overshadowed. Furthermore, the analysis so far has focused on the first stage of State aid analysis. Even in those cases where the effects of State aids on competitors bring a measure within the definition of aid, the final outcome will depend on the application of the exemptions, which is the issue addressed next.

3. The Administration of the Exemptions

The finding that a measure falls within the definition of aid triggers the general prohibition laid down by Article 107(1) TFEU. This means that the measure in question may not be implemented unless it meets one of the exemptions foreseen by Article 107(2) and (3) TFEU. As noted earlier, Article 107(2) TFEU defines

54 de Cecco (n 43) 121–22.

55 ibid, 117.

56 Case C-280/00 *Altmark Trans GmbH and Regierungspräsidium Magdeburg v Bundersverwaltungsgericht* [2003] ECR I-7747, paras 89–93.

57 ibid, para 93.

three mandatory but narrow exemptions (aid to individual consumers, aid for natural disasters and aid for the reunification of Germany), which are very rarely invoked.[58] This is the reason why the following paragraphs focus on Article 107(3) TFEU, which lists the exemptions that are at stake in most of the cases.

The exemptions listed in Article 107(3) TFEU leave ample space to depart from the general prohibition of Article 107(1) TFEU. This is because the conditions that justify a departure from the prohibition reflect economic and non-economic considerations alike. State aids may thus be deemed compatible where they contribute to the economic development of certain sectors or areas[59] but also, for instance, where they promote culture and heritage conservation.[60] This is in stark contrast with internal market rules, which foreclose the possibility to justify an obstacle to free movement on the basis of economic considerations.[61] It also contrasts with antitrust, 'in that [most Article 107(3) TFEU headings] can be ascribed to economic policy considerations, though—in contrast to competition policy—they are not based on economic efficiency or on consumer welfare'.[62]

The open texture of the exemptions defined by Article 107(3) TFEU stretches their breadth even further. Indeed, the vagueness of notions such as 'promote', 'facilitate', 'furthering' or 'common interest' means that their application is 'pre-programmed only in a very limited sense'.[63] The case law has coined some principles that bind the Commission in the application of Article 107(3) TFEU—such as the requirement for the Commission to administer the exemptions from a Community-wide perspective[64] or the principle of 'compensatory justification',[65] which requires that the aid be *necessary* to accomplish one of the goals of that provision[66]—but these principles are quite general and constrain the Commission only in a very loose way.

On the other hand, the operation of Article 107(3) TFEU constitutes a textbook example of classic discretion, in that the finding that a measure satisfies its conditions empowers but does not oblige the Commission to grant an exemption.[67] In order to get an idea of the principles that govern the administration of the exemptions, it is therefore necessary to go beyond the text of that provision and to look at the practice of the Commission. This endeavour is facilitated by the

[58] Bacon (n 37) 15.

[59] Article 107(3)(a) and (d) TFEU.

[60] Article 107(3)(e) TFEU.

[61] de Cecco (n 43) 50.

[62] ibid, 52.

[63] Marc Schweda, 'Compatibility of State Aid Pursuant to Article 87(3) EC' in Martin Heidenhain (ed), *European State Aid Law* (Munich: Verlag CH Beck, 2010) 153.

[64] Case 730/79 *Philip Morris Holland BV v Commission* [1980] ECR 2671, para 24.

[65] Stephen Martin and Andrew C Evans, 'Socially Acceptable Distortion of Competition: Community Policy on State Aid' (1991) 16 *European Law Review* 79, 90.

[66] Case 730/79 *Philip Morris Holland BV v Commission* [1980] ECR 2671, para 26. See also: Kamiel Mortelmans, 'The Compensatory Justification Criterion in the Practice of the Commission in Decisions on State Aids' (1984) 21 *Common Market Law Review* 405.

[67] It is, literally, a 'textbook' example: see Paul P Craig, *EU Administrative Law*, 2nd edn (Oxford: Oxford University Press, 2012) 430.

process of juridification undergone by State aid policy, which has resulted in the codification of the Commission's criteria to apply Article 107(3) TFEU in a miscellaneous collection of soft-law instruments that take the form of communications, frameworks or guidelines. This shift towards a 'rule-based system'[68] has reduced the margin of manoeuvre of the Commission itself and, as a corollary, the room available to authorise State aids in derogation from the general prohibition of Article 107(1) TFEU.[69] There are two aspects of this phenomenon that are particularly noteworthy for the purposes of this chapter.

The first aspect is the contraction of the panoply of reasons on the basis of which State aids may be authorised. The soft-law instruments adopted in this field are binding for the Commission itself, in the sense that they temper or even eliminate the discretionary character of the decision to authorise State aid plans that serve the objectives and meet any other requirement defined in these instruments.[70] Yet, in principle, they do not foreclose the possibility of authorising other plans, on the basis of an outright application of Article 107(3) TFEU. This will rarely be the case, however, because of the comprehensive aspiration of the superstructure of rules created by the Commission and, more importantly perhaps, because of the 'steering effect' associated with the 'information value' of these instruments, which shape the way in which Member States design their State aid policies in the first place.[71]

It follows that, in practice, the shift to a 'rule-based system' narrows down the exemptions defined by Article 107(3) TFEU. In this sense, the modern approach to this provision is characterised by a strong emphasis on efficiency as the chief reason to depart from the general prohibition of State aid, the idea being that the main justification for subsidies and subsidies-like measures is their contribution to correcting 'market failures' and thereby to 'improving the functioning of markets and enhancing European competitiveness'.[72] This is linked not only to the types of objectives that are deemed acceptable for State aid, which still include social policy objectives like the protection of the environment[73] or the promotion of underdeveloped regions,[74] but rather to the adoption of the 'balancing test' as a

[68] Francis Rawlinson, 'The Role of Policy Frameworks, Codes, and Guidelines in the Control of State Aid' in Ian Harden (ed), *State Aid: Community Law and Policy* (Cologne: Bundesanzeiger Verlagsgesellschaft, 1993) 53.

[69] See the historical account of Rawlinson, ibid, 53–55. See also Michelle Cini, 'The Soft Law Approach: Commission Rule-Making in the EU's State Aid Regime' (2001) 8 *Journal of European Public Policy* 192, 198–201; Michael Blauberger, 'Of "Good" and "Bad" Subsidies: European State Aid Control through Soft and Hard Law' (2009) 32 *West European Politics* 719, 726–29.

[70] Case C-351/98 *Spain v Commission* [2002] ECR I-8031, para 53.

[71] Herwig CH Hofmann, 'Administrative Governance in State Aid Policy' in Herwig CH Hofmann and Alexander H Türk (eds), *EU Administrative Governance* (Cheltenham: Edward Elgar, 2006) 196.

[72] 'State Aid Action Plan. Less and better targeted state aid: a roadmap for state aid reform 2005–2009' COM (2005) 107 final, para 10. See also 'Communication from the Commission to the European Parliament, the Council, the European Economic and Social Committee and the Committee of the Regions on EU State Aid Modernisation (SAM)' COM (2012) 209 final, para 12.

[73] 'Communication from the Commission—Guidelines on State aid for environmental protection and energy 2014–2020' OJ C200, 28.6.2014, p 1.

[74] 'Guidelines on regional State aid for 2014–2020' OJ C209, 23.7.2013, p 1.

method designed to ensure that all the exemptions are administered in a way that minimises their impact in terms of efficiency.

Indeed, the balancing test is one of the main components of the modern approach to Article 107(3) TFEU, which aspires to be informed by a 'refined economic approach'.[75] It was hinted at in the State Aid Action Plan (SAAP)[76] and then articulated by the then chief-economist of DG COMP in an academic paper,[77] before being endorsed by then Competition Commissioner Kroes and adopted by the Commission itself in its own practice and guidelines.[78] The test is supposed to be applicable across the board, irrespective of the nature of the justification put forward in support of the measure in question,[79] and its ultimate goal is to ensure that the impact of State aids on competition and trade is as limited as possible.[80]

The balancing test follows three steps.[81] The first step scrutinises the objective of the State aid, so as to ensure that it addresses 'a market failure or another objective of common interest'. The second step introduces a proportionality-like requirement, since it seeks to ensure that the measure is appropriate (ie, that there are not other better instruments to achieve the objective, in line with the idea that State aids are always a second-best option), that it has an 'incentive effect' (ie, that it is likely to 'change the behaviour of firms' as a precondition to be effective) and that the level of aid is kept to the minimum necessary to achieve its objectives. Finally, the last step considers the overall effects of the aid on competition and trade, with the aim of ensuring that the distortions that it generates are 'sufficiently limited, so that the overall balance is positive'.

Thus, the last step seeks to ensure that the side-effects brought about by otherwise legitimate State aids are kept to a minimum. The point to note is that this includes the effects of State aids on competitors, because the test is based on a broad welfare policy standard (the so-called 'social welfare standard') that takes account of consumer but also producer surplus.[82] This may come as a surprise to the reader familiar with modern antitrust—given its emphasis on the idea of protecting competition rather than competitors—but it can be justified given the different object of both disciplines. The reason why antitrust law is not concerned with business practices that harm competitors is because this is seen as the natural by-product of the competitive process, the idea being that there is an inherently destructive dimension to the quest for efficiency. From this perspective, there is nothing wrong with the fact that the actions of certain firms push competitors

[75] 'State Aid Action Plan' (n 72) para 18.

[76] ibid, para 11.

[77] Friederiszick, Röller and Verouden (n 4).

[78] Lorenzo Coppi, 'The Role of Economics in State Aid Analysis and the Balancing Test' in Erika Szyszczack (ed), *Research Handbook on European State Aid Law* (Cheltenham: Edward Elgar, 2011) 65.

[79] 'State Aid Action Plan' (n 72) para 11.

[80] ibid, para 22.

[81] Friederiszick, Röller and Verouden, (n 4) 165. See also: Communication on State Aid Modernisation (n 72) para 63.

[82] Phedon Nicolaides and Ioana Eleonora Rusu, 'The Binary Nature of the Economics of State Aid' (2010) 37 *Legal Issues of Economic Integration* 25, 30.

out of the market. It is at least questionable, however, whether the same rationale can justify harm to competitors when it is the result of actions taken by the state, rather than the result of spontaneous business practices.

While theoretically justifiable, the problem with this approach is that it renders the administration of the test an extremely difficult task. Not in vain, the main criticism raised by the test is that its actual operation involves no balancing, because 'quantification of the effects of aid is neither easy in theory, nor attempted in practice so far'.[83] This is the reason why it is not possible to specify the relative weight attached to the different considerations that are relevant at this stage of the analysis and, in particular, the weight attached to the potentially harmful effects of State aids on competitors.

It is nevertheless possible to take out certain ideas from this analysis. The first idea is that the administration of the exemptions of Article 107(3) TFEU is not completely deaf to the interest of competitors. The balancing test ensures that the negative effects of State aids are as limited as possible and this includes their potentially harmful effects on competitors. It follows that the impact of State aids on competitors has some relevance from the viewpoint of the theory of harm that informs the operation of Article 107(3) TFEU and hence, more generally, the application of the substantive rules on State aid.

The second idea is that the exemptions of Article 107(3) TFEU are nevertheless *not* administered *in the interest of* competitors. The claim that State aid law is concerned with fairness and with the protection of the level playing field may have some merit if one looks at the application of the general prohibition of Article 107(1) TFEU, but it clearly loses strength when the focus shifts to the second stage of the analysis. The compatibility of State aids depends at that stage on their potential to remedy a market failure or to contribute to an objective of common interest, which means that the benchmark used to administer the exemptions prioritises other considerations (namely, efficiency or the various socio-redistributive concerns hidden under the notion of objective of common interest) over the interest of competitors. The practical difficulties associated with the balancing test make it difficult to specify the relative weight assigned to these considerations, but there is no doubt that they can and do often override the interest of competitors.

4. Competitors and the Operation of the Rules on State Aid

The analysis carried out in this section shows that there is a *partial but imperfect alignment* between the interest of competitors in shielding their market position from the potentially distortionary effects of State aids and the public interest served by the rules on State aid. There is a *partial alignment* because the rules on State aid depart from a broad prohibition that limits the capacity of governments to adopt selective measures of financial assistance to firms. As a general rule, the

[83] ibid, 38.

application of Article 107(1) TFEU depends on a discrimination test that brings within the prohibition any measure that has an uneven impact across undertakings, sectors or regions. On its face, this 'selectivity' test does not look at the impact of State measures on the relative position of market operators. However, the test is broad enough to catch almost any measure that has a disparate impact on its beneficiaries and their competitors. Also, and albeit of secondary importance, the impact of State aids on competitors is in principle one of the factors that are to be considered at the second stage of the analysis, in order to decide whether any exemption is applicable.

The alignment is *imperfect*, however, and this for two reasons. First, the selectivity test adopts a different facet when applied to measures of State intervention in the market or to financial arrangements related to the provision of services of general economic interest. The tests applied in each of these scenarios take efficiency considerations on board, which means that this type of measure can escape the prohibition despite its potentially negative impact on competitors. Secondly, the prohibition of State aids is subject to a long list of exemptions. The administration of these exemptions has been transformed from a purely discretionary exercise into a structured, effects-based analysis that leaves ample space for the implementation of State aids that redress a market failure or that contribute—efficiently—to another objective of common interest. There is some discussion (both on a descriptive and normative levels) with regard to the relative weight assigned to these efficiency and socio-redistributive values in the administration of the exemptions, as opposed to other factors that include the distortionary effects caused by State aids on competitors. It is clear, however, that these considerations take precedence over the interest of competitors at the second stage of the analysis.

Conclusion

This chapter has considered the relevance that the theory of harm that informs the substantive rules on State aid assigns to the potentially negative effects of subsidies and subsidies-like measures on competitors. The first part of the chapter has shown that none of the theories that compete to explain the normative rationale of the system of State aid control rely on the need to protect competitors against the distortionary effects of State aid as their main motif. The second part of the chapter has further shown that this is not the main concern that fuels the operation of the rules on State aid, although it is certainly one of the factors that determines their application. This is the reason why the last part of the chapter has developed the claim that there is a certain but imperfect alignment between the interest of competitors and the public interest served by the rules on State aid. The next chapter explores the implications of this claim when it comes to defining the role of competitors in the enforcement of State aid law.

2

The Institutional Design of the System of State Aid Control

Introduction

The previous chapter looked at the treatment afforded to competitors by the substantive rules on State aid. The focus now shifts from the *substantive* to the *institutional* dimension of the system of State aid control, the aim of this chapter being to analyse the position reserved to competitors within that system.

The main conclusion to be drawn from the previous chapter is that there is a certain but imperfect alignment between the interest of competitors and the public interest served by the rules on State aid. The existence of this overlap implies that competitors can be thought of as the *beneficiaries of State aid regulation* (not to be confused with the beneficiaries of State aid themselves): they may not be the only nor the main reason why the EU is equipped with this set of rules, but they nevertheless derive some profit from their strict application.[1] This is because, in their eyes, the rules on State aid appear as a potential weapon to fight the distortionary effects caused by subsidies and the rest of subsidies-like measures covered by the notion of State aid.

The question that arises is how receptive the system of State aid control should be to the attempts of competitors to trigger or to steer the enforcement of its rules. This question touches upon the two issues identified in the Introduction to the book: it is as much about defining the permeability of the system of State aid control to the input of competitors (access) as it is about deciding the responsiveness of the system to their demands (leverage). The first part of this chapter shows that the answer to this question is contingent upon the role assigned to competitors in the enforcement of State aid law, which depends, in turn, on the relative weight attached to the two possible rationales for the involvement of competitors in State aid procedures: the 'instrumental' and the 'legal protection' rationales.

The second part of the chapter investigates the role assigned to competitors within the institutional design of the system of State aid control. More precisely,

[1] On regulatory beneficiaries in general, see Nina A Mendelson, 'Guidance Documents and Regulatory Beneficiaries' (2006) 31 *Administrative and Regulatory Law News* 8 and 'Regulatory Beneficiaries and Informal Agency Policymaking' (2007) 92 *Cornell Law Review* 397.

it looks at the institutional arrangements that support the 'public' and the 'private enforcement' sides of the system of State aid control and shows that they are seemingly informed by a strongly instrumental conception of the role of individuals (in general) and competitors (in particular) within that system. This analysis is only meant to set the background for the inquiry carried out in the rest of the book, which will revisit and test this characterisation.

I. The Involvement of Competitors in the Enforcement of State Aid Law

1. Harm to Competitors and State Aid Law

As noted earlier, the main conclusion to be drawn from the previous chapter is that there is a certain but imperfect alignment between the *interest of competitors* in shielding their market position from the potentially harmful effects of State aids and the *public interest* protected by the rules on State aid. The existence of a certain alignment is obvious, because the rules on State aid rest on a broad prohibition that limits the capacity of governments to adopt selective measures of financial assistance to firms that may have distortionary effects on the relative market position of different operators. The alignment is only *imperfect*, however, because the interest of competitors is not the ultimate litmus test to determine the compatibility of State aids. There are indeed other considerations that come into play and that may displace the concerns raised by the potentially harmful effects of State aids on competitors.

The existence of this mismatch means that the involvement of competitors in the administration of the rules on State aid cannot simply be grounded on a straightforward scope-of-protection type of argument (ie, the rules on State aid are designed to protect competitors, so competitors should be able to enforce these rules in order to prevent or redress the harmful effects of State aids). Indeed, the analysis carried out in the previous chapter reveals that the web of interests at stake is more complex than that. This is not to say that competitors should be kept completely apart from the administration of the rules on State aid, but this observation calls for a more elaborate theory to justify their involvement in State aid procedures.

This theory can be one of two types. The first theory justifies the involvement of competitors in the enforcement of State aid law on the basis of a utilitarian argument that focuses on the added value that they bring to the performance of the system of State aid control (instrumental rationale). The second theory is, so to speak, a narrow version of the scope-of-protection argument discarded above, which grounds their involvement on the need to afford competitors some form of legal protection within the area of overlap (legal protection rationale).[2] Besides

[2] See Hans P Nehl, '2013 Reform of EU State Aid Procedures: How to Exacerbate the Imbalance between Efficiency and Individual Protection' (2014) 13 *European State Aid Law Quarterly* 235, 236,

spelling out both theories, the following two sections explore the different implications that each of them has when it comes to defining the role of competitors in the enforcement of State aid law.

2. The Instrumental Rationale

(a) *Outline of the Theory*

The instrumental rationale to involve competitors in the supervision and enforcement of State aid law surfaces very often in the policy documents of the EU institutions.[3] It sees the involvement of competitors as a means to ensuring the effectiveness of the system of State aid control. The idea of effectiveness is a concern that runs across all areas of EU law,[4] mainly as a result of the perception that the EU suffers from an 'institutional deficit' that results from the 'mismatch between [its] highly complex and differentiated regulatory tasks and the available administrative instruments'.[5] Yet it is of particular concern in the area of State aid, where the risk of under-enforcement is taken to be particularly high given the Commission's limited investigatory powers.[6] This is the reason why the instrumental rationale is especially salient in this domain.

(b) *The Added Value of Competitors for the Enforcement of State Aid Law*

The following paragraphs reconstruct the instrumental theory that informs most of the policy documents of the Commission and (as the second part of the chapter will make clear) much of the case law. This theory is premised on the assumption that the enforcement of State aid law is the Commission's responsibility, which is why it justifies the involvement of competitors on the basis of their potential

who speaks of an 'instrumental' and a 'protective' rationale. On the broader theme of the 'instrumental' and 'essentialist' rationales for the participation of affected parties in administrative procedures, see Eric Barbier De La Serre, 'Procedural Justice in the European Community Case-Law Concerning the Rights of the Defence: Essentialist and Instrumental Trends' (2006) 12 *European Public Law* 225.

[3] See, eg, 'State Aid Action Plan. Less and better targeted state aid: a roadmap for state aid reform 2005–2009' COM (2005) 107 final, para 55: ('Private litigation in front of national courts could therefore provide increased discipline in the field of state aid') and Council Regulation (EU) No 734/2013 of 22 July 2013 amending Regulation (EC) No 659/1999 laying down detailed rules for the application of Article 93 of the EC Treaty (OJ L204, 31.7.2013, p 15) recital 13 ('complaints are an essential source of information for detecting infringements of the Union rules on State aid').

[4] Francis Snyder, 'The Effectiveness of European Community Law: Institutions, Processes, Tools and Techniques' (1993) 56 *The Modern Law Review* 19, 22.

[5] Giandomenico Majone, 'The Credibility Crisis of Community Regulation' (2000) 38 *Journal of Common Market Studies* 273, 279.

[6] Eric Morgan de Rivery, Sabine Thibault-Liger and Jacques Derenne, 'Procedure' in Jacques Derenne and Massimo Merola (eds), *Economic Analysis of State Aid Rules. Contributions and Limits* (Berlin: GCLC-Lexxion, 2007) 179; Themistoklis K Giannakopoulos, *Safeguarding Companies' Rights in Competition and Anti-dumping/Anti-subsidies Proceedings*, 2nd edn (Aalphen aan den Rijn: Wolters Kluwer, 2011) 471.

contribution to the three main tasks faced by the Commission in this field: the task of spotting State aids (*detection*), the task of telling apart good and bad State aid (*assessment*) and the task of ensuring compliance with its decisions (*follow-on enforcement*). The latter falls outside the scope of the book, which is concerned—as noted in the Introduction—with the role of competitors in the process that leads to the adoption of State aid decisions in the first place. For the sake of completeness, however, it will also be briefly discussed.

Detection

The system of State aid control relies on the obligation of Member States to notify in advance any plan to put into effect measures that meet the definition of aid of Article 107(1) TFEU. It is thus informed by a strong prophylactic concern that seeks to block State aids before they even see the light of day. Consequently, it further relies on a broad definition of State aid, which guarantees that all *potentially* harmful State aids go through the preventive control of the Commission. Thus, the first challenge raised by this system is to ensure that Member States actually comply with the standstill and notification obligations of Article 108(3) TFEU. In the jargon of the discipline, State aids granted in breach of these obligations are referred to as 'illegal' or 'unlawful'.

The detection of unlawful State aid is a very demanding task from the perspective of the Commission. The volume of State aid granted every year within the EU stays high. This is arguably the result of the political choices made at the national level, but also of the very design of the system, which relies on a sweeping definition of aid that brings within the purview of the Commission a broad and diverse set of measures.[7] The underlying policy choice in favour of over-inclusion at the jurisdictional stage, with the possibility of narrowing down the prohibition at the compatibility stage, adds to the complexity of the task. Furthermore, Member States often omit for strategic reasons the notification of those measures that are most likely to distort competition and trade.[8]

Faced with such an important challenge, and given its relatively 'weak administrative capacity',[9] it should come as no surprise that the Commission seeks to enlist competitors in the fulfilment of this task.[10] Their position as regulatory beneficiaries of the rules on State aid means that they have, a priori, the right

[7] See, eg, Luca Rubini, *The Definition of State Aid: WTO and EC Law in Comparative Perspective* (Oxford: Oxford University Press, 2010) 151–80.

[8] Michel Nolin, 'Les droits des plaignants dans le secteur des aides d'État', in Association Europénne des Avocats (ed), *Un rôle pour la défense dans les procédures communautaires de concurrence: Congrès organisé les 25 et 26 novembre* (Brussels: Bruylant, 1997) 142.

[9] R Daniel Kelemen, 'Adversarial Legalism and Administrative Law in the European Union', in Susan Rose-Ackerman and Peter L Lindseth (eds), *Comparative Administrative Law* (Cheltenham: Edward Elgar, 2010) 610.

[10] See, eg, 'Notice on the enforcement of State aid law by national courts' OJ C85, 9.4.2009, p 1) para 5, referring to the fact that the private enforcement of Article 108(3) TFEU before national courts can 'contribute to stronger overall State aid discipline'.

incentives to discharge this function. On the other hand, their participation on the same markets as State aid beneficiaries means that they are well placed to spot the advantages that they receive. The instrumental case for the involvement of competitors in the task of detecting aids is therefore based on the idea that they can act as 'watchdogs'[11] and bring to the attention of the Commission State aid measures that would otherwise go unnoticed.

Assessment

The second challenge raised by the system of State aid control is to assess the potential effects of the measures under scrutiny in order to tell apart good and bad State aid, something which can only be done on the basis of a reliable and complete information record. In this sense, excessive reliance on the information submitted by the concerned Member State may prove problematic, for it may be deficient—quantity- or quality-wise—or even biased,—given the presumed interest of the Member State in having its State aid plans approved.[12] It may also more simply reflect the capture of the Member State by the State aid beneficiary.[13]

The instrumental approach suggests that bringing competitors closer to the administration of the rules on State aid may avoid this problem. The argument applies to other actors as well. However, competitors occupy a distinctive position amongst the different sources of information to which the Commission may turn in its attempt to capture the widespread effects that State aids may produce. Again, this is because their participation in the same markets as State aid beneficiaries means that they are likely to have first-hand information on the likely effects of the measure under scrutiny[14] and because their interest in a strict enforcement of the prohibition of State aid means that they can help to compensate the pro-compatibility bias of the concerned Member State.

The involvement of competitors at this stage is all the more necessary given the hopes that modern State aid law places on the 'refined economic approach'.[15] The previous chapter noted some of the practical problems raised by the type of economic analysis required by this approach. There is no doubt, however, that this analysis can only be done on the basis of a substantial amount of complex information on the structure and functioning of the markets that are liable to be affected by the measures under scrutiny—that is, on the assumption that the new approach is to be taken seriously. 'Having the Commission communicate

[11] Christian Nordberg, 'Judicial Remedies for Private Parties under the State Aid Procedure' (1997) 24 *Legal Issues of Economic Integration* 35, 36.

[12] Herwig CH Hofmann and Alessandro Morini, 'Judicial Review of Commission Decisions in State Aid', in Erika Szyszczack (ed), *Research Handbook on European State Aid Law* (Cheltenham: Edward Elgar, 2011) 355.

[13] Hans W Friederiszick, Lars-Hendrik Röller and Vincent Verouden, 'European State Aid Control', in Paolo Buccirossi (ed), *Handbook of Antitrust Economics* (Boston, MA: MIT Press, 2007) 644.

[14] Morgan de Rivery, Thibault-Liger and Derenne (n 6) 188.

[15] 'State Aid Action Plan' (n 3) para 18.

with national administrations in order to obtain the necessary information about companies seems an awkward task to ask for'.[16] The recent reform of the Procedural Regulation in order to improve the 'market information tools' of the Commission confirms the value of market actors (in general) and competitors (in particular) in the assessment of State aid.[17]

Follow-on Enforcement

The last challenge raised by the system of State aid control is to ensure that the concerned Member State complies with the final decision of the Commission. This challenge arises when the outcome of the procedure is either a negative or a recovery decision. It also arises in connection with conditional decisions (which are positive decisions subject to conditions), but these can be assimilated to negative or recovery decisions from the perspective of the supervisory activity that they require. Negative and recovery decisions raise, however, different challenges.

In a way, negative decisions bring the Commission back to square one in the three-stage process described here. By definition, negative decisions are handed down before the implementation of the measure that they seek to block, which means that they basically impose an obligation of a negative kind—the obligation to refrain from implementing the State aid plan that the Commission deems incompatible with the common market. Consequently, the follow-up of negative decisions is very similar to the supervision required by the standstill clause of Article 108(3) TFEU, in the sense that the main challenge that they raise is also one of detection. It follows that competitors may at this stage perform the same monitoring function that makes them potentially useful allies at the detection stage, that is, in their role as watchdogs.

The challenge raised by recovery decisions is of a different kind. This is because of the type of obligation that they impose, which is the positive obligation to recover the amount of aid unlawfully granted. Compliance therefore requires an active commitment on the side of the Member State. Yet, due to the high economic and political stakes involved in State aids,[18] Member States may often prove unwilling to collaborate. This problem is further aggravated by the fact that the recovery task usually falls on the same authority that granted the aid in the first place.[19] Thus, the instrumental case for the involvement of competitors in the

[16] Andreas Bartosch, 'Editorial. The End of Procedural Reform: The Commission, the Member States and Third Parties = the Teams That Lose' (2008) 7 *European State Aid Law Quarterly* 1, 1.

[17] Council Regulation (EU) No 734/2013 of 22 July 2013 amending Regulation (EC) No 659/1999 laying down detailed rules for the application of Article 93 of the EC Treaty (OJ L204, 31.7.2013, p 15), which is informed, according to its 2nd recital, by the objective of 'ensur[ing] that the Commission has the power, for the purposes of enforcing the State aid rules, to request all necessary market information from any Member State, undertaking or association or undertakings'.

[18] Thomas Köster, 'Recovery of Unlawful State Aid' in Michael Sánchez Rydelski (ed), *The EC State Aid Regime: Distortive Effects of State Aid on Competition and Trade* (London: Cameron May, 2006) 654.

[19] Nuria Mariñas, 'Enforcement of State Aid Recovery Decisions' (2005) *Competition Policy Newsletter* 17, 18.

follow-on enforcement of State aid decisions is based on their capacity to perform two functions. The first function is to sound the alarm in the event that recovery is not effective and timely. The second function is to provide the impetus to launch the process of recovery in those cases where national authorities show no initiative to implement the order of the Commission. They may additionally smooth the actual process of recovery, assisting the national authorities in charge of identifying the undertakings that benefitted from the aid that is to be repaid[20] and helping to curb their resistance.[21] More generally, their main contribution to the effectiveness of the process of recovery may be the leverage that they provide to national authorities in controversial cases where the political and economic stakes are high and national public opinion leans against repayment.

(c) *The Instrumental Rationale and the Role of Competitors in the Enforcement of State Aid Law*

The preceding analysis confirms the strength of the instrumental case for the involvement of competitors in the enforcement of State aid law. It shows that competitors may be a valuable source of information for the Commission (at the detection and assessment stages) and, additionally, provide the necessary impetus (at the follow-on enforcement stage) to minimise the 'gap between rule prescription and enforcement'[22] caused by the Commission's limited powers and resources. In this sense, the instrumental theory rests on a conception of competitors as the Commission's 'allies' in the task of ensuring compliance with the rules on State aid.[23]

The point to note is that this conception has an impact on the role assigned to competitors in the enforcement of State aid law. This is because their role is dependent on the very needs of the Commission that justify their involvement in the first place. From the perspective of access, this means that their input may not always be necessary. From the perspective of leverage, it means that their input is only valuable to the extent that it serves the enforcement agenda of the Commission, which is why this theory does not draw any line of accountability from the Commission to competitors themselves. In sum, the instrumental rationale sees competitors as the Commission's allies, which is why it gives them some access but no leverage.

[20] Michela Angeli, 'The European Commission's "New Policy" on State Aid Control: Some Reflections on Public and Private Enforcement of Recovery of Illegal Aid' (2009) 30 *European Competition Law Review* 533, 536.

[21] Köster (n 18) 661.

[22] I borrow the phrase from Jody Freeman, 'The Private Role in Public Governance' (2000) 75 *New York University Law Review* 543, 662.

[23] Neelie Kroes, 'Reforming Europe's State Aid Regime: An Action Plan for Change' (Speech delivered at the University of Leiden Joint Conference on European State Aid Reform, 14.06.2005) 7.

3. The Legal Protection Rationale

(a) *Outline of the Theory*

The legal protection rationale rests on the idea that competitors deserve some form of protection against the distortionary effects of State aids: the impact of State aids on competitors may not be the touchstone of their compatibility, but competitors should nevertheless be able to stir the application of the rules on State aid to prevent or redress the harmful effects of subsidies (and subsidy-like measures) that happen to be in contravention of these rules.[24] This idea informs, in a more or less explicit way, the most critical branch of the legal scholarship on the position of third parties in State aid procedures.[25]

A priori, the legal protection rationale warrants a greater involvement of competitors in the enforcement of State aid law than its instrumental counterpart. This is because it focuses on the needs of competitors rather than on those of the Commission. Thus, it demands more both in terms of access (insofar as it is no longer conditional on the needs of the Commission) and, especially, of leverage (insofar as it introduces an element of accountability that is absent in the other theory). However, this theory faces a major problem when it comes to defining with some precision the position reserved to competitors within State aid procedures.

(b) *The Risks of Over-enforcement and Abuse*

The problem stems from the mismatch identified earlier between the interest of competitors and the public interest served by the rules on State aid. The existence of this mismatch raises two risks, which complicate the definition of the role of competitors within State aid procedures. If we think of the system of State aid control as a form of 'meta-regulation' (ie, as a mechanism that subjects to a systematic review the use by Member States of a particular set of regulatory instruments),[26] the first risk concerns the *meta-regulatory* layer (ie, the application of the rules on State aid) whereas the second risk concerns the *regulatory* layer (ie, the national ramifications of the application of the rules on State aid).

[24] For a similar argument in relation to the traditional reluctance of common law to let competitors have standing to complain about the injury caused by 'increased competition of someone else made possible by an allegedly illegal government act or subsidy', see Eric Stein and G. Joseph Vining, 'Citizen Access to Judicial Review of Administrative Action in a Transnational and Federal Context' (1976) 70 *The American Journal of International Law* 219, 230: 'There was never a self-evident logic to a position that because a business had no right to be free of competition it had no right to be free of illegally created competition'.

[25] See, eg, Nehl (n 2).

[26] Herwig CH Hofmann, 'State Aid Review in a Multi-level System' in Herwig CH Hofmann and Claire Micheau (eds), *State Aid Law of the European Union* (Oxford: Oxford University Press, 2016) 5. Note that the concept of meta-regulation normally refers to the rules that frame self-regulation. See, eg, Carol Harlow and Richard Rawlings, *Law and Administration*, 3rd edn (Cambridge: Cambridge University Press, 2009) 289. On the concept of meta-regulation as used here, see Bronwen M Morgan, 'The Economization of Politics: Meta-Regulation as a Form of Nonjudicial Legality' (2003) *Social and Legal Studies* 489, 490.

The first risk stems from the fact that the input brought by competitors is not necessarily a reliable signal when it comes to applying the rules on State aid. This is because it may be in their interest to over-enforce the rules on State aid, ie, to go beyond the optimum level of enforcement, as determined by the normative goals of the discipline itself. A similar problem exists in the field of antitrust and merger control, where competitors fare high in 'enforcement capability' but present some problems of 'incentive compatibility'[27] as a result of the risk of their using antitrust to protect themselves against more efficient firms.[28] In the field of State aid, it implies that competitors may push for over-inclusion in the application of the notion of aid (Article 107(1) TFEU) and for under-inclusion in the application of the exemptions (Article 107(3) TFEU).

This problem is heightened by the second risk, which does not concern the application of the rules on State aid themselves, but rather the ramifications of their application on the national regulatory processes on which they impinge. Indeed, the multi-level character of State aid control requires us to think of the effects that the empowerment of competitors at the meta-regulatory level has over the regulatory layer itself.[29] In other words, the challenge is to determine how much leverage competitors should have over the administration of the rules on State aid, but also how much leverage this gives them, indirectly, over the regulatory policies of Member States.

In order to fully grasp the problem, it is necessary to depart from the observation that State aid law and State aid control constitute a politically very sensitive form of regulatory review. This observation is grounded on at least three reasons. The first reason is that State aid control is a 'functional, cross-sectoral competence'[30] that empowers the Commission to control the use that Member States make of a particular set of regulatory tools irrespective of the policy that they serve, which means that it encroaches on a broad range of regulatory policies in most of which Member States have 'independent decision making powers'.[31] The second reason is that some of these policies are 'activities which, by their nature or prevalence, may be instrumental to success or failure of governments',[32] including, most notably,

[27] Joseph F. Brodley, 'Antitrust Standing in Private Merger Cases: Reconciling Private Incentives and Public Enforcement Goals' (1995) 94 *Michigan Law Review* 1, 26 and 28.

[28] William J. Baumol and Janusz A. Ordover, 'Use of Antitrust to Subvert Competition' (1985) 28 *Journal of Law and Economics* 247.

[29] See Herwig CH Hofmann, 'Private Participation in the Control of Public Spending—the Multi-Level Subsidy Regimes' (2003) *III Discussion Paper No 12*, who looks at the role of private parties at the different levels.

[30] Armin Von Bogdandy and Jürgen Bast, 'The Federal Order of Competences', in Armin Von Bogdandy and Jürgen Bast (eds), *Principles of European Constitutional Law*, 2nd edn (Oxford: Hart Publishing/Verlag CH Beck, 2009) 294.

[31] Jürgen Schwarze, *European Administrative Law*, Rev 1st edn (Luxembourg: Office for Official Publications of the European Communities/Sweet & Maxwell, 2006) 383. See also: Von Bogdandy and Bast (n 30) 294.

[32] Schwarze (n 31) 383–84. See, eg, Case C-63/14 *Commission v France* [2015], ECLI:EU:C:2015:458, para 51–52, where one of the arguments raised by France to resist recovery of State aid in favour of the

their industrial policy.[33] Finally, the third reason is that 'due to increasing harmonisation of law in the single market, states aids are often the last possibility of MS to enter into competition with each other, for example for investments'.[34]

It is precisely as a result of its political sensitivity that the power enjoyed by the Commission as the 'main actor in the control of State aid policies', with hardly any intervention from the Council and the European Parliament, is in itself a somewhat controversial issue.[35] The point to note is that this controversy also affects, more intensely perhaps, the capacity to interfere with national regulatory processes that competitors may acquire through the system of State aid control. The risk is to see competitors use the leverage provided to them by State aid procedures to promote their own agenda and, more generally, 'to influence national policy debates in their own favour'.[36]

(c) *The Legal Protection Theory and the Role of Competitors in the Enforcement of State Aid Law*

The preceding analysis shows that the legal protection rationale is not exempt from difficulties, as a result of the risks of over-enforcement and abuse opened up by the mismatch between the interest of competitors and the public interest served by the rules on State aid. Still, the legal protection rationale is more demanding than its instrumental counterpart, in that it dissociates the involvement of competitors from the needs of the Commission and in that it introduces an element of accountability to ensure that the Commission pays heed to the concerns voiced by competitors. In sum, the legal protection rationale sees competitors as agents of accountability rather than as the Commission's allies, which is why it gives them access and leverage.

4. The Instrumental and the Legal Protection Paradigms

The foregoing analysis has distilled the two main theories that may justify the involvement of competitors in the enforcement of State aid law: the instrumental rationale (which grounds their involvement on the added value that they bring

companies running the ferry service between Corsica and mainland France was 'the social unrest which might arise following the announcement of the compulsory liquidation of the [beneficiary], unrest which might undermine public order and also cause a break in the territorial continuity between Corsica with the mainland'. The Court rejected the argument.

[33] Michelle Cini, 'The Soft Law Approach: Commission Rule-Making in the EU's State Aid Regime' (2001) 8 *Journal of European Public Policy* 192, 198. See also: Mitchell P Smith, 'Integration in Small Steps: The European Commission and Member State Aid to Industry' (1996) 19 *West European Politics* 563, 572 ('The politics of State aid are explosive because in most cases jobs are at stake').

[34] Herwig CH Hofmann, 'Administrative Governance in State Aid Policy', in Herwig CH Hofmann and Alexander H Türk (eds), *EU Administrative Governance* (Cheltenham: Edward Elgar, 2006) 186.

[35] ibid, 202.

[36] ibid, 188.

to the Commission in its task of ensuring compliance with the rules on State aid) and the legal protection rationale (which grounds it instead on the need to afford competitors some protection against irregular State aid). The main idea to draw from the previous analysis is that both theories differ in the role that they assign to competitors in the enforcement of State aid law: they both demand that competitors be given some voice in State aid procedures (access), but they diverge on how much influence this should give them over the Commission's decisions (leverage). The instrumental rationale is only concerned with access, whereas the legal protection rationale additionally calls for leverage.

Granted, this analysis suffers from at least two limitations. First, the instrumental and the legal protection rationales are not as distant from each other as implied here. On the one hand, the recognition of the type of procedural guarantees required by the legal protection theory probably has an impact on the incentives of affected parties to collaborate with the Commission,[37] which means that a procedural regime that took the instrumental theory to its ultimate consequences (making access totally dependent on the Commission's will and withholding any type of procedural guarantee) would in all likelihood discourage participation and hence be self-defeating. On the other hand, it is possible to devise a broader instrumental theory than the one expounded here, one that focuses on the needs of the 'system' of State aid control as something higher than the needs of the Commission. From this perspective, one of the functions of competitors would be to spot the Commission's errors, which would require the articulation of the type of accountability mechanisms that have been associated here with the legal protection theory.[38]

Secondly, none of these theories is very useful when it comes to defining the exact status of competitors within State aid procedures. In its purest version, the instrumental theory is not concerned with the articulation of procedural guarantees in favour of affected parties, but this may be problematic (as was just noted) as a result of its impact on the incentives of affected parties to collaborate. As far as the legal protection theory is concerned, the risks of over-enforcement and abuse demand that the powers of competitors be somehow capped, but this is a rather general and nuanced prescription from which it is difficult to infer precise implications. The upshot is that, from a policy perspective, the challenge is to find a balance between these considerations.

However valid, these limitations should not overshadow the function of the two theories expounded in this section. The point to note is that each theory assigns a different role to competitors in the enforcement of State aid law (Commission's allies vs accountability agents) and that this has an impact on their procedural status

[37] Nehl (n 2) 238.

[38] See, eg, Sara Poli, 'The Legal Standing of Private Parties in the Area of States After the Appeal in *Commission v. Kronoply/Kronotex*' (2012) 39 *Legal Issues of Economic Integration* 357, 378: 'It is in the interest of the correct application of state aid law that private applicants are able to challenge the legality of the Commission decision at an early stage'.

(mere access vs access and leverage). Thus, the previous analysis provides two different paradigms to examine the way in which the system of State aid control operates in practice. The rest of the chapter shows that, in its inception at least, the system of State aid control seems to be informed by a strongly instrumental conception of the role of interested parties, which grants some voice but almost no leverage to competitors. The rest of the book will revisit and test this idea.

II. The Bilateral Design of the System of State Aid Control

1. Overview of the System of State Aid Control

The previous section has spelled out the two alternative theories on the basis of which the involvement of competitors in the enforcement of State aid law can be grounded, showing that each of them assigns to competitors a different role and, as a corollary, a different status within the system of State aid control. This section demonstrates that the institutional design of the system of State aid control is informed, in its inception at least, by an instrumental conception of the role of individuals (in general) and competitors (in particular). This claim is grounded on the observation of three aspects of the system of State aid control: the structure of State aid procedures, the mechanisms of accountability to which the Commission is subject in the administration of the rules on State aid, and the peculiar relationship between private and public enforcement in this field.

The system of State aid control can be defined as the sum of the different institutional arrangements designed to ensure that the general prohibition of Article 107(1) TFEU is respected and that, accordingly, no State aids reach the market outside the exceptional circumstances foreseen in Article 107(2) and (3) TFEU. It rests on two pillars: the central monitoring function assured by the Commission ('public enforcement') and the more discreet but nevertheless important role performed by national courts ('private enforcement').

The system of State aid control revolves around the central role of the Commission as the main institution in charge of monitoring the conformity of national subsidies and subsidies-like measures with the rules on State aid. In order to discharge this function, the Commission exercises various forms of supervision. There is, on the one hand, the control of new State aids, which is supposed to take place through the ex ante authorisation procedure laid down by Article 108(2) and (3) TFEU ('Procedure regarding notified aid'),[39] but also through the reactive procedure developed by the practice of the Commission and the case law of the

[39] Articles 2 to 11 of Council Regulation (EU) 2015/1589 of 13 July 2015 laying down detailed rules for the application of Article 108 of the Treaty on the Functioning of the European Union (OJ L248, 24.9.2015, p 9) ['Procedural Regulation' or 'PR'].

European Courts for unlawful State aid ('Procedure regarding unlawful aid').[40] There is, on the other hand, the permanent supervision of existing aid, which is governed by Article 108(1) and (2) TFEU ('Procedure regarding misuse of aid'[41] and 'Procedure regarding existing aid schemes').[42]

The system of State aid control also relies on national courts to ensure compliance with its rules. The judicial recognition of the direct effect of the last sentence of Article 108(3) TFEU[43] and the decentralisation process boosted by the Commission and the EU legislator[44] have involved national courts in the task of supervising and enforcing the rules on State aid. These developments add a second layer of supervision to the system of State aid control and simultaneously create an alternative channel for the enforcement of its provisions. Because the operation of this layer depends for the most part on the impulse of private litigants, this is what the book refers to as 'private enforcement' in contrast to the 'public enforcement' assured by the Commission itself.[45] The private enforcement of State aid law is discussed in more depth in Chapter 3; however, it is also considered here as one of the pieces that make up the system of State aid control.

2. The Bilateral Design of State Aid Procedures

This section unpacks the idea of bilaterality, which surfaces so often, in one way or another, to describe the structure of State aid procedures. The analysis focuses on the 'Procedure regarding notified aid' (hereinafter referred to, more simply, as the 'State aid procedure'), which is the main tool at the disposal of the Commission in order to ensure compliance with the rules on State aid, given its aspiration to filter all State aids granted within the EU. Yet most of the observations made here are also valid, *mutatis mutandis*, for the other procedures.

The bilateral characterisation of the State aid procedure is mostly based on the structure of its first phase, which is truly a 'dialogue exclusive to the Commission and the Member State concerned'.[46] However, the following paragraphs make the case that the idea of bilaterality captures quite well the overall structure of the procedure.

[40] Articles 12–16 PR.
[41] Article 20 PR.
[42] Articles 21–23 PR.
[43] Case 6/64 *Flaminio Costa v Enel* [1964] ECR 585, p 596 and Case 120/73 *Gebrüder Lorenz GmbH v Germany* [1973] ECR 1471, para 8.
[44] This process is analysed in more depth in the next chapter.
[45] Note that the concept of private enforcement in the field of State aid cannot be defined so narrowly as in antitrust. In the latter context, Assimakis P Komninos, *EC Private Antitrust Enforcement: Decentralised Application of EC Competition Law by National Courts* (Oxford: Hart Publishing, 2008) 2 defines 'private enforcement' as 'litigation, in which private parties advance independent civil claims or counterclaims based on EC competition provisions'. State aid actions are normally brought against the granting public authorities, which is why the term is used in this context with a broader meaning.
[46] Opinion of Advocate General Mengozzi in Case C-487/06 P *British Aggregates Association v Commission* [2008] ECR I-10515, para 74.

The bilateral character of the State aid procedure manifests itself at the very initiation stage, since 'It is apparent from the actual structure of Article [108(3) TFEU], which establishes a bilateral relationship between the Commission and the Member State, that only the Member States are under the obligation to notify'.[47] But it manifests itself more generally throughout the first phase of the procedure (ie, the so-called 'preliminary examination phase'), which is characterised by the total absence of information and participation rights for any actor other than the Member State concerned, including State aid beneficiaries and their competitors. Indeed, the Commission is under no obligation to publicise in any way the reception of a State aid notification[48] and the case law has explicitly recognised that, even in those cases where interested parties become aware of the existence of the procedure, they enjoy no right to submit comments before the opening of the second phase.[49]

Although in a less intense way, the bilateral character of the State aid procedure also manifests itself at the second stage of the procedure. The so-called 'formal investigation procedure' is structured around the consultation phase provided for by Article 108(2) TFEU, which requires the Commission to give notice to the 'parties concerned' and to invite them to submit comments whenever it contemplates the possibility of blocking a national plan to grant State aid. The insertion into the procedure of this participatory step certainly mitigates its purely bilateral character, since it gives voice to the full panoply of stakeholders that fall under the concept of 'parties concerned'.[50]

Yet it would be wrong to conclude that the existence of this participatory step fundamentally alters the bilateral character of the procedure. For one thing, the Commission is only bound to go through the consultation phase in certain cases, namely as a precondition to adopt a negative decision. More importantly, the consultation phase appears to be designed as an information-gathering device at the service of the Commission rather than as an opportunity for interested parties to defend their interests. As the Court famously put it in an early case, 'the sole aim of [the communication foreseen in current Article 108(2) TFEU] is to obtain from persons concerned all information required for the guidance of the Commission

[47] Joined Cases C-442/03 P and C-471/03 P *P&O European Ferries and Diputación Foral de Vizcaya v Commission* [2006] ECR I-4883, para 103.

[48] Joined Cases 91 and 127/83 *Heineken Brouwerijen BV v Inspecteur der Vennootschapsbelasting, Amsterdam and Utrecht* [1984] ECR 3435, para 15. See also Michael Niejahr and Tibor Scharf, 'Third Parties in State Aid Control: More Than Just a Source of Information?', in *EC State Aid Law/Le droit des aides d'État dans la CE. Liber Amicorum Francisco Santaolalla Gadea* (The Hague: Kluwer Law International, 2008) 347–68, 354; Ute Zinsmeister, 'The Role of Third Parties in State Aid Cases' in Association Europénne des Avocats (ed), *Un rôle pour la défense dans les procédures communautaires de concurrence: Congrès organisé les 25 et 26 novembre 1996* (Brussels: Bruylant, 1997) 257–66, 261.

[49] Case C-225/91 *Matra SA v Commission* [1993] ECR I-3203, para 51-4.

[50] The ECJ defined the notion of 'parties concerned' for the purposes of Article 108(2) TFEU in Case 323/82 *Intermills v Commission* [1984] ECR 3809, para 16. The definition was later codified in Article 1(h) PR, which refers instead to 'interested parties'. More on this in Chapter 5.

with regard to its future action'.[51] This is arguably the reason why it takes the form of a broad consultation phase, where the information rights of individuals are restricted to the publication of a general notice in the Official Journal of the European Union[52] and where their only participatory entitlement is a one-shot opportunity to submit comments, with no dialogue or follow-up contacts with the Commission.[53]

Finally, the decision that puts an end to the procedure further adds to its bilateral character, given the rule that it shall always be formally addressed to the concerned Member State. This should come as no surprise in the normal scenario, where the decision responds to the notification submitted by the Member State concerned in compliance with the standstill clause of Article 108(3) TFEU. But the same rule applies where the procedure is launched in response to a complaint (no decision addressed to the complainant) and where it results in an order to recover unlawful State aid from its beneficiaries (no decision addressed to the beneficiaries themselves).[54] By preventing individuals from relying on the more permissive rules of standing that apply to a decision's formal addressees, this rule limits the possibilities for third parties to seek judicial review and to affect, in this way, the final outcome of the procedure.

The preceding analysis shows that the bilateral design of the State aid procedure assigns a purely instrumental role to interested parties, including competitors. This is because it excludes them altogether from the first phase of the procedure. And because it only involves them in the second phase, when the Commission needs to rely on the information that they hold, so as to fully appreciate the likely effects of the measures under scrutiny.

3. The Elite Model of Accountability

The bilateral characterisation of the State aid procedure and the purely instrumental role that it assigns to interested parties is reminiscent of the general infringement procedure, with which it is often compared.[55] The design of the general infringement procedure is a widely studied topic in the literature on EU administrative

[51] See Case 70/72 *Commission v Germany* [1973] ECR 813, para 19. See, more recently, Case C-276/03 P *Scott SA v Commission* [2005] ECR I-8437, para 34: 'It is true that case-law has granted the beneficiary of aid certain procedural rights. However, those rights are designed to enable the beneficiary to provide information to the Commission and to put forward its arguments, but do not confer on it the status of a party to the procedure'.

[52] Case 323/82 *Intermills v Commission* [1984] ECR 3809, para 17; Joined Cases C-74 and 75/00 *Falck SpA and Acciaierie di Bolzano SpA v Commission* [2002] ECT I-7862, para 80.

[53] Case C-367/95 P *Commission v Sytraval and Brink's France SARL* [1998] ECR I-1719, para, 59; Joined Cases C-74 and 75/00 *Falck SpA and Acciaierie di Bolzano SpA v Commission* [2002] ECT I-7862, paras 80 and 82.

[54] Case C-367/95 P *Commission v Sytraval and Brink's France SARL* [1998] ECR I-1719, para 44.

[55] Case C-301/87 *France v Commission (Boussac)* [1990] ECR I-307, para 23: 'This [procedure] is in fact no more than a variant of the action for a declaration of failure to fulfil Treaty obligations, specifically adapted to the special problems which State aid poses for competition within the common

law.[56] One of the main difficulties raised by its design is, precisely, the totally peripheral role that it assigns to individuals, as mere 'information sources' for the Commission and, as such, devoid of any procedural rights.[57] This issue became especially topical in the early 2000s, as a result of the increasing value attached to participation and transparency by modern EU administrative law[58] and of the growing demands for complainants to have a greater voice, with the support of the European Ombudsman.[59] It is beyond the scope of this chapter to provide a complete account of the debates prompted by these developments, but some of the insights produced in that context are certainly useful for the present inquiry.

Indeed, one of the main contributions to that debate was the influential article by Harlow and Rawlings on 'Accountability and Law Enforcement', where they develop the distinction—hinted at in a previous article[60]—between an 'elite' model of accountability,—based on intergovernmental mechanisms of enforcement and on the delegation to an agent of the power to hold public actors accountable,—and a 'participatory' model of accountability—where the performance of public actors 'is evaluated by those affected by their actions'.[61] Their main claim is that the general infringement procedure responds to the first model and that 'the mere fact that the levers of the centralised infringement procedure are not available to "any citizen on a basis of equality" does not make it any less a public accountability system'.[62]

Harlow and Rawlings show that the general infringement procedure was conceived as a diplomatic device intended to facilitate the negotiation of compliance

market'. See also Alberto J Gil Ibáñez, 'Exceptions to Article 226: Alternative Administrative Procedures and the Pursuit of Member States' (2000) 6 *European Law Journal* 148, 150; Loïc Azoulai, *Les garanties procédurales en droit communautaire: recherches sur la procédure et le bon gouvernement* (Ph.D. Thesis) (Florence: European University Institute, 2000) 279.

[56] See, eg, Andrew C Evans, 'The Enforcement Procedure of Article 169 EEC: Commission Discretion' (1979) 4 *European Law Review* 442; Roberto Mastroianni, 'The Enforcement Procedure under Article 169 of the EC Treaty and the Powers of the European Commission: Quis Custodiet Custodes?' (1995) 1 *European Public Law* 535; Alfonso Mattera Ricigliano, 'La procédure de manquement et la protection des droits des citoyens et des opérateurs lésés' (1995) 3 *Revue du Marché Unique Européen* 123; Richard Rawlings, 'Engaged Elites: Citizen Action and Institutional Attitudes in Commission Enforcement' (2000) 6 *European Law Journal* 4; Ian Harden, 'What Future for the Centralized Enforcement of Community Law?' (2002) 55 *Current Legal Problems* 495; Carol Harlow and Richard Rawlings, 'Accountability and Law Enforcement: The Centralised EU Infringement Procedure' (2006) 31 *European Law Review* 447; Luca Prete and Ben Smulders, 'The Coming of Age of Infringement Proceedings' (2010) 47 *Common Market Law Review* 9. More generally, see Alberto J Gil Ibáñez, *The Administrative Supervision and Enforcement of EC Law: Powers, Procedures and Limits* (Oxford: Hart Publishing, 1999) and Melanie K Smith, *Centralised Enforcement, Legitimacy and Good Governance in the EU* (London: Routledge, 2010).

[57] See, eg, Case 247/87 *Star Fruit Company SA v Commission* [1989] ECR 291, paras 11–14, and the following discussion.

[58] See Francesca Bignami, 'Three Generations of Participation Rights before the European Commission' (2004) 68 *Law and Contemporary Problems* 61. This issue is discussed in more depth in Chapter 5.

[59] See, eg, cases discussed in Harlow and Rawlings (n 56) 465–71.

[60] Rawlings (n 56) 8–13.

[61] Harlow and Rawlings (n 56) 447–48.

[62] ibid, 449.

through a bargaining process between the Commission and Member States. This is the reason why the procedure is divided into two phases, the first of which only involves the Commission and the targeted Member State, with no participation or information rights for any other stakeholder. It is also the reason why the possibility of subjecting the dispute to the Court of Justice constitutes a weapon of last resort that is only used by the Commission in a small fraction of cases.[63]

This logic also explains the totally peripheral role assigned to individuals within the general infringement procedure, which responds to the need to prevent the Commission from being accountable to individuals.[64] This is because the elite model of accountability expects the Commission to lead Member States into compliance through a process of institutional bargaining that would be inoperative if the Commission were not given enough leeway. From this perspective, the intrusion of individuals represents a threat, for it 'generate[s] a subsidiary dimension of accountability of the Commission' itself.[65] The model does not exclude their access altogether, but it does assign to them a purely instrumental role. Provided they do not threaten the tight control of the Commission over the procedure, 'the mere fact that complaints are made by individuals does not bring them squarely within a participatory model of accountability'.[66]

The theoretical work of Harlow and Rawlings and their analysis of the general infringement procedure are useful to the present inquiry in two different ways. First of all, their analysis of the general infringement procedure as a paradigmatic example of the elite model of accountability casts light on the design of the State aid control procedure itself. The division of this procedure into two phases, the first of which is completely shielded from the input and the control of third parties, lays down the grounds for the type of inter-institutional bargaining that is typical of the first phase of the general infringement procedure.[67] Granted, the provision for the consultation of interested parties in the second phase of the procedure somewhat mitigates its strictly elite character, but this seems to be a type of individual involvement that the elite model can easily accommodate, for—as noted earlier—it does not threaten the tight control that the Commission holds over the procedure.

The work of Harlow and Rawlings is also useful on a different level. It makes it possible to contextualise the bilateral design of the State aid control procedure as a manifestation of a common model in EU administrative law. This model requires that individuals be kept at arm's length to avoid their interfering with the process of inter-institutional bargaining between the Commission and Member States. From this perspective, then, the purely instrumental role assigned to competitors

[63] ibid, 454–56.
[64] ibid, 449 and 474.
[65] ibid, 449.
[66] ibid.
[67] Raj S Chari and Francesco Cavotorta, 'Economic Actors' Political Activity in "Overlap Issues": Privatisation and EU State Aid Control' (2002) 25 *West European Politics* 119, 132: 'informal contacts' between Commission and MS are 'commonplace' after notification.

and other individuals by the original design of State aid procedures is anything but an anomaly. The second part of the book will revisit the bilateral characterisation of the State aid procedure and test the extent to which the role actually played by competitors responds to the instrumental logic suggested by this model. The analysis carried out here suggests that any move in the direction of a more protective logic is a departure from a model that transcends the boundaries of State aid governance.

4. The Subordination of Private to Public Enforcement

The two previous sections have unpacked the idea of bilaterality that dominates the legal discourse in the field of State aid procedures, connecting it to the 'elite model of accountability' that is so common in EU administrative law and showing that it is informed by a strongly instrumental conception of the role assigned to individuals (in general) and competitors (in particular) within that setting. The preceding analysis suggests that the State aid procedure is likely to provide competitors with some opportunities to voice their concerns (access) but with little chance of affecting their outcome (leverage).

This is because, in general, the bilateral/elite model that presides over the State aid procedure expects individuals to ventilate their claims through other routes. There are basically two options. The first option is to take an indirect route and to try to get to the Commission through its only valid interlocutors, namely Member States. Competitors may thus try to seek the support of their national governments, pushing them to defend their interests in the Commission's arena, yet this strategy depends heavily on the political will of national governments.[68] It may thus be the best strategy for national champions wishing to challenge foreign State aid programmes but is otherwise unlikely to yield good results.

The other option is to resort to national courts. In the framework of their scrutiny of the general infringement procedure, Harlow and Rawlings note that the Court firmly closed this avenue to individuals but 'move[d] decisively to open the legal process to private parties, … setting in place a separate route through national courts', which could 'then be used to justify retention of the elite model'.[69] The underlying idea seems to be that, in order to shield the Commission from the pressures coming from individuals, the elite model of accountability diverts their claims through national courts. Thus, the elite model of accountability limits the involvement of individuals in the 'public enforcement' procedures of the Commission and encourages them to protect their interests instead through 'private enforcement' channels.[70]

[68] Gerrit Schohe, 'Le statut du plaignant' in Mariana Dony and Catherine Smits (eds), *Aides d'État* (Brussels: Éditions de l'Université de Bruxelles, 2005) 215.

[69] Harlow and Rawlings (n 56) 474.

[70] See also Roland Bieber and Francesco Maiani, 'Enhancing Centralized Enforcement of EU Law: Pandora's Toolbox?' (2014) 51 *Common Market Law Review* 1057.

The diversion of individuals through national courts connects with a broader phenomenon in EU law, namely the process of 'constitutionalisation'[71] whereby some of the obligations assumed by Member States in the economic sphere have been transformed into individual, actionable rights that national courts are supposed to protect.[72] The origins of this process go back to the seminal *van Gend en Loos* case, where the ECJ laid down the foundations of the doctrine of direct effect.[73] It would later transcend the realm of economic regulation[74] and become one of the most characteristic legal developments in the emergence of the EU legal order.[75] It is yet another manifestation of the strongly decentralised design that presides over the EU legal order, with a small administration at the centre of the system and where the default rule is that the implementation and application of EU law corresponds to Member States.

There is a strong instrumental logic behind this phenomenon, insofar as 'direct effect creates a large number of "private attorneys general", who operate not only to vindicate their own private rights, but also to ensure that the norms of the [Treaty] are correctly applied by the Member States'.[76] The Court was well aware of this idea in its own ruling in *van Gend en Loos*, where it noted that 'The vigilance of individuals concerned to protect their rights amounts to an effective supervision in addition to the supervision entrusted by Articles [258 and 259 TFEU] to the diligence of the Commission and of the Member States'.[77] The recognition of rights in favour of individuals and the promotion of private litigation can thus be seen as a supplement to the relatively 'weak administrative capacity' of the EU,[78] which may in turn be the reason why the Court of Justice 'has never accepted that this Treaty-based scheme of institutional enforcement should be the only, nor even the principal means by which Community law may be enforced'.[79]

The point to note here is that the instrumental logic that informs the doctrine of direct effect and the private enforcement of EU law is 'even more pronounced' in the field of State aid.[80] This is because the prohibition of State aid of Article

[71] Joseph Weiler, 'The Transformation of Europe' (1991) 100 *Yale Law Journal* 2403, 2413–14.

[72] Bruno de Witte, 'Direct Effect, Primacy and the Nature of the Legal Order' in Paul P Craig and Gráinne De Búrca (eds), *The Evolution of EU Law* (Oxford: Oxford University Press, 2011) 358.

[73] Case 26/62 NV *Algemene Transport- en Expeditie Onderneming van Gend en Loos v Netherlands Inland Revenue Administration* [1963] ECR 3, p 12.

[74] Norbert Reich, '"System Der Subjectiven Öffentlichen Rechte" in the Union: A European Constitution for Citizens of Bits and Pieces' in *Collected Courses of the Academy of European Law*, VI (The Hague: Kluwer Law International/Martinus Nijhoff Publishers/Academy of European Law, EUI, 1995).

[75] Paul P Craig, 'Once Upon a Time in the West: Direct Effect and the Federalization of EEC Law' (1992) 12 *Oxford Journal of Legal Studies* 453, 453.

[76] ibid, 455.

[77] Case 26/62 NV *Algemene Transport- en Expeditie Onderneming van Gend en Loos v Netherlands Inland Revenue Administration* [1963] ECR 3, p 13.

[78] Kelemen (n 9) 610.

[79] Adam Tomkins, 'Of Institutions and Individuals: The Enforcement of EC Law' in Paul P Craig and Richard Rawlings (eds), *Law and Administration in Europe—Essays in Honour of Carol Harlow* (Oxford: Oxford University Press, 2003) 276.

[80] Francesco de Cecco, *State Aid and the European Economic Constitution* (Oxford: Hart Publishing, 2013) 45.

107(1) TFEU lacks direct effect.[81] The private enforcement of State aid law therefore rests on the last sentence of Article 108(3) TFEU, which provides that '[the Member State concerned shall not put its proposed measures into effect until [the State aid procedure] has resulted in a final decision'. It is thus

> in fact triggered by a breach by a Member State of its procedural duties under the Treaty rules on State aid, duties which, rather than laying the ground for a substantive right not to be harmed by State aid, give rise to an interest vis-a-vis the prescribed administrative procedure.[82]

Thus, the recognition of direct effect to the last sentence of Article 108(3) TFEU adds to rather than detracts from the purely instrumental role that the system of State aid control seems to assign to competitors. This provision affords competitors with a tool to fight unlawful State aid before national courts, but its content is such that, in so doing, competitors also act at the service of the Commission. This is because Article 108(3) TFEU does not create an alternative channel to challenge the compatibility of State aid, an issue that falls within the exclusive competence of the Commission.[83] It creates instead an additional layer of supervision to ensure that all State aids are detected and channelled through the hands of the Commission. The upshot is that competitors also act as the Commission's allies when they invoke the direct effect of Article 108(3) TFEU before national courts.[84]

Conclusion

There are two ideas to take out from this chapter. The first idea is that the observation that competitors are not at the core of the theory of harm that informs the rules on State aid does not imply that they should be barred from participating in its enforcement. Their involvement in the administration of the rules on State aid can indeed be grounded on two different theories, each of which provides us with a different paradigm to analyse and assess the position of competitors in State aid procedures. There is, on the one hand, the instrumental paradigm, which sees competitors as the Commission's allies and demands that they be given access but no leverage. There is, on the other hand, the legal protection paradigm, which recognises the need to provide competitors with the tools to protect themselves against irregular State aids and demands that they be given access but also leverage.

81 Case 77/72 *Capolongo v Azienda Agricola Maya* [1973] ECR 611, para 6.
82 de Cecco (n 80) 45–46.
83 Case 78/76 *Steinike & Weinlig v Germany* [1977] ECR 595, para 9.
84 In the same sense, see Jean-Paul Kepenne and Kilian Gross, 'Quelques considérations sur le rôle du juge national dans le contrôle des aides d'État', in *EC State Aid Law/Le droit des aides d'etat dans la CE. Liber Amicorum Francisco Santaolalla Gadea* (The Hague: Kluwer Law International, 2008) 408: 'dans le domaine des aides, le juge national agit davantage comme "bras armé" de la Commission que comme défenseur des droits des particuliers'.

The second idea developed in this chapter is that the institutional design of the system of State aid control responds to the instrumental paradigm, in that it provides competitors with various forms of access but with little chance of leverage. This observation is grounded on an analysis of the 'public' and the 'private enforcement' pillars of the system of State aid control. The 'public enforcement' pillar responds to a 'bilateral model' that is reminiscent of the 'elite model' that presides over the general infringement procedure, which is well known for the totally peripheral role that it assigns to individuals. On the other hand, the 'private enforcement' pillar rests on the direct effect of the standstill clause of Article 108(3) TFEU, rather than on the substantive prohibition of Article 107(1) TFEU. This means, in turn, that the possibility to invoke State aid law before national courts only affords competitors an opportunity to ensure that all State aids go through the preventive control of the Commission—and not an alternative channel for the enforcement of the rules on State aid.

As noted earlier, this characterisation of the system of State aid control is only meant to provide the framework for the analysis carried out in the rest of the book. The three chapters that make up the second part of the book will revisit the bilateral characterisation of the 'public enforcement' side of the system of State aid control, looking at the actual opportunities of leverage afforded to competitors by the three possibilities of access that they have in that context: the possibility to lodge complaints, the possibility to participate in the consultation phase of Article 108(2) TFEU and the possibility to seek judicial review of State aid decisions. Before that, however, the next chapter will look more closely at the opportunities afforded to competitors by the private enforcement of State aid law.

3

The Private Enforcement of State Aid Law

Introduction[1]

The previous chapter has revealed that the institutional design of the system of State aid control seems to be based on an instrumental conception of the role of competitors in the enforcement of its rules. This conception manifests itself in the idea of 'bilaterality' that informs the public enforcement side of the system of State aid control, but also in the very foundations of its private enforcement side. This is because the private enforcement of State aid law revolves around the direct effect of the standstill clause of Article 108(3) TFEU rather than of the substantive prohibition of Article 107(1) TFEU. This chapter investigates the significance that this peculiar arrangement has from the viewpoint of competitors.

The chapter unfolds as follows. Section I reviews the decentralisation process undergone by the system of antitrust enforcement in the early 2000s, which is a constant reference in the discussions on the private enforcement of State aid law. Sections II and III analyse the way in which the European Courts and the other EU institutions have favoured the private enforcement of State aid law. Section IV spells out the limitations of the machinery for private enforcement in the field of State aid. The main claim developed in that section is that none of the developments described in this chapter have fundamentally altered the subordination of private enforcement (and hence of national courts) to public enforcement (and hence to the Commission), which is the reason why the possibilities afforded to competitors by the former are necessarily limited if compared in comparison to other regulatory contexts such as antitrust.

I. The Private Enforcement of EU Antitrust Law

It is difficult to survey the mechanisms to challenge State aids available to competitors at the national level without discussing the process of decentralisation undergone

[1] A previous version of this chapter was published in Fernando Pastor-Merchante, 'La aplicación privada de la normativa sobre ayudas de Estado' 55 (2015) *Revista española de derecho europeo* 13.

by the system of antitrust supervision and enforcement in the early 2000s.[2] There is certainly a fundamental difference between State aid and antitrust law, as a result of their different objects, which are to police the regulatory policies of Member States—in the case of the former—and to discipline the market conduct of private firms—in the case of the latter. Yet there are two reasons why it is apposite to look at the channels for the decentralised enforcement of antitrust as a prelude to the analysis of the same issue in relation to State aids. The first reason is that the developments that have occurred in the field of antitrust have had an important influence over the State aid policy of the EU institutions. As the following paragraphs will make clear, there are important parallels between the approach followed by the EU institutions and scholarship with regard to the issue of decentralisation in both fields—which is probably due to the fact that both fields share a common epistemic and practising community. The second reason is methodological: the comparison will spotlight the differences between both sets of rules and hence the limitations faced by the decentralised enforcement of State aid law.

Prior to the adoption of Regulation 1/2003,[3] the enforcement of EU antitrust law presented some similarities with the system of State aid control. Granted, the supervision of the rules on antitrust was not subject to a general authorisation system like the one we find in State aid, because national courts and national competition authorities were empowered to apply current Article 101(1) TFEU. This meant that they could declare void any restrictive agreement falling within its scope, as foreseen in Article 101(2) TFEU. It also meant that they could order the compensation of any damage caused by its infringement, in accordance with the case law of the Court.[4] In principle, then, the old system of antitrust supervision was much more decentralised than the current system of State aid control.

In practice, however, the decentralised application of antitrust faced a major obstacle, which was the monopoly that the Commission had over the application of the exemptions laid down by Article 101(3) TFEU.[5] This monopoly had two implications. The first implication was that the parties to possibly anticompetitive agreements had an incentive to notify them to the Commission so as to check their legality before their conclusion. The second implication was that national courts and national competition authorities would lose their jurisdiction over a case as soon as the controversial agreement was notified to the Commission. They were thus prevented from applying Article 101 TFEU in full, which in turn reduced the incentives for competitors to enforce this provision before national courts.

[2] Malcom Ross, 'Decentralization, Effectiveness and Modernization: Contradictions in Terms?' in Andrea Biondi, Piet Eeckhout and James Flynn (eds), *The Law of State Aid in the European Union* (Oxford: Oxford University Press, 2004) 86.

[3] Council Regulation (EC) No 1/2003 of 16 December 2002 on the implementation of the rules on competition laid down in Articles 81 and 82 of the Treaty (OJ L1, 4.01.2003, p 1).

[4] Case C-453/99 *Courage v Crehan* [2001] ECR I-6297, para 26.

[5] Article 9(1) of Council Regulation (EEC) No 17 of 6 February 1962 First Regulation implementing Articles 85 and 86 of the Treaty (OJ 13, 21.02.1962, p 204) provided that 'Subject to review of its decision by the Court of Justice, the Commission shall have sole power to declare Article 85(1) inapplicable pursuant to Article 85(3) of the Treaty'.

The upshot is that the *actual* operation of the old system of antitrust looked quite similar to the centralised and ex ante type of control that is typical of State aid law.

The strong centralisation of the old antitrust system allowed the Commission to develop its own competition policy and to ensure its uniform application throughout the common market.[6] However, it also placed an important burden on the Commission, which was 'forced into a reactive posture, with its limited staff resources being diverted by agreements parties had chosen to notify, instead of being wholly focused on the proactive pursuit of its own enforcement agenda'.[7] The Commission took some initiatives to alleviate this problem, such as the adoption of block exemption regulations and the administrative practice of issuing comfort letters rather than formal decisions. However, the 'gigantic administrative bottleneck' caused by the flood of exemption requests submitted to the Commission came to be seen as a major threat for the effectiveness of the system.[8]

It is against this background that the Commission launched its decentralisation programme, with the publication in 1999 of the White Paper on Modernisation.[9] The objective was to articulate 'a more efficient and simpler system of control', 'so as to relieve companies from unnecessary bureaucracy, to allow the Commission to become more active in the pursuit of serious competition infringements and to increase and stimulate enforcement at national level'.[10] The main proposal made by the Commission was to put an end to the monopoly of the Commission over the application of the exemptions, which was perceived to be 'One of the causes of the Commission's difficulty in focusing its action on cases involving a real Community interest'.[11] The introduction of this 'directly applicable exception system' would follow three axes: 'the ending of the system of notification and authorisation, decentralised application of the competition rules, and intensified ex post control'.[12] This project resulted in the submission in 2000 of the proposal at the origin of Regulation 1/2003.[13]

The entry into force of Regulation 1/2003 completely transformed the administration of the rules on antitrust laid down by the Treaty. It basically put into effect the proposals made in the White Paper on modernisation, empowering national courts and national competition authorities to apply in full Article 101 TFEU. The abolition of the notification and authorisation mechanism relieved the Commission of the heavy administrative burden represented by the previous system. The

[6] Giorgio Monti, *EC Competition Law* (Cambridge: Cambridge University Press, 2007) 396.

[7] James S Venit, 'Brave New World: The Modernization and Decentralization of Enforcement under Articles 81 and 82 of the EC Treaty' (2003) 40 *Common Market Law Review* 545, 550.

[8] Damien Geradin, 'Competition between Rules and Rules of Competition: A Legal and Economic Analysis of the Proposed Modernization of the Enforcement of EC Competition Law' (2003) 9 *Columbia Journal of European Law* 1, 13.

[9] 'White Paper on the Modernisation of the Rules Implementing Articles 85 and 86 of the EC Treaty' COM (1999) 101 final.

[10] ibid, para 10.

[11] ibid, para 58.

[12] ibid, para 75.

[13] Proposal for a Council Regulation on the implementation of the rules on competition laid down in Articles 81 and 82 of the Treaty and amending Regulations (EEC) No 1017/68, (EEC) No 2988/74, (EEC) No 4056/86 and (EEC) No 3975/87 (COM (2000) 582 final).

Commission was still expected to watch over the operation of the system, but it would do so through a system of ex post rather than ex ante supervision. The new Regulation strengthened its fact-gathering and inspection powers to ensure that it would perform this task effectively.[14]

One of the goals of the reform was to promote private enforcement as a complement to the supervisory function exercised by the Commission. The idea was that, by putting an end to the 'procedural bifurcation of Article 81',[15] private actors would be more eager to take action before their national competition authorities and courts and, thus, to contribute to the enforcement of the rules on antitrust.[16]

More than 10 years after the adoption of Regulation 1/2003, it seems that the reform was partially successful. National competition authorities routinely apply EU antitrust rules, often at the request of affected market actors. However, as foreseen by some commentators,[17] private enforcement before national courts has not acquired the same importance that it has in other jurisdictions.[18] As Advocate General Mazak put it:

> While no de jure hierarchy has been established, at present the role of the Commission and national competition authorities is, in my view, of far greater importance than private actions for damages in ensuring compliance with Articles 101 and 102 TFEU. Indeed so reduced is the current role of private actions for damages in that regard that I would hesitate in overly using the term 'private enforcement'.[19]

This explains the recent efforts made by the Commission to stimulate the compensation of damages for antitrust violations,[20] which are based on the observation that 'most victims of infringements of EU competition rules in practice do not obtain compensation for the harm suffered'.[21]

[14] Articles 17 to 22 of Council Regulation (EC) No 1/2003 of 16 December 2002 on the implementation of the rules on competition laid down in Articles 81 and 82 of the Treaty (OJ L1, 04.01.2003, p 1).

[15] Venit (n 7) 548.

[16] White Paper on Modernisation (n 9) paras 25, 36–39 and 46. See also Recital 7 of Regulation 1/2003: 'National courts have an essential part to play in applying the Community competition rules. When deciding disputes between private individuals, they protect the subjective rights under Community law, for example by awarding damages to the victims of infringements. The role of the national courts here complements that of the competition authorities of the Member States. They should therefore be allowed to apply Articles 81 and 82 of the Treaty in full'.

[17] Venit (n 7) 570.

[18] Renato Nazzini and Ali Nikpay, 'Private Actions in EC Competition Law' (2008) 4 *Competition Policy International* 107, 108; Enrico Camilleri, 'A Decade of EU Antitrust Private Enforcement: Chronicle of a Failure Foretold?' (2013) 34 *European Competition Law Review* 531, 531.

[19] Opinion of Advocate General Mazák in Case C-360/09 *Pfleiderer AG v Bundeskartellamt* [2011] ECR I-5106, para 40.

[20] Directive 2014/104/EU of the European Parliament and of the Council of 26 November 2014 on certain rules governing actions for damages under national law for infringements of the competition law provisions of the Member States and of the European Union Text with EEA relevance (OJ L349, 5.12.2014, p 1).

[21] 'Proposal for a Directive of the European Parliament and of the Council on certain rules governing actions for damages under national law for infringements of the competition law provisions of the Member States and of the European Union' COM (2013) 404 final, 4. See also Camilleri (n 18) 531, and Nazzini and Nikpay (n 18) 108.

Whether 'the tide' is finally coming in for private enforcement of competition rules in Europe is open to question.[22] Some authors raise objections of principle to the very idea that there should be more private enforcement of the EU rules on antitrust.[23] The point to note, however, is that the push for the decentralisation of State aid enforcement was preceded by a similar movement in antitrust. This move was prompted by the concern that the old system of antitrust enforcement relied too much on the supervision of the Commission and too little on national courts and national competition authorities. The main element of the reform was the elimination of the procedural bifurcation that prevented any actor other than the Commission from applying in full the rules on antitrust. The reform was undoubtedly successful in liberating Commission resources that could be put to better use. It was also successful in involving national competition authorities in the task of supervising and enforcing the EU rules on antitrust. On the other hand, it may have been a necessary but insufficient step if the objective was to generate a high volume of private antitrust enforcement.

II. The Foundations for the Private Enforcement of State Aid Law

1. The Direct Effect of Article 108(3) TFEU

The system of State aid control confers a prominent position to the Commission, which is entrusted with the task of verifying ex ante the compatibility with the common market of all the new State aid plans designed by Member States. This prominence notwithstanding, the interpretation of the Treaty made by the Court leaves some space for the decentralised enforcement of some of its provisions. This section reviews the case law on the direct effect of the standstill clause laid down by Article 108(3) TFEU, which opens an avenue for competitors to challenge unlawful State aids before national courts.

The Court of Justice recognised for the first time the direct effect of this clause in its seminal *Costa v Enel* ruling, despite its not being in question in that case.[24] It was then confirmed in *Lorenz*, where the Court declared that 'the prohibition on implementation referred to in the last sentence of Article [108(3) TFEU] has a direct effect and gives rise to rights in favour of individuals, which national courts

[22] Roger Gamble, 'Whether Neap or Spring, the Tide Turns for Private Enforcement: The EU Proposal for a Directive on Damages Examined' (2013) 34 *European Competition Law Review* 611, 611.

[23] See, eg, Wouter PJ Wils, 'Should Private Antitrust Enforcement Be Encouraged in Europe?' (2003) 26 *World Competition* 473.

[24] Case 6/64 *Flaminio Costa v Enel* [1964] ECR 585, p 596: 'the States have entered into an obligation with the Community, which binds them as states but creates no individual rights except in the case of the final provision of article [108(3) TFEU], which is not in question in the present case'.

are bound to safeguard' and that 'the direct effect of the prohibition extends to all aid which has been implemented without being notified and, in the event of notification, operates during the preliminary period, and where the Commission sets in motion the contentious procedure, up to the final decision'.[25] By empowering individuals to invoke—and national courts to enforce—the standstill clause of Article 108(3) TFEU, *Lorenz* paved the way for the development of a system of private enforcement in the field of State aid.

In *Steinike & Weinlig*, decided only three years later, the Court would revisit this issue and tackle more squarely the role of national courts in the enforcement of State aid law. It held, first, that the assessment of the compatibility of State aids with the common market falls within the exclusive purview of the Commission,[26] which means that 'The parties concerned cannot ... challenge the compatibility of an aid with Community law before national courts or ask them to decide as to any compatibility'.[27] It further held that national courts 'may [however] have cause to interpret and apply the concept of aid contained in Article [107 TFEU] in order to determine whether State aid introduced without observance of the preliminary examination procedure provided for in Article [108(3) TFEU] ought to have been subject to this procedure'.[28]

The allocation of powers between the Commission and national courts in the enforcement of State aid law would thus be governed by two basic principles. The first principle holds that national courts have the power to enforce the standstill clause of Article 108(3) TFEU and that, in order to do so, they also have the power to interpret the definition of aid of Article 107(1) TFEU, for they would otherwise not be able to determine whether the measures complained of are actually subject to the standstill clause. However, the second principle holds that national courts have no power to enforce the prohibition embodied in Article 107(1) TFEU because the task of declaring the incompatibility of State aid with the common market is reserved to the Commission.[29] The upshot is that national courts are expected to confine their analysis to the *procedural* regularity of State aids and to refrain from assessing, additionally, their *substantive* regularity—that is, their compatibility with the common market.

Lorenz and *Steinike & Weinlig* set the bedrock for the development of a system of private enforcement in the field of State aid. In its subsequent case law, the Court has had occasion to define more precisely some of the features of this system. The point to note is that, in general, the Court has been eager to strengthen the role assigned to national courts in the enforcement of State aid law. The rest

[25] Case 120/73 *Gebrüder Lorenz GmbH v Germany* [1973] ECR 1471, para 8.
[26] Case 78/76 *Steinike & Weinlig v Germany* [1977] ECR 595, para 9.
[27] ibid, para 10.
[28] ibid, para 14.
[29] ibid, para 9; Case C-354/90 *Fédération Nationale du Commerce Extérieur des Produits Alimentaires (FNCEPA) and Syndicat National des Négociants et Transformateurs de Saumon v France* [1991] ECR I-5505, para 15; and Case C-39/94 *Syndicat Français de l'Express international (SFEI) v La Poste and others* [1996] ECRI I-3547, para 42.

of this section reviews two jurisprudential developments that back this claim. The first development is the case law on the remedies that national courts are supposed to grant in response to the infringement of Article 108(3) TFEU, which has favoured an extensive interpretation of the legal consequences attached to the breach of the standstill obligation. The second development is the case law on the allocation of powers between the Commission and national courts, which has underlined that their respective tasks are not only different but also independent of each other.

2. Remedies for Breach of the Standstill Clause

The rulings of the Court in *Lorenz* and *Steinike & Weinlig* associated national courts with the task of enforcing the rules on State aid. They did not specify, however, the remedies that they were expected to administer in the fulfilment of this task. The Court formulated the general rule in that regard in the *French Saumon* case, where it held that

> national courts must offer to individuals in a position to rely on such breach the certain prospect that all the necessary inferences will be drawn, in accordance with their national law, as regards the validity of measures giving effect to the aid, the recovery of financial support granted in disregard of that provision and possible interim measures.[30]

This formulation encapsulates the main ideas that run across the case law on this issue. First, the use of the verb 'must' conveys the idea that the imposition of the right remedies to redress the infringement of Article 108(3) TFEU is a duty rather than a prerogative for national courts.[31] Second, the reference to national law indicates that 'The appropriate consequential measures to be taken by the national courts are not in principle dictated by Community law but depend on the kinds of remedy available in domestic law';[32] and that they are to be adopted in accordance with the national rules on procedure, subject to the principles of equivalence and effectiveness.[33] Finally, the reference to the 'validity of the measures' signals that the role of national courts 'goes beyond that of a judge ruling on an application for interim relief',[34] which is why they may order the interim suspension of the

[30] Case C-354/90 *Fédération Nationale du Commerce Extérieur des Produits Alimentaires (FNCEPA) and Syndicat National des Négociants et Transformateurs de Saumon v France* [1991] ECR I-5505, para 12. See, more recently Case C-672/13 *OTP Bank Nyrt v Magyar Állam*, ECLI:EU:C:2015:185, para 69.

[31] Case C-39/94 *Syndicat Français de l'Express international (SFEI) v La Poste and others* [1996] ECRI I-3547, para 67.

[32] Opinion of Advocate General Jacobs in Case C-368/04 *Transalpine Ölleitung in Österreich GmbH and others v Finanzlandesdirektion für Tirol and others* [2006] ECR I-9957, para 61.

[33] Case C-368/04 *Transalpine Ölleitung in Österreich GmbH and Others v Finanzlandesdirektion für Tirol and others* [2006] ECR I-9957, para 45.

[34] Case C-39/94 *Syndicat Français de l'Express international (SFEI) v La Poste and others* [1996] ECRI I-3547, para 67.

unlawful aid, but also its full recovery[35] and the compensation of damage caused by its premature implementation.[36]

In developing these principles, the Court has embraced an extensive interpretation of the remedial powers of national courts. Indeed, it has stressed the non-exhaustive character of the remedial toolkit that appears most often in its judgments (suspension, recovery and damages), inviting national courts to explore other options. This is particularly salient in the cases related to fiscal State aids, where the Court has recognised, for instance, the possibility of suspending the collection of the charges used to finance unlawful State aid.[37] It is also evident in the cases that deal with the possibility of recovering the illegality interest in lieu of the full amount of the unlawful aid, where the latter is eventually declared compatible by the Commission.[38] The underlying idea, in all these cases, is that national courts should 'take any steps which appear necessary in the circumstances to nullify the effects of the breach'.[39]

Furthermore, the Court has repeatedly invited national courts to go beyond the restorative function with which they are entrusted as a matter of EU law. The idea is that national courts may decide to draw other inferences, on top of the minimum remedial requirements imposed by the need to eliminate the effects of the procedural irregularity. The approach to the issue of damages in the *SFEI* ruling is a good illustration thereof. The Court could not escape the conclusion that the Treaty is not a sufficient legal basis to found an action for damages against the beneficiary of the aid, because the obligations imposed by Article 108(3) TFEU are directed to the granting Member State.[40] Yet the Court immediately added that the principle of non-discrimination may require, in certain circumstances, that the inferences drawn by national courts go beyond what is strictly required by Community law, if stricter consequences are attached to the breach of a similar national provision.[41] The Court was thus inviting national courts to uphold the actions for damages addressed against State aid beneficiaries if such a remedy could be grounded on national law.

[35] Case C-368/04 *Transalpine Ölleitung in Österreich GmbH and Others v Finanzlandesdirektion für Tirol and others* [2006] ECR I-9957, para 56.

[36] Case C-39/94 *Syndicat Français de l'Express international (SFEI) v La Poste and others* [1996] ECRI I-3547, para 75; Case C-199/06 *Centre d'éxportation du livre Français (CELF) v Société internationale de diffusion et d'édition (SIDE)* [2008] ECR I-469, para 55.

[37] Joined Cases C-34 to 38/01 *Enirisorse SpA v Ministero delle Finanze* [2003] ECR I-14243, para 45.

[38] Case C-199/06 *Centre d'éxportation du livre Français (CELF) v Société internationale de diffusion et d'édition (SIDE)* [2008] ECR I-469, para 52.

[39] Opinion of Advocate General Jacobs in Case C-354/90 *Fédération Nationale du Commerce Extérieur des Produits Alimentaires (FNCEPA) and Syndicat National des Négociants et Transformateurs de Saumon v France* [1991] ECR I-5505, para 27.

[40] Case C-39/94 *Syndicat Français de l'Express international (SFEI) v La Poste and others* [1996] ECRI I-3547, para 74.

[41] ibid, para 75.

3. The Independence of National Courts

There is a second development in the case law of the Court that shows its commitment to enhancing the role of national courts in the enforcement of State aid law. As noted earlier, the *Steinike & Weinlig* ruling emphasised the different nature of the functions assigned to the Commission and to national courts in the administration of the rules on State aid: it is for national courts to assess the procedural regularity of State aids and for the Commission to examine their substantive compatibility with the common market.[42] This scheme implies that two different institutions may be called to intervene in the assessment of the same State aid plan, which raises the question of the relationship between their respective procedures and determinations. The Court has declared in later cases that their respective roles are 'complementary *but* separate' (emphasis added).[43] In so doing, the Court has underscored the independence of the task performed by national courts and thus consolidated their position within the system of State aid control.

There are two dimensions to the independence of national courts. The first dimension is procedural. It stems from the ruling of the Court in *SFEI*, where it held that

> the initiation by the Commission of a preliminary examination procedure under [Article 108(3) TFEU] or the consultative examination procedure under Article [108(2) TFEU] cannot release national courts from their duty to safeguard the rights of individuals in the event of a breach of the requirement to give prior notification.[44]

Later cases have stressed even more strongly that national courts 'may not stay' proceedings where the Commission undertakes the examination of the allegedly unlawful aid, irrespective of the existence of indicia suggesting that the Commission will clear the aid.[45] The Court has therefore embraced in State aid procedures the opposite rule from that in antitrust: whereas in antitrust national courts are supposed to stay proceedings where the Commission takes up a case,[46] they are prohibited from doing so when State aids are at stake.

[42] Case 78/76 *Steinike & Weinlig v Germany* [1977] ECR 595, paras 9–14.

[43] Case C-284/12 *Deutsche Lufthansa AG v Flughafen Frankfurt-Hahn GmbH* ECLI:EU:C:2013:755, para 27; Case C-505/14 *Klausner Holz Niedersachsen GmbH v Land Nordrhein-Westfalen* ECLI:EU:C:2015:742, para 20. Note that in previous cases the Court used to define their roles as 'complementary *and* separate', following the formulation of Case C-39/94 *Syndicat Français de l'Express international (SFEI) v La Poste and others* [1996] ECRI I-3547, para 41. Arguably, the new formulation stresses this point even more strongly.

[44] Case C-39/94 *Syndicat Français de l'Express international (SFEI) v La Poste and others* [1996] ECRI I-3547, para 44; Case C-284/12 *Deutsche Lufthansa AG v Flughafen Frankfurt-Hahn GmbH* ECLI:EU:C:2013:755, para 32.

[45] Case C-1/09 *Centre de l'exportation du livre Français (CELF) v Société internationale de diffusion et d'édition (SIDE)* [2010] ECR I-2099, para 40, where the Community judicature had previously annulled an initial positive decision.

[46] Case C-234/89 *Stergios Delimitis v Henninger Bräu AG* [1991] ECR I-935, paras 53–54.

The second dimension is substantive. It implies that the determinations made by the Commission and national courts do not affect each other. This independence runs both ways. The Court held in *Boussac* that the Commission may not declare the incompatibility of a State aid on the sole ground that it was granted in breach of the standstill and notification obligations.[47] More importantly for the purposes of this chapter, it then held in the *French Saumon* case that a final positive decision by the Commission 'does not have the effect of regularizing ex post facto the implementing measures which were invalid because they had been taken in breach of the prohibition laid down by the last sentence of [Article 108(3) TFEU]'.[48] In sum, the substantive compatibility of State aids is not blemished by their procedural irregularity, and their procedural irregularity is not cured by the determination that they are compatible with the common market.

This solution essentially rules out the application of a 'harmless error' type of reasoning to justify the procedural breaches committed by Member States in the implementation of their State aid plans. Thus, it implies that national courts may be called on to assess the procedural regularity of State aids whose substantive compatibility with the common market has previously been established by the Commission. The remedial toolkit that national courts are expected to administer in this scenario is governed by the same principles that apply to standard cases, with the particularity that their restorative function only requires the effects produced by the illegal implementation of the aid up to its clearance by the Commission to be redressed. This is the reason why they are bound to order the repayment of the 'interest in respect of the period of unlawfulness' and 'to uphold claims from compensation for damage caused by reason of the unlawful nature of the aid',[49] although nothing prevents them from going beyond these minimum remedial requirements and ordering full recovery.[50]

The case law of the Court on the independence of national courts makes it clear that the rationale behind this scheme is linked to the objective of ensuring the effectiveness of Article 108(3) TFEU. This is true for the substantive as well as for the procedural dimension. As far as the substantive dimension is concerned, the Court held in *SFEI* that 'the effectiveness of Article [108(3) TFEU] would be weakened if the fact that the Commission was seized of the matter were to prevent the national courts from drawing all the appropriate conclusions from the infringement of that provision'.[51] Similarly, the *French Saumon* Court grounded its

[47] Case C-301/87 *France v Commission (Boussac)* [1990] ECR I-307, paras 12–24.

[48] C-354/90 *Fédération Nationale du Commerce Extérieur des Produits Alimentaires (FNCEPA) and Syndicat National des Négociants et Transformateurs de Saumon v France* [1991] ECR I-5505, para 16; Case C-368/04 *Transalpine Ölleitung in Österreich GmbH and Others v Finanzlandesdirektion für Tirol and others* [2006] ECR I-9957, para 54.

[49] Case C-199/06 *Centre d'éxportation du livre Français (CELF) v Société internationale de diffusion et d'édition (SIDE)* [2008] ECR I-469, para 55.

[50] Case C-368/04 *Transalpine Ölleitung in Österreich GmbH and Others v Finanzlandesdirektion für Tirol and others* [2006] ECR I-9957, para 56.

[51] Case C-39/94 *Syndicat Français de l'Express international (SFEI) v La Poste and others* [1996] ECRI I-3547, para 45. See also Case C-1/09 *Centre de l'exportation du livre Français (CELF) v Société*

holding that positive decisions do not cure the procedural irregularity of State aids on the observation that 'Any other interpretation would have the effect of according a favourable outcome to the non-observance by the Member State concerned of the last sentence of Article [108(3)TFEU] and would deprive that provision of its effectiveness'.[52]

The Court has stressed in other cases that the need to ensure the effectiveness of Article 108(3) TFEU responds to the fact that it is central to the machinery of review entrusted to the Commission, 'which, in turn, is essential for protecting the proper functioning of the common market'.[53] It follows that the ultimate rationale for the independence of national courts is their contribution to protecting the central role of the Commission in the supervision of State aids. It should be noted, however, that the effect of this scheme is to consolidate the position of national of courts themselves within the system of State aid supervision, for it means that their task is not directly subservient to that of the Commission. Thus, by stressing the independence of the role played by national courts in the enforcement of State aid law (both in procedural and in substantive terms), the case law of the Court affords private enforcement a life of its own.

The stance taken by the Court raises, however, certain difficulties. The main one is the risk of parallel proceedings leading to contradictory outcomes.[54] In principle, the rules applied by the Commission and national courts are different (Article 108(3) TFEU vs Article 107(2) and (3) TFEU), which means that there can be no contradiction between their findings. Indeed, *Boussac* and the *French Saumon* case imply that there is no contradiction in the finding that a State aid is *unlawful* but *compatible* with the common market. It should be noted, however, that the Commission and national courts alike need to determine as a preliminary question whether the measures that they scrutinise match the definition of aid laid down by Article 107(1) TFEU—and this is where their findings may clash. Two basic scenarios need to be distinguished.

The first scenario is that in which a national court finds that a measure constitutes State aid granted in breach of the standstill provision but the Commission adopts a decision that there is no aid (rather than a decision declaring that the measure under scrutiny constitutes State aid but is compatible with the common

internationale de diffusion et d'édition (SIDE) [2010] ECR I-2099, para 32 ('the national court cannot stay the proceedings without rendering Article [108(3) TFEU] ineffective, contrary to the principle of effectiveness of the applicable national procedures').

[52] Case C-354/90 *Fédération Nationale du Commerce Extérieur des Produits Alimentaires (FNCEPA) and Syndicat National des Négociants et Transformateurs de Saumon v France* [1991] ECR I-5505, para 6. See also Joined Cases 261 and 262/01 *Belgium v Van Calster and Cleeren* [2003] ECR I-12249, para 63, and Case C-368/04 *Transalpine Ölleitung in Österreich GmbH and others v Finanzlandesdirektion für Tirol and others* [2006] ECR I-9957, para 41.

[53] Case 171/83 R *Commission v France* [1983] ECR 2621, para 12 and Joined Cases 91 and 127/83 *Heineken Brouwerijen BV v Inspecteur der Vennootschapsbelasting, Amsterdam and Utrecht* [1984] ECR-3435, para 20.

[54] Martin Köhler, 'Private Enforcement of State Aid Law—Problems of Guaranteeing EU Rights by Means of National (Procedural) Law' (2012) 11 *European State Aid Law Quarterly* 369, 381.

market). The case law of the Court implies that this scenario is not problematic because of the error bias encoded into the Treaty, which favours false positives in the application of Article 108(3) TFEU. This is the idea behind the observation that the deferral of the implementation of State aid plans until the Commission rules on their compatibility 'is based on the preservative purpose of ensuring that an incompatible aid will *never* be implemented' (emphasis added).[55] It implies that the overreach of Article 108(3) TFEU is deliberate, its goal being to prevent false negatives—ie, State aids that go unnoticed.

In the second scenario, it is the Commission but not the national court which concludes that a measure constitutes State aid. It is this hypothesis that is worrisome from the perspective of the system of State aid control, for it implies a failure on the part of the national mechanisms of enforcement to fulfil their prophylactic function. This is the reason why the Court has declared that the finding of the Commission takes precedence, no matter whether it is provisional (if embodied in a decision to open the formal investigation procedure) or final (if embodied in a decision taken at the end of the formal investigation phase).

The second hypothesis (ie, contradiction caused by a final decision) is less problematic in doctrinal terms. The power of national courts to apply the definition of aid is ancillary to their power to enforce the standstill clause, which means that, in principle, this is a task for the Commission. It follows that the duty of national courts to abide by the finding that a measure constitutes State aid embodied in a final Commission's decision can easily be justified on the basis of the principle of primacy. In *Lucchini*, the Court resorted to the principle of primacy to justify its finding that the principle of *res judicata* could not prevent the recovery of a State aid 'which has been found to be incompatible with the common market in a decision of the Commission which has become final'.[56] In *Lucchini*, the clash between the Commission and the Italian judicature concerned the compatibility of the State aid in question, but the same reasoning would justify the precedence of the Commission's finding concerning the existence of aid over that of the national courts.

The first hypothesis (ie, contradiction caused by the provisional assessment embodied in a decision to open the formal investigation procedure) was considered in the *Lufthansa* case.[57] The preliminary question at the origin of the case was whether a national court is bound by the Commission's preliminary assessment that a measure constitutes State aid that is implicit in the adoption of a decision to initiate the formal investigation procedure. Once again, the

[55] Case C-199/06 *Centre d'éxportation du livre Français (CELF) v Société internationale de diffusion et d'édition (SIDE)* [2008] ECR I-469, para 47 and Case C-1/09 *Centre de l'exportation du livre Français (CELF) v Société internationale de diffusion et d'édition (SIDE)* [2010] ECR I-2099, para 29.

[56] Case C-119/05 *Ministero dell'Industria, del Commercio e dell'Artigianato v Lucchini SpA* [2007] ECR I-6199, para 63.

[57] Case C-284/12 *Deutsche Lufthansa AG v Flughafen Frankfurt-Hahn GmbH* ECLI:EU:C:2013:755.

Court framed its inquiry against the principle of effectiveness, which would be frustrated

> if national courts were able to hold that a measure does not constitute aid within the meaning of Article 107(1) TFEU and, therefore, not to suspend its implementation, even though the Commission had just stated in its decision to initiate the formal examination procedure that that measure was capable of presenting aid elements.[58]

The Court conceded that the assessments embodied in this type of decision are 'preliminary in nature'.[59] However, it dismissed the problem of imposing on national courts the duty to follow a preliminary determination that is open to change in the course of the procedure on the basis of the 'preventive aim of the State aid control system'[60]—in other words, on the basis of the error bias encoded into the system. The Court also resorted to the duty of sincere cooperation to ground its conclusion.[61]

The decision of the Court in the *Lufthansa* case is no doubt controversial, if only because it erodes the independence of national courts in the application of the rules on State aid.[62] However, the point to note is that it actually promotes State aid litigation, providing competitors and other third parties with a powerful tool to block the implementation of any measure preliminarily characterised by the Commission as State aid. In this sense, it is consistent with the relentless efforts made by the European judicature to strengthen the private enforcement side of the system of State aid control.

III. The Role of the Commission in Fostering the Private Enforcement of State Aid Law

1. The Policy Preferences of the Commission

The previous section reviewed the case law of the Court of Justice on the direct effect of the last sentence of Article 108(3) TFEU, which laid down the foundations for the development of a system of private enforcement in the field of State aid law. The analysis highlighted the moves made by the Court to consolidate the powers of national courts and the opportunities offered to competitors and other

[58] ibid, para 38.
[59] ibid, para 37.
[60] ibid, para 40.
[61] ibid, para 41.
[62] Thomas Lübbig and Tom Morgan, 'State Aid, National Courts and the Separation of Powers: Should Judges be Bound to the European Commission's Unfinished State Aid Business?' (2014) 5 *Journal of European Competition Law & Practice* 256, 257. But see Pierre de Bandt, 'Lufthansa: A New Era for State Aid Enforcement?' (2014) 5 *Journal of European Competition Law & Practice* 206.

private litigants by the decentralised mechanisms of State aid enforcement. This section looks at the reaction of the other EU institutions to these moves. More precisely, it surveys the policy followed by the Commission, which stands out as the main promoter of private enforcement in this area.

The Commission came on the scene in 1995, with the adoption of the first Notice on cooperation between national courts and the Commission in this field.[63] The adoption of the Notice was prompted by the case law of the Court, which had assigned to national courts their own role in the system of State aid supervision.[64] Most of the Notice was actually devoted to summarising the case law on the allocation of tasks between the Commission and national courts in the system of State aid supervision.[65] Yet the Notice also evinced the willingness of the Commission to foster the decentralised enforcement of State aid law. Its basic assumption was that

> [w]hile the Commission is not always in a position to act promptly to safeguard the interests of third parties in State aid matters, national courts may be better placed to ensure that breaches of the last sentence of Article [108(3) TFEU] are dealt with and remedied.[66]

Accordingly, it set itself the objective of working 'towards closer cooperation with national courts'.[67] Its policy would follow two axes. First, it would commit itself to 'a policy of openness and transparency' aimed at facilitating the knowledge of the rules on State aid;[68] the Notice itself was a first step in that direction. Secondly, it would set two specific channels of cooperation with national courts, namely, the possibility of requesting information from the Commission in order to determine whether it has taken up specific cases[69] and the possibility of asking the Commission for guidance on the application of the definition of aid.[70]

The Commission took up the issue again in its State Aid Action Plan, a consultation document aimed at launching a comprehensive reform of the system of State aid control.[71] The SAAP shared certain traits with the programme of reforms initiated a few years earlier in the field of antitrust. For one thing, it also presented itself as a modernisation project inspired by the need to adjust the focus of the Commission's policy so as to give priority to the most distortive cases.[72] In order to achieve this objective, the Commission proposed the adoption of a general block exemption regulation, which would bring together the dispersed regulations which

[63] Notice on cooperation between national courts and the Commission in the State aid field (OJ C312, 23.11.1995, p 8).
[64] ibid, para 3.
[65] ibid, paras 4–22.
[66] ibid, para 3.
[67] ibid, para 26.
[68] ibid, para 27.
[69] ibid, para 28.
[70] ibid, para 29.
[71] State Aid Action Plan. 'Less and better targeted state aid: a roadmap for state aid reform 2005–2009' COM (2005) 107 final, para 2.
[72] ibid, para 17.

were already in force and define new categories of exempted aid.[73] The Commission also announced that it would additionally engage in a policy of advocacy and transparency, so as to enrol private stakeholders and national judges in the task of ensuring compliance with the rules on State aid.[74] The underlying idea was that the curtailment of the systematic and preventive control of the Commission required a reinvigoration of other forms of supervision, including the mobilisation of private parties and national courts in the task of detecting and fighting illegal State aids.

The last modernisation plan adopted by the Commission in this area insisted on the idea of moving towards a more focused system of control and, as a corollary, on the need to build up the effectiveness of the decentralised mechanisms of supervision. Indeed, one of the three main goals of the SAM project was 'to focus Commission ex ante scrutiny on cases with the biggest impact on internal market whilst strengthening the Member States cooperation in State aid enforcement'.[75] Accordingly, and in line with the SAAP, the SAM proposed a new revision of the *de minimis* and block exemption regulations.[76] Although it did not launch any specific initiative in that regard, the SAM also noted that an increase in the size and scope of exempted measures would result in an increase of the 'responsibilities of Member States for ensuring the correct enforcement of State aid rules'.[77] Less ex ante/centralised control necessarily meant more ex post/decentralised supervision, private enforcement being an important part of the latter, as the communication expressly recognised.[78]

Although the details and the priorities of these different initiatives are not identical, there seems to be a common theme in all of them. Indeed, the Commission shows a strong preference for an ever-more decentralised system of State aid control, as a means of ensuring that its limited resources are used efficiently and that it is the measures that entail more risks which attract closer scrutiny. This seems to be the only way, in the Commission's view, of meeting another second-level objective, which is the one of steering the system of State aid control in a way that favours growth and the macroeconomic fitness of the EU.

Thus, the decentralisation policy of the Commission rests on two pillars. It rests, first of all, on the instruments through which certain State aids are freed from the preventive control of the Commission: the *de minimis* and block exemption regulations considered in the next section. It rests, secondly, on a set of peripheral mechanisms of supervision designed to ensure that only those measures that satisfy the appropriate formal and substantive criteria avoid the prophylactic control of the Commission. Although private enforcement through national courts is only

[73] ibid, para 35.
[74] ibid, paras 55–56.
[75] 'Communication from the Commission to the European Parliament, the Council, the European Economic and Social Committee and the Committee of the Regions on EU State Aid Modernisation (SAM)' COM/2012/0209 final, para 8.
[76] ibid, para 20.
[77] ibid, para 21.
[78] ibid.

one of these mechanisms, it is an important one—hence the attempt to mobilise market actors and national courts through various advocacy and transparency initiatives, an issue considered below.

2. The *De Minimis* and Block Exemption Regulations

The Commission's decentralisation policy rests on the possibilities offered by Article 109 TFEU, which empowers the Council to 'determine the conditions under which Article 108(3) shall apply and the categories of aid exempted from this procedure'. It was on the basis of this provision that the Council adopted in 1999 the so-called Enabling Regulation (ER).[79]

Article 1 ER empowered the Commission to declare, by means of regulations, that certain categories of aids 'should be compatible with the common market and shall not be subject to the notification requirements of Article [108(3) TFEU]'. Originally, the categories of aid that could be exempted were aid in favour of small and medium-sized enterprises; research and development; environmental protection; and employment and training. The Commission made use of this power for the first time in 2001, with the adoption of the Regulation on training aid,[80] the Regulation on *de minimis* aid[81] and the Regulation on State aid to Small and Medium Enterprises.[82] This package was later complemented by the Regulation on State aid for employment,[83] the Regulations on State aid for SMEs active in the agricultural and fisheries sectors[84] and the Regulation on *de minimis* aid in

[79] Council Regulation (EC) No 994/98 of 7 May 1998 on the application of Articles 92 and 93 of the Treaty establishing the European Community to certain categories of horizontal State aid (OJ L142, 14.5.1998, p 1) amended by Council Regulation (EU) No 733/2013 of 22 July 2013 amending Regulation (EC) No 994/98 on the application of Articles 92 and 93 of the Treaty establishing the European Community to certain categories of horizontal State aid (OJ L204, 31.7.2013, p 11).

[80] Commission Regulation (EC) No 68/2001, on the application of Articles 87 and 88 of the EC Treaty to training aid (OJ L10, 13.1.2001, p 20) amended by Commission Regulation (EC) No 1040/2006 of 7 July 2006 amending Regulations (EC) No 2204/2002, (EC) No 70/2001 and (EC) No 68/2001 as regards period of application (OJ L187, 8.7.2006, p 8).

[81] Commission Regulation (EC) No 69/2001 on the application of Articles 87 and 88 of the EC Treaty to de minimis aid (OJ L10, 13.1.2001, p 30).

[82] Commission Regulation (EC) No 70/2001 of 12 January 2001 on the application of Articles 87 and 88 of the EC Treaty to State aid to small and medium-sized enterprises (OJL 10, 13.1.2001, p 33) amended by Commission Regulation (EC) No 1040/2006 of 7 July 2006 amending Regulations (EC) No 2204/2002, (EC) No 70/2001 and (EC) No 68/2001 as regards period of application (OJ L187, 8.7.2006, p 8).

[83] Commission Regulation (EC) No 2204/2002 of 12 December 2002 on the application of Articles 87 and 88 of the EC Treaty to State aid for employment (OJ L337, 13.12.2002, p 3) amended by Commission Regulation (EC) No 1040/2006 of 7 July 2006 amending Regulations (EC) No 2204/2002, (EC) No 70/2001 and (EC) No 68/2001 as regards period of application (OJ L187, 8.7.2006, p 8).

[84] Commission Regulation (EC) No 1/2004 of 23 December 2003 on the application of Articles 87 and 88 of the EC Treaty to State aid to small and medium-sized enterprises active in the production, processing and marketing of agricultural products (OJL 1, 3.1.2004, p 1) and Commission Regulation (EC) No 1595/2004 of 8 September 2004 on the application of Articles 87 and 88 of the EC Treaty to State aid to small and medium-sized enterprises active in the production, processing and marketing of fisheries products (OJ L291, 14.9.2004, p 3).

the agricultural and fisheries sectors.[85] All of them were later replaced by the General Block Exemption Regulation adopted in 2008,[86] which was in turn recently replaced in 2014 by the SAM version.[87]

Article 2 ER, on the other hand, empowered the Commission to decide, also by means of regulations, that

> certain aids do not meet all the criteria of Article [107(1) TFEU] and that they are therefore exempted from the notification procedure provided for in Article [108(3) TFEU], provided that aid granted to the same undertaking over a given period of time does not exceed a certain fixed amount.

This is the legal basis for the successive *de minimis* regulations that the Commission has adopted in the field of State aid,[88] the one in force as recently as in 2013.[89] The threshold currently in force is €200,000, for a single recipient, over any period of three fiscal years.[90]

The *de minimis* and the block exemption regulations widen the scope for the decentralised application and enforcement of the rules on State aids.[91] This is because they allow the implementation of certain aids without going through the centralised authorisation procedure and because, as a corollary, they redefine the role of all the parties involved in the system of State aid control.[92] First, the *de minimis* and block exemption regulations exempt the Commission from the task of systematically revising the compatibility of State aid plans prior to their implementation. In relation to the measures covered by these regulations, the Commission is simply expected to exercise its general ex post monitoring function. Second, the role of national courts is no longer restricted to applying the definition of aid in order to verify that Article 108(3) TFEU has been complied with; they are additionally expected to verify that the conditions for the application of

[85] Commission Regulation (EC) No 1860/2004 of 6 October 2004 on the application of Articles 87 and 88 of the EC Treaty to de minimis aid in the agriculture and fisheries sectors (OJ L325, 28.10.2004, p 4).

[86] Commission Regulation (EC) No 800/2008 of 6 August 2008 declaring certain categories of aid compatible with the common market in application of Article 87 and 88 of the Treaty (General Block Exemption Regulation) (OJ L214, 9.8.2008, p 3).

[87] Commission Regulation (EU) No 651/2014 of 17 June 2014 declaring certain categories of aid compatible with the internal market in application of Articles 107 and 108 of the Treaty (General Block Exemption Regulation) (OJ L187, 26.6.2014, p 1).

[88] Commission Regulation (EC) No 69/2001 on the application of Articles 87 and 88 of the EC Treaty to de minimis aid (OJ L10, 13.1.2001, p 30) and Commission Regulation (EC) No 1998/2006 of 15 December 2006 on the application of Articles 87 and 88 of the Treaty to de minimis aid (OJ L379, 28.12.2006, p 1).

[89] Commission Regulation (EU) No 1407/2013 of 18 December 2013 on the application of Articles 107 and 108 of the Treaty on the Functioning of the European Union to de minimis aid (OJ L352, 14.12.2013, p 1).

[90] ibid, Article 3(2).

[91] Adinda Sinnaeve, 'Block Exemptions for State Aid: More Scope for State Aid Control by Member States and Competitors' (2001) 38 *Common Market Law Review* 1479, 1480; Michael Berghofer, 'The General Block Exemption Regulation: A Giant on Feet of Clay' (2009) 8 *European State Aid Law Quarterly* 323, 334.

[92] Sinnaeve (n 91) 1500; Berghofer (n 91) 327.

the *de minimis* and block exemption regulations are actually met.[93] Finally, 'the competitor is encouraged and expected to—actively—monitor any aid granted to its competitors closely and challenge any potentially illegal aid before the national courts', which will have to 'apply the regulation to decide whether the aid in question is covered'.[94] The implications of these developments are discussed at the end of this chapter.

3. Advocacy and Transparency

The second aspect of the Commission's decentralisation is the advocacy in favour of the use of the decentralised channels of enforcement in the fight against State aid. This idea was already implicit in its Notice on cooperation, but it became even clearer in the SAAP. The Commission pinned high hopes on private litigation as a means to increasing compliance in this field. Accordingly, it announced its intention to continue its strategy of advocacy in order to strengthen the general awareness of the rules on State aid.[95] One of its main targets would be national judges.[96]

Pursuant to the SAAP, the Commission requested a study on the enforcement of State aid law by national courts.[97] The study was published in 2006 and its results indicated that 'classical private enforcement' (ie, 'actions by private parties against member States or aid recipients alleging that the aid granted in a specific case was unlawful') had played a limited role in this field.[98] The rules on State aid were mostly invoked as a shield to resist the payment of discriminatory taxes; they were also routinely invoked by State aid beneficiaries to resist recovery. But the evidence indicated that they were rarely if ever used to attack unlawful State aid (use as a sword), hence the claim that the 'private enforcement of State aid law [was] still in its infancy'.[99] One of the recommendations put forward by the study was the adoption of a new Notice on cooperation, 'which should address all aspects of the application of EC State aid law by Member States' courts' and, in particular, 'should clarify that pursuant to most recent case law of the European Court of Justice … competitors and other parties affected by a measure granting aid must be granted a remedy in national courts'.[100]

The Commission followed this recommendation and adopted in 2009 a new Notice on cooperation aimed at providing national courts with an updated summary of the rules on the enforcement of State aid law.[101] The new Notice replaced

[93] Sinnaeve (n 91) 1495.
[94] Berghofer (n 91) 328.
[95] 'State Aid Action Plan', n 71, para 55.
[96] ibid, para 56.
[97] Thomas Jestaedt, Jacques Derenne and Tom Ottervanger, *Study on the Enforcement of State Aid Law at National Level* (Brussels: Jones Day, Lovells, Allen & Overy, 2006).
[98] ibid, 33.
[99] ibid, 34.
[100] ibid, 35.
[101] Notice on the enforcement of State aid law by national courts (OJ C85, 9.4.2009, p 1) para 6.

the previous one,[102] but its content was similar, in that it reviewed the relevant case law of the Court of Justice and laid down the same cooperation mechanisms, namely information and opinion requests.[103] This Notice would be followed by other related policy documents, such as the Notice on recovery (which sought to achieve the same pedagogical function in relation to the rules on the enforcement of recovery decisions)[104] and the State Aid Manual of Procedures (an internal working document of the Commission which was made public on the website of the Commission).[105] The advocacy strategy of the Commission has taken other forms, including the compilation and diffusion of information in the form of State Aid Scoreboards, a State aid register and a State aid weekly e-newsletter,[106] as well as the subsidisation of training programmes for national judges.[107]

Some of the initiatives adopted in the wake of the SAM programme are also inspired by the objective of enhancing transparency in this area. One of its flagship initiatives was the adoption of the Notice on the notion of State aid, which sets out the Commission's understanding of Article 107(1) of the Treaty, as interpreted by the European Courts, 'with a view to contributing to an easier, more transparent and more consistent application of this notion across the Union'.[108] However, the most important move was the insertion of Article 9(1)(c) into the General Block Exemption Regulation, which requires Member States to publish a long list of information (including the identity of the beneficiary and the objective of the measure) for any State aid award above €500,000, a measure that seeks to facilitate the task of market actors in ensuring that their competitors do not benefit from illegal government support.[109]

This brief review of the Commission's policy over the last 20 years shows a clear commitment on its part to decentralise the system of State aid control, reducing

[102] ibid, para 7.

[103] The recent reform of the Procedural Regulation has incorporated these mechanisms into that instrument. See Article 23(a) PR, introduced by Council Regulation (EU) No 734/2013 of 22 July 2013 amending Regulation (EC) No 659/1999 laying down detailed rules for the application of Article 93 of the EC Treaty (OJ L204, 31.7.2013, p 15).

[104] Notice from the Commission—Towards an effective implementation of Commission decisions ordering Member States to recover unlawful and incompatible State aid (OJ C272, 15.11.2007, p 4) para 6.

[105] *State Aid. Manual of Procedures. Internal DG Competition Working Documents for the Application of Articles 107 and 108 TFEU* (Luxembourg: Publication Office of the European Union, 2013).

[106] Erika M Szyszczak, *The Regulation of the State in Competitive Markets in the EU* (Oxford: Hart Publishing, 2007) 25: 'The greater openness of EC Commission behaviour allows competitors and consumers to understand where state aid is being used and also contributes to a normative understanding of how state aid decisions are made'.

[107] See calls periodically published on the website of the Commission (http://ec.europa.eu/competition/court/training.html).

[108] Commission Notice on the notion of State aid as referred to in Article 107(1) of the Treaty on the Functioning of the European Union (OJ C 262, 19.7.2016, p 1) para 1.

[109] See Albert Sánchez-Graells, 'Digging Itself Out of the Hole? A Critical Assessment of the European Commission's Attempt to Revitalize State Aid Enforcement After the Crisis' (2016) 2 *Journal of Antitrust Enforcement* 157, who is sceptical about the effect that this increased transparency will have on the number of challenges or complaints.

the volume of measures that go through its systematic and preventive control (through the progressive expansion of the scope of the *de minimis* and block exemption regulations) and strengthening the peripheral mechanisms of supervision (inter alia, fostering the role of market actors as watchdogs and the private enforcement of the rules on State aid).

IV. The Limitations of the System of Private Enforcement of State Aid Law

1. The Underuse of Private Enforcement in the Field of State Aid Law

Despite its strongly centralised character, the system of State aid control partially relies on private enforcement as a means to ensuring compliance with its rules. As the two previous sections have shown, the case law of the European Court and the policy of the Commission have made the most of the space left by the Treaty for the decentralised application and enforcement of State aid law. The result has been the consolidation of the position of national courts within the system of State aid enforcement and, hence, the expansion of the opportunities of redress that they offer to competitors and other private litigants.

The evidence indicates, however, that private litigants have failed to make full use of these opportunities. As noted earlier, this was the main conclusion of the Study on the enforcement of State aid law conducted at the request of the Commission in 2006. Another Study carried out in 2009 noted a certain increase in the number of State aid cases brought before national courts, although the numbers were still low in relation to claims for damages.[110] More generally, most commentators share the perception that private enforcement has not completely taken off.[111]

This section inquires into the reasons that explain the underuse of the channels for the private enforcement of State aid law. I review the main practical obstacles identified by the literature on the private enforcement of State aid law and use the

[110] Jacques Derennne (dir), *2009 Update of the 2006 Study on the Enforcement of State Aid Rules at National Level. Final Report* (Brussels: Lovells, 2009) 2.

[111] See, eg, Adinda Sinnaeve, 'Editorial: What to Expect from National Courts in the Fight against Unlawful State Aid?' (2005) 4 *European State Aid Law Quarterly* 1, 1 ('the national route has not been a success-story so far'); Jacques Derenne and Cédric Kaczmarek, 'La récupération des Aides illégales: le rôle du juge national dans le "private enforcement" du droit des aides d'état' (2009) 10 *ERA Forum* 251, 264; James Flynn, 'The Role of National Courts' in Andrea Biondi, Piet Eeckhout and James Flynn (eds), *The Law of State Aid in the European Union* (Oxford: Oxford University Press, 2004) 323, 332. But see Barbara Brandtner, Thierry Beranger and Christof Lessenich, 'Private State Aid Enforcement' (2010) 9 *European State Aid Law Quarterly* 23, 23: 'more and more cases are brought before national courts, and they cover an increasing variety of issues', a claim that they ground on the 2009 Study.

old system of antitrust to argue that the main problem lies elsewhere, namely in the peculiar procedural bifurcation that affects State aids.

2. Obstacles to the Private Enforcement of State Aid Law

The literature on the private enforcement of State aid law has identified several reasons that may account for the paucity of cases brought before national courts. They can basically be grouped into three different problems.

There is, first of all, the problem of knowledge and transparency.[112] The alleged problem stems from the fact that the rules on State aid are complex and relatively little known. It follows, so the argument goes, that private parties are not always aware of the possibilities opened up by this set of rules and that national courts are not always willing to entertain claims based on a body of law they know little about. This problem may partially account for the low level of private State aid enforcement. However, it is a problem that should disappear over time, as national courts and market operators become aware of and familiar with the rules on State aid.[113] Also, it happens to be the main problem addressed by the Commission through its policy of transparency, reviewed above.[114]

There are, in the second place, the general difficulties associated with cross-border litigation.[115] Potential claimants in State aid cases often come from a foreign jurisdiction, which increases the cost and the uncertainty of litigating. Some commentators have suggested that this problem is magnified by the fact that State aid actions are addressed against public authorities,[116] although litigation against the State seems to be such a routine phenomenon that it is hard to believe that this really constitutes a discouraging factor.[117] Both factors may have some weight, however, when it comes to deciding on the course of action to follow (ie, complaint before the Commission vs action before a national court).[118]

There is, finally, the problem of building a successful claim for the damage arising out of the unlawful implementation of State aid. Although the possibilities of redress offered to competitors by the private enforcement of State aid law are

[112] Flynn (n 111) 330–31; Derenne and Kaczmarek (n 111) 264–65; Sinnaeve (n 111) 1–2; Ross (n 2) 87.

[113] Ingeborg Simonsson, 'On the Emerging Obligation for Member State Authorities to Supervise and Enforce EC State Aid Law, and the Resulting Need to Consider Decentralisation' in Nils Wahl and Per Cramér (eds), *Swedish Studies in European Law* (Oxford: Hart Publishing, 2006) 253–54.

[114] Notice on the enforcement of State aid law by national courts (OJ C85, 9.4.2009, p 1) para 6.

[115] Derenne and Kaczmarek (n 111) 264.

[116] Flynn (n 111) 332.

[117] Simonsson (n 113) 250.

[118] See Francis G Jacobs and Thomas Deisenhofer, 'Procedural Aspects of the Effective Private Antitrust Enforcement of EC Competition Rules: A Community Perspective' in Claus-Dieter Ehlermann and Isabela Atanasiu (eds), *European Competition Law Annual 2001: Effective Private Enforcement of EC Antitrust Law* (Oxford: Hart Publishing, 2003) 187, for an analysis of the 'incentives and disincentives' that may inform the decision to engage in 'civil litigation' rather than to take action before 'administrative enforcement authorities' in the context of antitrust.

not restricted to the compensation of damage, this is perceived to be one their strongest incentives to take this route, especially if compared with the alternative of lodging a complaint before the Commission.[119] The problem allegedly lies in the difficulties raised by the need to establish loss as a consequence of the procedurally irregular implementation of a State aid.[120]

The liability of Member States for infringement of EU law is governed by the three-step test laid down by *Francovich*,[121] as refined in *Brasserie/Factortame*,[122] which provides that

> the rule of law infringed must be intended to confer rights on individuals; the breach must be sufficiently serious; and there must be a direct causal link between the breach of the obligation resting on the State and the damage sustained by the injured parties.[123]

The case law of the Court of Justice in the field of State aid facilitates the fulfilment of the two first conditions insofar as it suffices to establish the infringement of a procedural rule to trigger the potential responsibility of the granting Member State.[124] However, it does not facilitate in any way the fulfilment of the third condition, which is arguably particularly problematic in this domain, given the need to prove financial loss as a result of irregular implementation of the State aid.[125]

Section III explained that the main remedies available to redress the infringement of Article 108(3) TFEU are the recovery of unlawful State aid and the award of damages. This analysis suggests that, in practice, the last remedy is rarely available, which leaves the suspension of the aid and its recovery as the main remedies that private litigants may secure through this channel. This is problematic in two ways. First, it means that one of the main incentives for competitors to enforce State aid law (namely, the possibility of obtaining financial compensation for the harm suffered as a result of State aid) is rarely effective. Second, it means that the main advantage involved in bringing an action before a national court rather than a complaint before the Commission is only rarely available, which further reduces (in relative terms) the incentives to follow the national pathway.

3. The Bifurcation Between *Substantive* and *Procedural* Regularity in State Aid

The rest of this chapter develops the claim that the practical difficulties identified above reflect only part of the problem. In order to illustrate this point, it is useful

[119] Notice on the enforcement of State aid law by national courts (OJ C85, 9.4.2009, p 1) para 5 and 26.

[120] Brandtner, Beranger and Lessenich (n 111) 26; Flynn (n 111) 332; Derenne and Kaczmarek (n 111) 259.

[121] Joined Cases C-6 and 9/90 *Andrea Francovich and others v Italy* [1991] ECR I-5357, para 40.

[122] Joined Cases C-46 and 48/93 *Brasserie du Pêcheur SA v Germany and others* [1996] ECR I-1029.

[123] ibid, para 51.

[124] Notice on the enforcement of State aid law by national courts (OJ C85, 9.4.2009, p 1) paras 46–47.

[125] Brandtner, Beranger and Lessenich (n 111) 26.

to go back to the developments that have occurred in the field of antitrust, where the main aspect of the process of decentralisation fostered by the 2003 reform was the end of the 'procedural bifurcation' that characterised the old system. It will be recalled that the cause of this bifurcation was the Commission's monopoly over the administration of the exemptions, which prevented national courts from applying in full the rules on collusive agreements. By breaking the monopoly of the Commission, Regulation 1/2003 removed one of the main obstacles that complicated the private enforcement of the EU rules on antitrust. Recent developments suggest that this was not the only obstacle. But there is little doubt that the empowerment of national courts to apply Article 101 TFEU *in full* was a necessary condition for the development of private enforcement in that area.

The antitrust reference is helpful because it suggests a plausible explanation for the underuse of private enforcement in the field of State aid. This is because a similar bifurcation affects the operation of the rules on State aid, albeit with two important differences. The first difference is that the bifurcation operates along different lines in each field. Whereas in the old system of antitrust the bifurcation affected the application of the prohibition and the administration of its exemptions, it is the procedural and the substantive assessment of State aids that are separated in this field. Indeed, the monopoly of the Commission is not restricted to applying the exemptions of Article 107(2) and (3) TFEU, for it also includes the application of the prohibition of Article 107(1) TFEU. As noted earlier, national courts may need to apply the definition of aid laid down therein, but only as a preliminary condition to enforce the standstill clause of Article 108(3) TFEU. Their role is thus restricted to verifying the procedural regularity of State aids and to ensuring their notification, so that the Commission exercises its exclusive powers.

The second difference concerns the origin of the bifurcation. In the case of the old system of antitrust, the bifurcation was imposed by a piece of secondary legislation. This is the reason why it was possible to eliminate it through a legislative reform that replaced Regulation 17 with Regulation 1/2003. On the contrary, the monopoly of the Commission over the substantive assessment of State aids is enshrined in the Treaty. It stems from the lack of direct effect of the rules laid down by Article 107 TFEU,[126] which is in turn a result of the existence of a special procedure that reserves for the Commission the application of these rules.[127] It follows that the bifurcation between the procedural and the substantive assessment of State aids has a sort of 'constitutional' dimension, which conditions its possible reform.

[126] Case 77/72 *Capolongo v Azienda Agricola Maya* [1973] ECR 611, para 6. See Pieter J Slot, 'Procedural Aspects of State Aids: The Guardian of Competition Versus the Subsidy Villains?' (1990) 27 *Common Market Law Review* 741, 756: 'The regime for state aids differs clearly from the competition rules of Articles [101 and 102 TFEU] as far as the question of direct effect of the substantive norm, that is Article [107 TFEU], is concerned. Article [101(2) TFEU] gives national courts the power to declare anti-competitive arrangements void. There are no such powers for national courts in the area of state aids'.

[127] Case 78/76 *Steinike & Weinlig v Germany* [1977] ECR 595, paras 8–10.

It is certainly the case that the Treaty itself partially de-constitutionalises this issue. By empowering the Council to determine the categories of aid that shall be exempted from the notification procedure, Article 109 TFEU opens the door for the curtailment of the system of ex ante control through a simple legislative reform. And, as the previous section has shown, this is a possibility that the EU legislator has made increased use of, to the point that the number of State aids granted each year under the block exemption regulations is greater than the number of State aids that go through the authorisation procedure.[128] This analysis suggests that the constitutional entrenchment of the system of ex ante control is not an insurmountable obstacle, as shown by the fact that the exception (ex post control) has almost superseded the general rule (ex ante control).

However, the point to note is that the process of decentralisation nurtured by these legislative reforms has not completely eliminated the procedural bifurcation that prevents national courts from assessing, in full, the validity of State aid measures. This is not so much because of the limited scope of the *de minimis* and block exemption regulations, which cover—as noted earlier—a very significant proportion of the volume of State aid granted each year within the EU, but rather because of the asymmetrical character of the powers that these regulations assign to national courts. Indeed, the *de minimis* and block exemption regulations empower national courts to authorise the implementation of those measures that satisfy the conditions defined by their provisions. When this is the case, national courts may thus give a final judgment on the procedural and substantive regularity of State aids, without consulting in any way with the Commission. But this power is unidirectional, in the sense that it only operates to clear State aids. This is because neither the *de minimis* nor the block exemption regulations empower national courts to quash State aids on substantive grounds (read: to declare their incompatibility with the common market). As soon as they conclude that the regulations are not applicable, national courts fall back into their standard role in the system of State aid control, which is to assess the procedural regularity of State aids and to defer to the Commission when it comes to ruling on their substantive compatibility with the common market.

The persistence of this bifurcation implies that the role of national courts within the system of State aid control remains limited. The case law of the European Courts and the legislative developments considered in this chapter have certainly strengthened their position, but none of these developments has affected the exclusive power of the Commission to enforce the prohibition of Article 107(1) TFEU. Although the possibilities of redress offered by national courts may often be sufficient for competitors, especially as a strategy to win time and to postpone the implementation of pernicious State aid, the preceding analysis suggests that their last hope always lies in the Commission. This is the reason why, in some cases, they may prefer to bypass national courts and to resort directly to

[128] 2015 State Aid Scoreboard (http://ec.europa.eu/competition/state_aid/scoreboard/index_en.html).

the Commission—a possibility discussed in the next chapter, which deals with the issue of complaints in State aid cases. More generally, this is the reason why any strategy seeking to block for good the implementation of State aid measures needs to involve the Commission. The rest of the book examines the different ways in which this can be done.

Conclusion

To sum up, the institutional design for the control of State aids confers a prominent position on the Commission, which has the exclusive power to declare State aids incompatible with the common market. This is not altered by the direct effect of Article 108(3) TFEU and by the decentralising bent of the case law developed by the Court on the basis of that provision. It is not altered either by the decentralising policies fostered by the Commission and the EU legislator, which have not empowered national courts to carry out a full assessment of the regularity of State aids. The upshot is that the developments described in this chapter have not redressed the subordination of the system of private enforcement before national courts to the machinery of public enforcement controlled by the Commission. This is the reason why the rest of the book looks at the possibilities offered to competitors within that machinery.

PART II

4

The Position of Complainants in State Aid Procedures

Introduction

The previous chapter has brought to light the limitations that the private enforcement of State aid law presents from the viewpoint of competitors. As a result of the pivotal position occupied by the Commission in this field, competitors may decide to bypass national courts and to resort directly to the Commission when it comes to challenging State measures of financial assistance to other firms. This chapter is therefore concerned with complaints as a vehicle for competitors to fight State aids.

The definition of the status of complainants within State aid procedures faces two basic difficulties. The first one is the need to take account of the general dilemma posed by the embedment of complaints within any regulatory scheme: complainants act as watchdogs and, as such, increase the likelihood of detecting infringements; but they also challenge the autonomy of the regulator to set priorities and follow its own enforcement agenda. The first part of this chapter spells out this problem and describes the way in which EU administrative law has generally responded to it, releasing the Commission from the obligation to investigate and respond to every complaint that it receives.

The second problem stems from the peculiar design of the system of State aid supervision, which rests on the obligation of Member States to notify any plan to grant State aid before putting it into place. Chapter 2 noted that the bilateral character of the State aid procedure is particularly strong at the initiation stage, given its design as an authorisation procedure in which the role of the Commission is to respond to the requests for clearance made by Member States. The question that arises, then, is how to embed complaints within a system to which they are in principle alien. The second part of the chapter deals with this issue (ie, the issue of access), describing the different jurisprudential and legislative moves that opened the State aid procedure to the input of complainants.

Finally, the last part of the chapter addresses the issue of leverage. It shows that the status of complainants in State aid cases is not governed by the general regime outlined in the first part of the chapter, which means that they have more bite. This is because, besides securing access, the European Courts (first) and the legislator (later) have provided complainants in State aid matters with a right that they seldom enjoy in other contexts, namely the right to a response on the merits of their allegations. The chapter concludes with an assessment of the significance that this right has for the inquiry carried out in this book.

I. The Position of Complainants in EU Administrative Law

1. Administrative Authorities, Complaints and Enforcement Discretion

As noted in Chapter 2, the system of State aid control places great emphasis on the need to detect every measure that falls within the definition of aid of Article 107(1) TFEU, irrespective of their eligibility to the exemptions listed in Article 107(2) and (3) TFEU. This is the result of the constitutional choice in favour of a system of ex ante control that places the ultimate decision on the implementation of national State aid plans in the hands of the Commission. The challenge is to detect those measures that meet the definition of State aid but are implemented without going through the Commission—'unlawful' or 'illegal' State aid in the jargon of the discipline.

The reader is referred to the second chapter for a more elaborate discussion of the added value that competitors bring to the system of State aid control in terms of detection, be it when they rely on the direct effect of the standstill provision before national courts or when they lodge complaints with the Commission. This chapter is concerned with the latter scenario, which raises some problems of its own. These problems are not specific to the realm of State aid control, nor, in fact, to the EU administration itself. They affect the relationship between complainants and supervisory authorities at large, which is why it may be useful to take one step back and to look at them from a more general perspective.

The ultimate cause of these problems lies in the necessarily limited character of any administrative authority's resources. It is this limitation that makes complaints a potentially useful device, insofar as they add strength to the authority's detection capacity. Yet it is also this limitation that turns complaints into a double-edged sword. This is because they challenge the authority's capacity to carry out a 'proactive' rather than 'reactive' policy of enforcement.[1]

In the 'reactive mode',[2] supervisory authorities are complaints driven and hence in the position that is typical of courts.[3] The main drawback of this approach is

[1] Robert A. Kagan, 'On Regulatory Inspectorates and Police' in Keith Hawkins and John M Thomas (eds), *Enforcing Regulation* (Boston, MA: Kluwer/Nijhoff Publishing, 1984) 40.

[2] ibid.

[3] For a general discussion of the problems raised by 'case based policy making', see Frederick Schauer and Richard Zeckhauser, 'The Trouble with Cases' in Daniel P Kessler (ed), *Regulation versus Litigation. Perspectives from Economics and Law* (Chicago, IL: University of Chicago Press, 2011) 61.

that 'Responding to complaints ... often diverts enforcement personnel to comparatively low-priority problems',[4] hence the need for some degree of proactive enforcement. The challenge then is to figure out how to allocate the available resources so that they provide the most 'value added',[5] ie, to determine the criteria that are to inform 'an ordered policy of selective enforcement'.[6] This is certainly no easy task.[7] Particular attention may be devoted to the most important or common infringements, or to those that raise particular difficulties as a result of their novelty or complexity.[8] In any event, the kernel of this strategy is that the regulator retains control over its own enforcement agenda.

The challenge is thus to find 'the optimum balance of reactive and proactive strategies'.[9] It is in order to achieve this balance that supervisory authorities are normally endowed with some degree of 'enforcement discretion'—ie, with 'the authority to turn a blind eye to legal violations'.[10] What this means is that complaints are welcome as a useful source of information, but that the enforcer is given leeway in the selection of complaints that it decides to investigate. It may therefore refrain from investigating certain complaints, despite their being in appearance well founded, and focus its resources instead on those allegations that match its own enforcement priorities. The other side of the coin is that complainants are entitled neither to an investigation of their allegations nor to a response on the merits of their claims. The following two sections illustrate how these principles work in EU administrative law.

2. The Enforcement Discretion of the Commission Under EU Administrative Law

Article 17(1) TEU entrusts the Commission with the mission of ensuring the application of the Treaties. In order to fulfil this task, the Commission has at its disposal several mechanisms. It has, on the one hand, the *general* procedure for the enforcement of EU law, laid down by Articles 258 and 259 TFEU, which empower

[4] Kagan (n 1) 40.

[5] ibid, 41.

[6] Richard Rawlings, 'Engaged Elites: Citizen Action and Institutional Attitudes in Commission Enforcement' (2000) 6 *European Law Journal* 4, 28.

[7] Rodolphe Muñoz, 'The Monitoring of the Application of Community Law: The Need to Improve the Current Tools and an Obligation to Innovate' (2006) 4 *Jean Monnet Working Paper Series*, 9.

[8] For an example of the way in which the Commission sets its own priorities in the framework of its general supervisory task see, eg, 'Commission Communication—Better monitoring of the application of Community law' COM (2002) 725 final, and 'Commission Communication—A Europe of results. Applying Community law' COM (2007) 502 final. In the field of antitrust, see 'Communication from the Commission—Guidance on the Commission's enforcement priorities in applying Article 82 of the EC Treaty to abusive exclusionary conduct by dominant undertakings' (OJ C45, 24.2.2009, p 7).

[9] Kagan (n 1) 41.

[10] I borrow the phrase from Zachary S Price, 'Enforcement Discretion and Executive Duty' (2014) 67 *Vanderbilt Law Review* 671, 673, who uses it in a different context.

the Commission to sue before the Court of Justice any Member State that fails to abide by one of its reasoned opinions. It has, on the other hand, several *special* procedures for the enforcement of particular provisions of the Treaty. These special procedures empower the Commission to declare that an infringement has occurred and to record this finding in a binding decision, without going through the Court. It is on the basis of this power that the Commission may enforce the rules on competition against private undertakings[11] and Member States.[12]

From the very early days, the Commission has sought the assistance of citizens and undertakings in its task of monitoring the application of EU law.[13] The Commission has been very successful in its endeavour to promote complaints.[14] However, it has had to face a growing number of judicial challenges by 'disappointed complainants'[15] as well as increasing demands 'for greater "voice" or more participatory elements in the procedure'.[16]

As a result of this pressure, the position of complainants in the procedures for the enforcement of EU law has undergone some changes. Their position within the general infringement procedure has attracted the attention of the Commission in several soft-law instruments, which have articulated certain procedural guarantees such as the systematic registration of complaints and the establishment of certain time limits.[17] The status of complainants within competition procedures has been developed by secondary law.[18] Finally, the establishment of a European Ombudsman has created a new instrument to bring to light the most flagrant examples of maladministration committed by the Commission in the handling of complaints.[19]

It is beyond the scope of this chapter to describe in detail these developments. The point to note is that none of them has called into question the power of the Commission to allocate its enforcement resources as it deems best—that is to say, the idea that the Commission enjoys some degree of enforcement discretion on

[11] Article 105 TFEU and Council Regulation (EC) No 1/2003 of 16 December 2002 on the implementation of the rules on competition laid down in Articles 81 and 82 of the Treaty (OJ L1, 4.1.2003, p 1).

[12] Article 106(3) TFEU.

[13] Ignace Maselis and Hans M Gilliams, 'Rights of Complainants in Community Law' (1997) 22 *European Law Review* 103, 103.

[14] See the historical account of Ludwig Krämer, 'The Environmental Complaint in EU Law' (2009) 6 *Journal for European Environmental & Planning Law* 13.

[15] Maselis and Gilliams (n 13) 103.

[16] Carol Harlow and Richard Rawlings, 'Accountability and Law Enforcement: The Centralised EU Infringement Procedure' (2006) 31 *European Law Review* 447, 466.

[17] 'Commission Communication on the relations with the complainant in respect of infringements of Community law' COM (2002) 141 final; 'Communication from the Commission to the Council and the European Parliament. Updating the handling of relations with the complainant in respect of the application of Union law' COM (2012) 154 final.

[18] Article 27 of Council Regulation (EC) No 1/2003 of 16 December 2002 on the implementation of the rules on competition laid down in Articles 81 and 82 of the Treaty (OJ L1, 4.01.2003, p. 1) and Articles 5 to 9 of Commission Regulation (EC) No 773/2004, of 7 April 2004, relating to the conduct of proceedings by the Commission pursuant to Articles 81 and 82 of the EC Treaty (OJ L123, 27.4.2004, p 18).

[19] For a critical account of the role played by the EU in some salient cases related to complaints, see Harlow and Rawlings (n 16) 465–72.

the basis of which it can refrain from investigating certain complaints and that, as a corollary, complaints enjoy no right to a response on the merits of their allegations.

Within the framework of the general infringement procedure, the issue has arisen in two types of cases. It has arisen within the framework of actions of annulment brought by complainants against the act—typically a letter—whereby the Commission informed them of its intention to drop the investigation of their complaint. The question then was whether the act in question was actionable, ie, whether the decision to discontinue the investigation was subject to judicial review. The issue has also arisen within the framework of actions for failure to act brought by complainants pursuant to the refusal of the Commission to issue a reasoned opinion and/or to bring the subject matter of their complaint before the Court of Justice. The question then was whether the Commission was under an obligation to act in response to their complaint. A clear and common principle has arisen in both types of cases: the Commission enjoys under current Article 258 TFEU 'a discretion which excludes the right of individuals to require that institution to adopt a specific position' on their complaint.[20]

The European Courts have embraced the same principle (albeit with some qualifications)[21] in the context of the special procedures for the enforcement of the competition rules of the Treaty.[22] As far as the rules on antitrust are concerned, the CFI held in its landmark *Automec II* judgment that neither the Treaty nor secondary legislation confer upon complainants the right to obtain a decision as regards the existence or inexistence of any alleged infringement,[23] a principle that has been confirmed by the ECJ in later cases.[24] The same conclusion was reached in the *max.mobil* case, which concerned the enforcement of the rules on competition against a Member State through Article 106 TFEU. The ECJ held that under that provision 'individuals cannot require the Commission to take a position in a specific case'.[25]

The preceding analysis suggests that the default rule in EU administrative law is that, in the fulfilment of its general supervisory authority, the Commission is under no obligation to investigate every complaint that it receives. Needless to say, this principle is not without limits. These limits are considered next.

[20] Case 247/87 *Star Fruit Company SA v Commission* [1989] ECR 291, para 11 (action for failure to act) and Case C-87/89 *Sonito and others v Commission* [1990] ECR I-1981, para 6 (action of annulment).

[21] See next section.

[22] For a broader discussion of the issue see, eg, Wouter PJ Wils, 'Discretion and Prioritisation in Public Antitrust Enforcement, in Particular EU Antitrust Enforcement' (2011) 34 *World Competition* 353.

[23] Case T-24/90 *Automec Srl v Commission* [1992] ECR II-2223, para 75.

[24] See, eg, Case C-119/97 P *Ufex v Commission* [1999] ECR I-1341, para 88: the Commission 'is entitled to give differing degrees of priorities to complaints before it'.

[25] Case C-141/02 *Commission v T-Mobile Austria* [2005] ECR I-1283, para 69.

3. Limits: The Principle of Good Administration

Article 41(1) of the Charter of Fundamental Rights of the European Union recognises, under the head of the right to good administration, the right of every person to have one's affairs 'handled impartially, fairly and within a reasonable time by the institutions and bodies of the Union'. The explanation to the Charter provided by the Convention's *Praesidium* provides that 'Article 41 is based on the existence of a Community subject to the rule of law whose characteristics were developed in the case law which enshrined inter alia the principle of good administration'.[26] More specifically, Article 41(1) of the Charter builds on the case law of the European Courts on the duty of careful and impartial examination, whose implications for the enforcement discretion of the Commission are explored in the following.[27]

The duty of careful and impartial examination (also referred to as 'the principle of care' or 'principle of due diligence')[28] emerged as a standard to review the administrative action of the Commission in cases like *Nolle I*[29] and *Technische Universität München*,[30] where it was used to counterbalance the Commission's wide power of appraisal in antidumping procedures involving 'complex technical evaluations'.[31] It was then also applied to review the legality of decisions involving 'complex economic matters', be it in antitrust cases, like *Asia Motor France*,[32] or in State aid cases, like *Sytraval*.[33] In both types of case, the European Courts used the duty of careful and impartial examination to censure the way in which the Commission carried out its investigations. Thus, in *Asia Motor France*, the CFI held that

> once it decides to proceed with the investigation, [the Commission] must ... conduct it with the requisite care, seriousness and diligence so as to be able to assess with full knowledge of the case the factual and legal particulars submitted for its appraisal by the complainants.[34]

A different function was assigned to the duty of careful and impartial examination in the seminal *Automec II* case, where it was used to censure the decision of

[26] 'Draft Charter of Fundamental Rights of the European Union. Text of the explanations relating to the complete text of the Charter as set out in CHARTE 4487/00 CONVENT 50' (CHARTE 4473 CONVENT 49) 36.

[27] On the different genesis and functions of good administration as a general principle and as a specific procedural right, see Loïc Azoulai, 'Le principe de bonne administration' in Jean-Bernard Auby and Jacqueline Dutheil de la Rochère (eds), *Droit administratif européen* (Brussels: Bruylant, 2007); Hans P Nehl, 'Good Administration as Procedural Right and/or General Principle?' in Herwig CH Hofmann and Alexander H Türk (eds), *Legal Challenges in EU Administrative Law. Towards an Integrated Administration* (Cheltenham: Edward Elgar, 2009).

[28] Hans P Nehl, *Principles of Administrative Procedure in EC Law* (Oxford: Hart Publishing, 1999) 103.

[29] Case C-16/90 *Detlef Nölle, trading as 'Eugen Nölle' v Hauptzollamt Bremen-Freihafen* [1991] ECR I-5163.

[30] Case C-269/90 *Technische Universität München v Hauptzollamt München-Mitte* [1990] ECR I-5469.

[31] Case T-24/90 *Automec Srl v Commission* [1992] ECR II-2223, para 14.

[32] Case T-7/92 *Asia Motor France SA and others v Commission* [1993] ECR II-669.

[33] Case C-367/95 P *Commission v Sytraval and Brink's France* [1998] ECR I-1719.

[34] Case T-7/92 *Asia Motor France SA and others v Commission* [1993] ECR II-669, para 36.

the Commission to refrain from investigating certain cases.[35] It is this aspect of the principle that is relevant for the purposes of this chapter. As noted earlier, one of the main contributions of the *Automec II* judgment was that it cemented the enforcement discretion of the Commission in the handling of complaints. The same judgment made it clear, however, that the broad margin of manoeuvre recognised to the Commission was not boundless. The Commission would have to decide whether to investigate or to refrain from investigating complaints on the basis of a careful and impartial examination of the 'factual and legal particulars brought to its notice by the complainant',[36] and this decision would be subject to judicial review on the basis of two standards: the duty of careful and impartial examination itself and the duty to provide reasons, which required the Commission to justify its decision 'in light of the Community interest'.[37]

When applying these principles to the facts of the case, the *Automec II* Court concluded that the Commission had lived up to these standards, which is why it ruled in its favour. However, it would soon reach the opposite conclusion and quash a similar decision in another case concerning the car industry,[38] thereby dispelling any doubts with regard to its willingness to scrutinise very closely the handling of complaints by the Commission.[39]

This line of cases brings to the fore the relationship between the principle of care and the enforcement discretion of the Commission. It suggests that the principle now enshrined in Article 41(1) of the Charter does not exclude a priori the enforcement discretion of the Commission, but that it does impose certain formal constraints on its exercise. It should be noted, however, that the *Automec II* Court derived these constraints from the 'procedural safeguards' provided for by secondary law, namely the right to submit complaints in antitrust matters recognised—at that time—by Regulation No 17.[40] It follows, or so it seems, that in the absence of an explicit recognition by the legislator of the right to submit complaints, the duty of careful and impartial examination does not limit in any way the enforcement discretion of the Commission.[41]

This is confirmed by the case law of the European Courts on the position of complainants under Article 106 TFEU, which empowers the Commission to ensure compliance with the competition rules of the Treaty by the Member States themselves. Article 106(3) TFEU authorises the Commission to record its findings in decisions addressed against Member States, but the details of the procedure that it must follow have not been developed by secondary law. In the *Ladbroke* and *German accountants* cases, the CFI and the ECJ took the position that the Commission

[35] Nehl (n 28) 140.
[36] Case T-24/90 *Automec Srl v Commission* [1992] ECR II-2223, para 79.
[37] ibid, para 81.
[38] Case T-37/92 *BEUC v Commission* [1994] ECR II-285.
[39] Tim Frazer and Peter Holmes, 'Self-restraint: Cars, Complaints and the Commission' (1995) 1 *European Public Law* 85, 88.
[40] Case T-24/90 *Automec Srl v Commission* [1992] ECR II-2223, para 79.
[41] Maselis and Gilliams (n 13) 106.

was under no obligation to take action in response to complaints brought under Article 106 TFEU.[42] Yet in the latter case the ECJ added, obiter, that

> exceptional circumstances might exist where an individual or, possibly, an association constituted for the defence of the collective interests of a class of individuals has standing to bring proceedings against a refusal by the Commission to adopt a decision pursuant to its supervisory functions under Article [106 TFEU].[43]

In *max.mobil*, the CFI clung to this possibility and made a far-reaching interpretation of the duty of careful and impartial examination, using it to restrict the enforcement discretion of the Commission under Article 106 TFEU in a similar way as in *Automec II*. The CFI was well aware of the link that the case law had so far established between the duty of careful and impartial examination and 'the existence of procedural rights expressly recognised by the Treaty or by provisions of secondary law in order to account for the Commission's obligation to undertake an examination'.[44] However, it decided to test a broader conception of the scope of this duty, according to which 'the existence of [the] obligation to undertake a diligent and impartial examination is also justified by the general duty of supervision to which the Commission is subject'.[45]

The CFI relied on this idea to hold that the action for failure to act was admissible, but then dismissed it on the merits. The Commission was nevertheless unsatisfied and appealed the judgment out of fear of the far-reaching implications that the interpretation put forward by the Court could have in later cases.[46] It was successful in convincing the ECJ that the CFI should have dismissed the action as inadmissible in the first place, because 'the Commission is not obliged to bring proceedings within the terms of [Article 106 TFEU], as individuals cannot require the Commission to take a position in specific case'.[47] This is how the ECJ came to clarify, more generally, that this is not contrary to the principle of good administration for 'no general principle of Community law requires that an undertaking be recognised as having standing before the Community judicature to challenge a refusal by the Commission to bring proceedings against a Member State on the basis of Article [106(3) TFEU]'.[48]

The judgment of the ECJ in *max.mobil* has been described as a 'severe' one,[49] because it confirms that the duty of careful and impartial examination does not

[42] Case T-32/93 *Ladbroke Racing v Commission* [1994] ECR II-1015, para 38; Case C-107/95 P *Bundesverband der Bilanzbuchhalter v Commission* [1997] ECR I-947, paras 26–27.

[43] Case C-107/95 P *Bundesverband der Bilanzbuchhalter v Commission* [1997] ECR I-947, para 25.

[44] Case T-54/99 *max.mobil v Commission* [2002] ECR II-313, para 50.

[45] ibid, para 52.

[46] Melanie K Smith, *Centralised Enforcement, Legitimacy and Good Governance in the EU* (London: Routledge, 2010) 42.

[47] Case C-141/02 P *Commission v max.mobil Telekommunikation Service GmbH* [2005] I-1283, para 69.

[48] ibid, para 72.

[49] Jill Wakefield, *The Right to Good Administration* (Alphen aan den Rijn: Kluwer Law International, 2007) 157.

by itself curtail the enforcement discretion of the Commission in the handling of complaints. This is an important insight for the inquiry carried out in this chapter. It confirms that the general rule in EU administrative law is that the Commission enjoys a wide margin of discretion in the definition of its enforcement priorities and, as a corollary, in the selection of the complaints that it investigates. It also confirms that the Commission is subject to certain constraints in the exercise of this discretion, but only where primary or secondary law impose upon it (in one way or another) the obligation to examine complaints in the first place. And, even then, these constraints come down to the obligation to record its refusal to investigate in a duly reasoned decision. It is against this background that the rest of the chapter analyses the status of complainants in State aid cases.

II. The Road to the Adoption of the Procedural Regulation

1. The Opening of the State Aid Procedure to Complainants

The Treaty foresees a single mechanism to set the State aid procedure in motion, which is the notification made by Member States in compliance with Article 108(3) TFEU. The first question that arises is whether it is possible at all to embed complaints within a system imprinted with such a strong bilateral character. Although obvious for the modern State aid lawyer, there was a time when the answer to this question was open to doubt.[50] This is because the possibility of bringing complaints was never explicitly recognised in the Treaties but also, more importantly, because the role of the Commission itself in fighting unlawful State aid was not always as clear as it is today. There were indeed two possible interpretations of the courses of action that were open to the Commission in this endeavour.

The first interpretation was that the State aid procedure was not an appropriate device to enforce the rules on State aid against non-notified measures. This interpretation was favoured by several Advocates General, who saw 'no reason for regarding it as implicit in Article [108 TFEU] that the procedure is available also in a case where the question is whether a Member State has introduced or altered an aid in contravention of the prohibition in paragraph (3)'.[51] The main implication of this reading was that the Commission would have to treat the implementation of State aid in breach of the standstill and notification obligation as any other

[50] See, eg, David R Gilmour, 'The Enforcement of Community Law by the Commission in the Context of State Aids: The Relationship between Article 93 and 169 and the Choice of Remedies' (1981) 18 *Common Market Law Review* 63.

[51] Opinion of Advocate General Warner in Case 173/73 *Italy v Commission* [1974] ECR 709, p 724. See also Opinion of Advocate General Lagrange in Case 6/64 *Flaminio Costa v ENEL* [1964] ECR 585.

infringement of the Treaty and, hence, to try to redress it through the general infringement procedure.[52] This interpretation did not completely rule out the possibility of bringing complaints in State aid matters, but it did imply that these complaints would have the same status as any other complaint lodged under the rules of the general infringement procedure, which is to say (as noted earlier) hardly any status at all.

The second interpretation was that the State aid procedure was an appropriate tool to fight unlawful State aid, which meant that the Commission could enforce State aid law against Member States in breach of their procedural obligations, without necessarily going through the general infringement procedure. According to this reading, the Commission was empowered to initiate of its own motion the State aid procedure whenever adverted of the existence of allegedly unlawful State aid and, as a corollary, to adopt a final decision without having to go through the Court. By segregating the fight of unlawful State aid from the general infringement procedure, this interpretation made some room—in principle at least—for the involvement of complainants in the State aid procedure itself.

The question was settled in *Italy v Commission*, where the ECJ endorsed the latter interpretation.[53] The Italian government challenged the decision of the Commission to declare the incompatibility with the common market of several measures of support to the textile industry that were never notified. In fact, none of the pleas put forward by Italy called into question the power of the Commission to launch the State aid procedure against unlawful measures. However, the ECJ grasped the opportunity to clarify that, in order to fight this type of State aid, 'the means of recourse open to the Commission are not restricted to the more complicated procedure under Article [258 TFEU]'.[54] This statement wiped out any possible doubts with regard to the power of the Commission to enforce on its own the rules on State aid in the absence of prior notification, a power that it would start using very actively in the early 1980s.[55]

No complaint was involved in the administrative procedure at the origin of this dispute, because the Commission took cognisance of the controversial measures through its own means. Yet, by recognising the power of the Commission to enforce the rules on State aid against non-notified measures, the judgment of the ECJ in *Italy v Commission* paved the way for the association of complainants with State aid procedures.

It is difficult to pinpoint the precise moment when this happened, because the possibility of bringing complaints emerged 'as a general administrative practice', without any explicit recognition in primary or secondary law.[56] The truth is, however,

[52] Alberto J. Gil Ibáñez, 'Exceptions to Article 226: Alternative Administrative Procedures and the Pursuit of Member States' (2000) 6 *European Law Journal* 148, 151.

[53] Case 173/73 *Italy v Commission* [1974] ECR 709.

[54] ibid, para 9.

[55] Johannes A Winter, 'The Rights of Complainants in State Aid Cases: Judicial Review of Commission Decisions Adopted under Article 88 (Ex 93)' (1999) 36 *Common Market Law Review* 521, 522.

[56] Pieter J Slot, 'Administrative Procedure' in Leigh Hancher, Tom Ottervanger and Pieter J Slot (eds), *EU State Aids* (London: Sweet & Maxwell, 2012) 947.

that it was a smooth process, as shown by the fact that the cases reviewed in the following section did not discuss in any way the possibility of lodging complaints in State aid matters, but only the implications that these complaints had from the viewpoint of the procedural status of the applicants and of the enforcement discretion of the Commission. In other words, the problem was not *whether* complaints had any role to play in State aid procedures (*access*), but rather *what* role they would play (*leverage*).

2. State Aid Complainants Before the European Courts

The European Courts were confronted with this problem in several cases brought by complainants who had failed to secure, in the course of the administrative procedure, the outcome that they were looking for. In one way or another, these cases called, in essence, for a clarification of the two main problems raised by the definition of the status of complainants within EU administrative procedures: the degree of enforcement discretion of the Commission in the handling of these complaints and, if any, the limits imposed upon its exercise.

In general, the Courts stuck to the bilateral definition of the procedure and to the idea that private parties do not acquire a special position as a result of their acting as complainants.[57] Their stance on this issue rested on the theory that the rationale for the involvement of private actors in State aid proceedings is instrumental to the information needs of the Commission, which means that it is for the Commission to decide, on a case-by-case basis, what use to make of the allegations put forward by complainants.[58] Whilst clinging to this conventional theory, however, the European Courts made some moves that could indicate a certain departure from the purely bilateral paradigm.

(a) *The Right to Challenge the Premature Closure of the State Aid Procedure* (Cook)

The first move was the empowerment of complainants to challenge the decision of the Commission to discontinue the investigation of their allegations at the preliminary stage of the procedure.

The standard that determines the legality of positive decisions adopted at the end of the preliminary phase ('decision to raise no objections') was spelled out by the ECJ in *Germany v Commission*.[59] Following a challenge brought by Germany against the decision of the Commission to raise no objections to a State aid plan notified by Belgium, the ECJ held that the decision to clear a State aid at the preliminary stage of the procedure is subject to judicial scrutiny, the standard of

[57] See, eg, Case T-613/97 *Ufex and others v Commission* [2000] ECR II-4055, para 86.
[58] ibid, para 89.
[59] Case 84/82 *Germany v Commission* [1984] ECR 1451.

review being the so-called 'serious difficulties test'.[60] The operation of this test is analysed in more depth in Chapter 6. Suffice it to say here that it is premised on the idea that the Commission is bound to open the second phase of the procedure 'when [it] has serious difficulties in determining whether a plan to grant aid is compatible with the common market';[61] and that the existence or inexistence of 'serious difficulties' is done on the basis of a cursory but objective assessment of the information available to the Commission at the time of its decision. Insofar as it forecloses the possibility to drop a case at the first stage of the procedure on the basis of opportunistic considerations, this test represents a sort of 'procedural trap' for the Commission, which is thus bound to go through both phases of the procedure unless a case is really straightforward.

The administrative procedure at the origin of *Germany v Commission* was initiated in response to a notification, rather than a complaint; all the actors involved in the dispute were actually Member States. The judgment matters, however, because the ECJ grounded its holding on the observation that the second phase of the procedure 'guarantees the other Member States and the sectors concerned an opportunity to make their views known', the idea being that this guarantee can only be effective if the opening of the consultation phase is deemed to be compulsory 'when the Commission has serious difficulties in determining whether a plan to grant an aid is compatible with the common market'.[62] In *Germany v Commission* it was a third-party Member State that relied on this guarantee, but the reference to the 'sectors concerned' suggested that the same course of action was open to competitors and other interested parties.

This was confirmed by the rulings of the ECJ in *CIRFS*[63] and in *Cook*, where the serious difficulties test was applied to strike down a decision not to raise objections adopted pursuant to a complaint.[64] The judgment of the ECJ in *Cook* will surface very often in this book, for its significance lies in the fact that it both sanctions the right of competitors to participate in the second phase of State aid procedures[65] and that it articulates a special rule of standing to enforce this right through the European judicature.[66] The point to note here is that the Court did not hide behind the fact that the procedure had its origin in a complaint to avoid rendering the Commission accountable for its decision to clear a State aid without exhausting the two phases of the procedure.

Insofar as it allows competitors to follow up their complaints and to challenge the premature closure of their file, the possibility of invoking the serious difficulties test can be seen as a first departure from the purely bilateral paradigm. Granted,

[60] ibid, para 13.
[61] ibid.
[62] ibid.
[63] Case 313/90 *Comité International de la Rayonne et des Fibres Synthétiques (CIRFS) and others v Commission* [1993] ECR I-1125, paras 26–27.
[64] Case C-198/91 *William Cook plc v Commission* [1993] ECR I-2487, para 29.
[65] See Chapter 5.
[66] See Chapter 6.

the serious difficulties test sets a relatively low standard for the Commission, since it leaves some room for the clearance of State aids without a fully fledged analysis of their likely effects. Still, it subjects any such decision to an objective standard of legality that prevents the Commission from relying on its own enforcement priorities to dispose of complaints at the preliminary stage of the procedure.

Yet the significance of this move should not be overestimated. This is because the possibility of invoking the serious difficulties test enables complainants to challenge the legality of State aid decisions adopted at the end of the preliminary phase, but leaves them powerless in the face of the Commission's inaction. The test is indeed relevant to determine whether the Commission was entitled to close the procedure without following it through to the end. However, it does not seem to provide any criterion to determine whether the Commission was under an obligation to initiate the procedure in the first place. If this analysis is correct, the move made by the Court in *Cook* left the Commission's enforcement discretion intact.

*(b) Procedural Rights of Complainants (*Sytraval*)*

Whereas the first move implied the empowerment of complainants to enforce the procedural rights that they enjoy in the second phase of the procedure, the second and third moves consisted instead in the recognition of certain procedural guarantees within the preliminary procedure itself. Let us start with the second one, which was famously made by the CFI in its controversial *Sytraval* judgment.[67]

The dispute at the origin of this case concerned the relationship between the French postal service operator (La Poste) and the commercial subsidiary that was set up to contract out the transportation of its moneys and valuables. Various companies operating in this sector (and an association reuniting them) lodged a complaint with the Commission alleging that the creation and operation of the subsidiary concealed several measures of unlawful aid. Despite having initially recognised that the complaint raised 'a number of important points of principle calling, in this instance, for an in-depth investigation',[68] the Commission eventually decided to close the file at the preliminary stage with a decision holding that there was no aid. The CFI upheld the action of annulment that the complainants brought against that decision, finding that the statement of reasons put forward by the Commission was not sufficient to support the conclusion that the contested measures did not constitute State aid.[69]

What is remarkable, however, is that the CFI inferred from the general duty to provide reasons the existence of three procedural obligations that the Commission had, in its view, completely disregarded. The CFI held, first, that the Commission is 'obliged to give a reasoned answer to each of the objections raised in the complaint, if only by referring where appropriate to the *de minimis* rule where the

[67] Case T-95/94 *Sytraval and Brink's France SARL v Commission* [1995] ECR-II 2651.

[68] ibid, para 11.

[69] ibid, para 86.

point in question is so insignificant as not to warrant the Commission spending any time on it'[70] (*reasoned response requirement*). The CFI held, secondly, that the Commission is obliged 'to examine the objection which the complainant would certainly have raised if it had been given the opportunity of taking cognizance of [the information at the disposal of the Commission]', whenever it dismisses a complaint without allowing the complainant to comment[71] (*synoptic requirement*).[72] It further held, finally, that 'the Commission's obligation to state reasons for its decisions may in certain circumstances require an exchange of views and arguments with the complainant [in order to] ascertain what view the complainant takes of the information gathered by the Commission in the course of its inquiry'[73] (*dialogue requirement*). The latter obligation was 'a necessary extension of the Commission's obligation to deal diligently and impartially with its inquiry into the matter'.[74]

The judgment of the CFI in *Sytraval* altered dramatically the position of complainants in State aid procedures. It represented an outright departure from the bilateral model and was therefore seen as a silent but genuine revolution.[75] It was, however, a short-lived one, since the ECJ would eventually tone down the interpretation of the rights of complainants made by the CFI. On appeal, the ECJ also found that the reasoning of the Commission's decision was defective,[76] but it clearly distanced itself from the views of the CFI with regard to the position of complainants in State aid procedures. Indeed, it rejected the existence of an obligation to conduct 'an exchange of views and arguments with the complainant' or to give complainants an opportunity to 'state their views'.[77] It also rejected the synoptic requirement and simply conceded that the obligation of the Commission to conduct a diligent and impartial examination 'may make it necessary for it to examine matters not expressly raised by the complainant'.[78] Finally, it loosened the reasons-giving requirement, releasing the Commission from the obligation to give an answer to each of the objections raised by complainants and relying instead on the oft-cited proposition that 'The requirements to be satisfied by the statement of reasons depend on the circumstances of each case'.[79] The move made by the CFI in *Sytraval* was thus redressed by the ECJ.

[70] ibid, para 62.
[71] ibid, para 66.
[72] I borrow the label from Martin Shapiro, 'Two Transformations in Administrative Law: American and European?' in Karl-Heinz Ladeur (ed), *The Europeanisation of Administrative Law: Transforming National Decision-Making Procedures* (Aldershot: Ashgate, 2002) 16.
[73] Case T-95/94 *Sytraval and Brink's France SARL v Commission* [1995] ECR-II 2651, para 78.
[74] ibid.
[75] Hans P Nehl, 'Judicial Protection of Complainants in EC State Aid Law: A Silent Revolution?' (2009) 8 *European State Aid Law Quarterly* 401, 408.
[76] Case C-367/95 P *Commission v Sytraval and Brink's France* [1998] ECR I-1719, paras 73–78.
[77] ibid, paras 58–59.
[78] ibid, para 62.
[79] ibid, para 63.

(c) Time Limits (Television Cases)

The third move concerns the time limits faced by the Commission to conclude the preliminary phase of the State aid procedure. The general rule in that regard was adopted in the *Lorenz* case, where the ECJ held that the Commission was under a duty to define its position on the compatibility of notified aids 'within a reasonable period'.[80] Given the silence of the Treaty on this issue, the Court applied by analogy the time limits that govern the conduct of the general infringement procedure, holding that the Commission was under a duty to define its position within two months from the notification.[81] This time limit would be later codified in the Procedural Regulation (PR).[82]

The foundation of such a duty was the need to 'take account of the interest of Member States of being informed of the position quickly',[83] which is why it was not possible to transpose this rule automatically to complaint-triggered procedures, as the CFI explicitly acknowledged in *Gestevisión*.[84] *Gestevisión* concerned an action for failure to act brought by a competitor of the alleged beneficiary more than two years after the submission of a complaint. Yet the unavailability of the *Lorenz* rule did not prevent the Court from holding that the Commission was obliged to act within a reasonable time and that it could not 'prolong indefinitely its preliminary investigation into measures that have been the object of complaints'.[85] The CFI found, on the facts of the case, that the duration of the investigation had not been reasonable and, accordingly, ruled in favour of the complainant. The same principle was applied, with the same result, in *TF1*.[86]

These two television cases represent a second inroad into the purely bilateral character of the procedure, insofar as they impose on the Commission the obligation to take a position on complaints within a reasonable time. Again, however, this claim cannot be taken too far, since in both cases the CFI expressly pointed out that the requirement to adopt a position within a reasonable time operates where the Commission 'has, as in this case, agreed to initiate such an investigation'.[87] This qualification suggests that the Commission can avoid the obligation to adopt a position within a reasonable time if it simply refrains from taking any action on the basis of the complaint, a reading that preserves the enforcement discretion of

80 Case 120/73 *Gebrüder Lorenz GmbH v Germany* [1973] ECR 1471, para 4.
81 ibid.
82 Article 4(5) PR.
83 Case 120/73 *Gebrüder Lorenz GmbH v Germany* [1973] ECR 1471, para 4.
84 Case T-95/96 *Gestevisión Telecinco v Commission* [1998] ECR II-3407, paras 76–79.
85 ibid, paras 73–74.
86 Case T-17/96 *TF1 v Commission* [1999] ECR II-1757, paras 72–81.
87 Case T-95/96 *Gestevisión Telecinco v Commission* [1998] ECR II-3407, para 74: 'the Commission cannot prolong indefinitely its preliminary investigation into State measures in relation to which there has been a complaint under Article 92(1) of the Treaty *where it has, as in this case, agreed to initiate such an investigation*' (emphasis added) reproduced in Case T-17/96 *TF1 v Commission* [1999] ECR II-1757, para 74.

the Commission and its power to decide whether to initiate the State aid procedure in the first place.[88]

(d) The Departure From the Bilateral Paradigm in State Aid Procedures

The preceding analysis has identified three moves in which the EU judicature departed from the bilateral paradigm according to which complainants are completely alien to the State aid procedure. The ruling of the CFI in *Sytraval* made a far-reaching interpretation of the rights of complainants in the State aid procedure, which included a right to a reasoned response that left little room for the Commission to carry out a selective policy of enforcement—on appeal, however, this interpretation was rejected by the ECJ. *Cook* and the television cases, on the other hand, allowed complainants to benefit from a set of procedural guarantees initially recognised in favour of Member States—the right to challenge the preliminary closure of the State aid procedure and the right to a decision within a reasonable time.

However, none of these cases went so far as to impose upon the Commission the duty to investigate and adopt a position on every complaint, since they were based on the assumption that the Commission had adopted a position in response to a complaint—the *Cook* line of cases—or that it had decided to launch an investigation but failed to adopt a position within a reasonable time—the television cases. Insofar as they got around this problem, these developments seemed to suggest that the default rule in EU administrative law was also applicable in the context of State aid procedures and that the Commission was therefore invested, in this field as in all others, with a broad margin of enforcement discretion in the handling of complaints.

3. The Position of Complainants Under the Original Procedural Regulation

The judgments of the ECJ in *Sytraval* and of the CFI in *Gestevisión* were issued in 1998, just a few months before the adoption and entry into force of the PR.[89] This regulation was adopted on the basis of ex-Article 89 EC (current Article 109 TFEU), which empowers 'The Council, on a proposal from the Commission and after consulting the European Parliament, [to] make any appropriate regulations for the application of Articles 107 and 108'. It was the first attempt to lay out in a piece of secondary legislation the rules that govern the conduct of State aid procedures.

[88] Adinda Sinnaeve, 'State Aid Procedures: Developments since the Entry into Force of the Procedural Regulation' (2007) 44 *Common Market Law Review* 965, 1026.

[89] Note that the ruling of the CFI in *TF1* was issued after the adoption of the PR, but reviewed a procedure pre-dating the PR, which was therefore not applicable.

The jurisprudential developments described in the previous section were not unconnected to the adoption of the PR. During the first four decades of State aid policy, the Commission had sat on Article 89 EC and its precedents, without producing any proposal to legislate in this field—save for two proposals elaborated in the 1960s and 1970s that failed to be approved by the Council.[90] According to some commentators, one of the reasons why the Commission decided to change gear and to push for the adoption of the PR was the perceived threat represented by some of the jurisprudential moves described above, and most notably by the CFI's judgment in *Sytraval*.[91] As Bartosch puts it:

> Looking at the timetable of these *Sytraval* judgments (at both the CFI and the ECJ level) and the stages of the adoption of Regulation No. 659/1999, i.e. judgement of the CFI in *Sytraval* on 28 September 1995, proposal of a Procedural Regulation on 18 February 1998, judgement of the ECJ in *Sytraval* on 2 April 1998, final adoption of the Procedural Regulation on 22 March 1999, it seems that the Commission—possibly intimidated by the first ruling in *Sytraval*—felt finally compelled to take up the various appeals made—at least implicitly—by the Community Courts to lay down the rules for its administrative procedure in State aid matters rather than have them elaborated on a case-by-case basis by its Luxembourg watchdogs.[92]

Although the ECJ would eventually step in and impose a much more restrictive reading of the position of complainants in State aid cases, the judgment of the CFI in *Sytraval* may thus have sufficed to convince the Commission of the need to have clear procedural rules capable of countering the pro-competitor stance of the European Courts in some of their rulings.

As originally adopted, the PR basically codified the rules that had been developed through the combination of the administrative practice of the Commission and the case law of the European Courts. In relation to the involvement of complainants, it confirmed the possibility for the Commission to rely on complaints to initiate the State aid procedure. This was done implicitly as the original draft of the PR did not contain a single reference to complaints or complainants. It did, however, devote a whole chapter to the procedure for the review of unlawful aids, thus confirming the adequacy of the State aid procedure to assess non-notified measures.[93] And it did recognise the right of interested parties to 'inform the Commission of any alleged unlawful aid'.[94]

By omission, the PR also endorsed the restrictive vision of the ECJ in *Sytraval* with regard to the role of complainants in the development of the State aid procedure. The absence of any reference to any participatory opportunity available

[90] Adinda Sinnaeve and Pieter J Slot, 'The New Regulation on State Aid Procedures' (1999) 36 *Common Market Law Review* 1153, 1153.

[91] ibid, 1154.

[92] Andreas Bartosch, 'The Procedural Regulation in State Aid Matters. A Case for Profound Reform' (2007) 6 *European State Aid Law Quarterly* 474, 477.

[93] Chapter III, Articles 10 to 15 PR.

[94] Article 20(2) PR.

to complainants—that is, besides the initial submission of the complaint and the subsequent submission of comments in the context of the consultation phase foreseen by Article 108(2) TFEU—ruled out the existence of any dialogue requirement of the type read by the CFI into the preliminary procedure. In general, there was therefore little doubt that the original PR took 'its cue from the judgment in the *Sytraval* appeal, and not the judgment of the CFI (now General Court) in the same case, which … gave the complainant considerable rights'.[95] The only exception was the right of complainants to be sent a copy of any decision taken on the basis of the information supplied,[96] which is of utmost importance given the possibility of challenging that decision opened up by *Cook*[97]—and which had been praised as a matter of good administrative practice but declared groundless by the ECJ.[98]

As a result of the codifying approach taken in its elaboration, the PR was silent on some of the issues that had been left open by the previous case law. One of these issues was, precisely, the degree of enforcement discretion that the Commission enjoyed in relation to complaints. Indeed, whilst entrenching the right of competitors and other interested parties to denounce unlawful aids, the PR did not explicitly address the central question raised by the involvement of complainants in State aid procedures, namely the extent to which they place the Commission under an obligation to investigate and adopt a position on the merits of their claims. If 'interpreted conservatively', it was thus difficult to escape the conclusion that the silence of the PR left intact the enforcement discretion of the Commission.[99]

An alternative reading was, however, possible. Some commentators argued that the PR did in fact provide an implicit answer to the question of the enforcement discretion of the Commission, ruling out the existence of any such discretion in the handling of State aid complaints.[100] This claim was based, in essence, on the combined interpretation of three of its provisions—namely, Articles 10(1), 13(1) and 20(2) of the original PR.

Article 10(1) PR stated that 'Where the Commission has in its possession information from whatever source regarding alleged unlawful aid, it *shall* examine that information without delay' (emphasis added).[101] The mandatory language used

[95] Slot (n 56) 967.

[96] Article 20(2) PR, *in fine.*

[97] Slot (n 56) 953.

[98] Case C-367/95 P *Commission v Sytraval and Brink's France* [1998] ECR I-1719, paras 45–46. But see: Slot, (n 56) 953, who considers that the right only exists where the decision is taken pursuant to the formal investigation phase.

[99] Massimo Merola and Leonardo Armati, 'Complainants' Rights in State Aid Matters. Lost in Modernisation?' in Inge Govaere and Dominik Hanf (eds), *Scrutinizing Internal and External Dimensions of European Law. Liber Amicorum Paul Demaret* (Brussels: Peter Lang, 2013) 569, 580.

[100] Adinda Sinnaeve, 'Rights of Interested Parties' in Martin Heidenhain (ed), *European State Aid Law* (Munich: Verlag CH Beck, 2010) 685, who bases his assertion on Article 10(1) read in conjunction with Article 20 PR. See also: Bartosch (n 92) 480, who bases his claim on Article 13(1) PR.

[101] Article 10(1) PR, original drafting.

by that provision made it clear that the Commission was under a duty to devote a minimum of attention to any piece of information pointing to a possibly unlawful aid. That complaints were an appropriate vehicle to bring this information to the attention of the Commission was beyond doubt, given the content of Article 20(2) of the original PR. The question was whether Article 10(1) PR allowed the Commission to discontinue the investigation of some complaints, after a mere cursory examination of their content, in accordance with its own enforcement priorities. This interpretation faced two obstacles.

The first obstacle was that Article 13(1) PR listed the type of decisions to which the examination of unlawful aid could give rise: a decision that there is no aid, a decision to raise no objections or a decision to open the formal investigation phase.[102] This list made no room for the adoption of an *Automec*-type of decision, ie, a formal decision embodying the reasoned refusal of the Commission to investigate a complaint. To be more precise, nothing in the PR itself prevented a 'decision to raise no objections' from having this content, but the procedural trap represented by *Cook* did imply that any such decision would be subject to the serious difficulties test and hence to an objective assessment that forecloses the closure of an investigation on the basis of the type of considerations that are relevant under *Automec II*.

If the PR left any margin of enforcement discretion to the Commission, the only way to exercise it would thus be through its own inaction—by refraining from taking any decision on complaints. This possibility fit uneasily, however, with the wording of Article 20(2) PR, whose original drafting provided that 'Any interested party may inform the Commission of any alleged unlawful aid' and that 'Where the Commission considers that on the basis of the information in its possession there are insufficient grounds for taking a view on the case, it shall inform the interested party thereof.' Although this provision left a door open for the Commission to escape the need to take a decision on every complaint, it seemed to subject this course of action to an objective condition, namely, the existence of insufficient grounds for taking a view on the case. Outside this hypothesis, it seemed to imply that the Commission was bound to carry out a proper investigation of every complaint.

There were thus various reasons to conclude that the PR denied the Commission any margin of enforcement discretion in the treatment of complaints. Yet, its hermeneutic appeal notwithstanding, this reasoning led to a somewhat paradoxical result—namely, the reinforcement of the position of complainants in State aid cases. Could this really be the effect intended by a regulation adopted in response to the generosity shown by the European judicature vis-à-vis complainants? One may of course discuss whether this was the objective of the Commission or plainly call into question the significance of the reasons behind the proposal to adopt a PR. Even so, it would still be paradoxical if the effect of a regulation that was silent

[102] Article 13(1) PR read in conjunction with Article 4 PR.

on the status of complainants, despite its adoption in the wake of a momentous case like *Sytraval*, was to provide them with a power that they do not have under any other branch of EU administrative law.

III. The Status of Complainants in State Aid Procedures

The previous section has traced the evolution of the status of complainants in State aid procedures up to the adoption of the PR. There are two ideas to take out from that analysis. The first idea is that there was a clear rejection on the part of the European Courts and of the legislator alike of providing complainants with any sort of participatory right other than the very submission of their allegations. The second idea is that neither the European Courts nor the legislator squarely addressed the issue of the enforcement discretion of the Commission in this field. Although it was possible to assume that this situation triggered the default rule in EU administrative law (enforcement discretion in the handling of complaints), there were also reasons to understand that the PR enshrined the exact opposite solution (obligation to respond to the merits of complaints).

This section reviews the position taken by the European Courts and the legislator on this issue after the adoption of the PR. The review starts with an analysis of the judgment of the ECJ in *Athinaïki Techniki*, where the ECJ seems to endorse the latter interpretation, and then moves on to consider its aftermath.

1. The *Athinaïki Techniki* Case

The facts of the case go back to October 2001, when the Greek authorities initiated a procedure for the award of a public contract with a view to disposing of 49 per cent of the capital of a casino. Athinaïki Techniki AE challenged the procedure before the Commission after the contract was awarded to its competing tenderer. It lodged two different complaints. The first one, lodged with DG Internal Market, challenged the tender in light of the EU public procurement rules. The second one, lodged with DG Competition, challenged the award to its competing undertaking on the ground that it involved unlawful and incompatible State aid. DG Competition decided to await the outcome of the other complaint, arguing that the disposal of a public asset in the context of a tendering procedure does not constitute State aid where the procedure has been carried out transparently and without discrimination. After the closure of the file by DG Internal Market, DG Competition sent a letter to the complainant informing it that there were insufficient grounds to take a view on the case and that it would therefore close the file.

Athinaïki Techniki AE brought an action of annulment against the decision to take no further action on its complaint. The CFI dismissed the action as inadmissible on the ground that the letter did not constitute 'a decision' within the meaning of the PR and therefore lacked 'legal effect'.[103] The judgment of the CFI was then overturned, on appeal, by the ECJ, which took the opposite view and considered that the letter was a decision within the meaning of Article 4 PR and was therefore open to challenge.[104] Accordingly, the ECJ set aside the order of the CFI and enjoined the lower Court to give a judgment on the merits of the pleas put forward by the applicant. Although the construction of the letter as an actionable act was outcome determinative, it does not actually represent a significant novelty. It confirms the stance taken by the CFI in *Deutsche Bahn*[105] and also happens to be in line with the un-formalistic approach generally adopted by the European Courts with regard to the conditions that an act needs to fulfil in order to be liable to form the basis of an action of annulment, an issue that is developed in more length in the last chapter of this book.

(a) The Procedure to Reject Complaints Read into the Procedural Regulation

Before reaching this conclusion, however, the ECJ took the opportunity to spell out the obligations of the Commission with regard to State aid complaints, and it is this aspect of the judgment that is relevant for the purposes of this chapter. In considering this issue, the ECJ basically drew a distinction between two scenarios, the distinctive criterion being the degree of completeness of the complaint.

The first scenario is that in which the information provided by the complainant is sufficient to assess the merits of the complaint; where this is the case, the ruling of the ECJ deems the procedure automatically initiated. Indeed, it reads former Articles 10(1) and 20(2) PR as

> grant[ing] to a person concerned the right to set in motion the preliminary stage ... by sending information regarding any allegedly unlawful aid to the Commission, which is then obliged to examine, without delay, the possible existence of aid and its compatibility with the common market.[106]

As explained earlier, the corollary of this interpretation is that the Commission is prevented from putting into effect any type of selective enforcement agenda for, once the procedure is set in motion, *Cook* and the serious difficulties test operate as a trap from which the Commission can only escape through a decision on the merits.

The second scenario covers those instances in which the Commission deems the information provided by complainants to be insufficient to assess the merits of their case. When this is the case, the ECJ considers that the Commission is

[103] Case T-94/05 *Athinaïki Techniki AE v Commission* [2006] ECR II-73, para 30.

[104] Case C-521/06 P *Athinaïki Techniki AE v Commission* [2008] ECR I-5829, para 60.

[105] Case T-351/02 *Deutsche Bahn v Commission* [2006] ECR II-1047, para 63. See comment in Carsten Nowak, 'Judicial Protection of Complainants in the Scope of EC State Aid Law: New Developments and Question Marks' (2006) 5 *European State Aid Law Quarterly* 621.

[106] Case C-521/06 P *Athinaïki Techniki AE v Commission* [2008] ECR I-5829, para 37.

under an obligation to allow complainants 'to submit additional comments within a reasonable period',[107] an obligation that it grounds on their 'right to be associated with [the procedure] in an adequate manner'.[108] This is remarkable in itself, because it implies that the Commission may not rely on Article 20(2) PR (Article 24 of the codified version) to avoid taking a decision without giving the applicant an opportunity to complete its initial submission. And this means, in turn, that persistent complainants have the tools to overcome the Commission's initial reluctance to look into their case.

Yet the most remarkable aspect of the ruling is that it precludes the possibility that this process be repeated without end. The ECJ considers, indeed, that 'Once those comments have been lodged, or the reasonable period expired, Article 13(1) [PR] obliges the Commission to close the preliminary examination with a formal decision'. The upshot is that 'the Commission is not authorised to persist in its failure to act during the preliminary examination stage',[109] or, as the Court has recently put it, that the 'the preliminary examination stage … *ultimately* obliges the Commission to take a position' (emphasis added).[110] Hence the claim made by some commentators that *Athinaïki Techniki* involved 'a de facto "abrogation" of the second sentence of Article 20(2) of the Procedural Regulation, in the sense that such a letter can no longer be viewed as a means available to the Commission for closing the file'.[111]

This abrogation is important, for it prevents the Commission from abusing the possibility foreseen in former Article 20(2) PR (Article 24 of the codified version) in order to leave complainants in limbo, with neither an investigation of their claims nor a decision to challenge. It is all the more important given the difficulties that private parties often face in compiling all the information that they need to build a strong complaint in State aid matters. The CFI pointed to this problem in its *Sytraval* ruling in order to reject one of the defences put forward by the Commission, which was based on the 'flimsiness of the evidence put forward by the complainants'.[112] Although the position taken on this issue by the CFI is no longer good law, the underlying institutional analysis still holds:

> It is very much more difficult for the complainants than it is for the Commission to gather the information and evidence needed in order to verify the validity of a complaint … Complainants are generally faced with the administrative obstacles inherent in steps of this kind, since they have to obtain confirmation of their objections from the very authorities whom they suspect of having infringed the Community rules on State aid,

[107] ibid, para 39.
[108] ibid, para 38.
[109] ibid, para 40.
[110] Case C-615/11 P *Commission v Ryanair*, ECLI:EU:C:2013:310, para 31.
[111] Edoardo Gambaro and Francesco Mazzocchi, 'Case C-521/06 P, Athinaïki Techniki v. Commission, Judgment of the Court of Justice (Fourth Chamber) of 17 July 2008, [2008] ECR I-5829; Case C-322/09 P, NDSHT v. Commission, Judgment of the Court of Justice (Third Chamber) of 18 November 2010, nyr; Case C-362/09 P, Athinaïki Techniki v. Commission, Judgment of the Court of Justice (Third Chamber) of 16 December 2010, nyr' (2011) 48 *Common Market Law Review* 2083.
[112] Case T-95/94 *Sytraval and Brink's France SARL v Commission* [1995] ECR II-2651, para 77.

without having any means of coercion at their disposal. The Commission, on the other hand, has at its disposal more effective and appropriate means of gathering the information necessary for a detailed and impartial investigation of the complaint.[113]

(b) Implications for the Enforcement Discretion of the Commission

In the course of its analysis of the second scenario, the ECJ draws a parallel with *Guérin*,[114] which is a leading case on the status of complainants in the field of antitrust.[115] This should come as no surprise, for what the Court essentially does in *Athinaïki Techniki* comes down to importing to the realm of State aid law the procedure that governs the handling of complaints in antitrust. This procedure is now defined by Article 7 of Regulation 773/2004,[116] which provides that:

> Where the Commission considers that on the basis of the information in its possession there are insufficient grounds for acting on a complaint, it shall inform the complainant of its reasons and set a time-limit within which the complainant may make known its views in writing.

This Article further provides that the Commission shall reject the complaint by a decision if the additional written submissions of the complainant are not convincing,[117] or deem the complaint withdrawn if no further information is submitted.[118]

In antitrust, the obligation of the Commission to give an opportunity for the complainant to provide additional information before rejecting its complaint, and the obligation to do so by means of a formal decision, are compatible with the enforcement discretion explicitly recognised to the Commission in the *Automec II* case. They may actually be seen as a procedural device at the service of the Commission's obligation to comply with the second aspect of *Automec II*, ie, with the duty to embody the refusal to investigate in a formal decision that invokes a valid reason of community interest in order to satisfy the requirements of the principle of care.

Yet the transplant of the very same scheme to the State aid procedure yields the opposite result. This is not so much because of the structure of the procedure itself (which does not exclude a priori the possibility of refraining from investigating complaints on grounds of administrative convenience), but rather because of the obligation imposed on the Commission to bring the procedure to an end with the adoption of a formal decision. As noted earlier, any such decision in the field of State aid triggers the serious difficulties test, which prevents the Commission from relying on the type of reasons that it can proffer in the field of antitrust to justify

[113] ibid.

[114] Case 282/95 P *Guérin automobiles v Commission* [1997] ECR I-1503.

[115] Case C-521/06 P *Athinaïki Techniki AE v Commission* [2008] ECR I-5829, para 40.

[116] Commission Regulation (EC) No 773/2004 of 7 April 2004 relating to the conduct of proceedings by the Commission pursuant to Articles 81 and 82 of the EC Treaty (OJ L123, 27.4.2004, p 18).

[117] Article 7(2).

[118] Article 7(3).

its refusal to investigate complaints. The effect of *Athinaïki Techniki* is, thus, to uphold the pro-complainants' reading of the PR, according to which the Commission enjoys no enforcement discretion in the field of State aid.

Granted, the judgment of the ECJ in *Athinaïki Techniki* could have been more explicit in that regard—and the same can be said of its later judgment in *NDSHT*, where it reiterated the same interpretation of the obligations borne by the Commission in relation to State aid complaints.[119] This is probably the reason why the Commission has tried to argue in later cases—as the CFI noted with disapproval in a recent judgment—that

> in reaction to a complaint concerning State aid, it has the option either to open the preliminary examination stage which leads to a decision within the meaning of Article 4 [PR], or, if it considers that there are insufficient grounds to rule on the case, to close the complaint without opening the preliminary stage.[120]

The same judgment of the CFI makes clear, however, that 'That position has been invalidated by the case-law of the Court of Justice',[121] because *Athinaïki Techniki* and NDSHT imply that 'the examination of a complaint on State aid necessarily gives rise to the opening of the preliminary examination stage which the Commission is obliged to close by adopting a decision pursuant to Article 4 [PR]'.[122] This judgment was issued in early 2013, before the approval of the reform of the PR, which was passed in the same year. Yet, as the following section explains, the reform has basically codified the findings of the ECJ in *Athinaïki Techniki*, with some small adjustments that have no impact on the rule that deprives the Commission of enforcement discretion in the field of State aid.

2. The Reform of the Procedural Regulation

It was in the context of the State Aid Modernisation programme (SAM) launched by Commissioner Almunia in 2012[123] that the PR was reformed in 2013.[124] The ultimate goal of the SAM was to turn State aid control into yet another instrument at the service of the Europe 2020 objective of 'making Europe a smart, sustainable

[119] Case C-322/09 *NDSHT v Commission* [2010] ECR I-11911, para 50.
[120] Case T-182/10 *AISCAT v Commission*, ECLI:EU:T:2013:9.
[121] ibid, para 26.
[122] ibid, para 27. See also: Case C-615/11 P *Ryanair v Commission*, ECLI:EU:C:2013:310, paras 26–40.
[123] 'Communication from the Commission to the European Parliament, the Council, the European Economic and Social Committee and the Committee of the Regions on EU State Aid Modernisation (SAM)' COM (2012) 209 final.
[124] Council Regulation (EU) No 734/2013 of 22 July 2013 amending Regulation (EC) No 659/1999 laying down detailed rules for the application of Article 93 of the EC Treaty (OJ L204, 31.7.2013, p 15. See codified version: Council Regulation (EU) 2015/1589 of 13 July 2015 laying down detailed rules for the application of Article 108 of the Treaty on the Functioning of the European Union (OJ L248, 24.9.2015, p 9).

and inclusive economy'.[125] In order to achieve this ambitious goal, the SAM proposed more down-to-earth measures aimed at increasing the 'quality of the Commission's scrutiny' in the field of State aid control.[126] These measures were informed by the idea that it was necessary to prioritise and to move towards a 'better targeted' system of State aid control.[127]

There were two axes to the prioritisation strategy pioneered by the Commission in the SAM. The first axis involved expanding the decentralisation process analysed in the previous chapter so as 'to focus Commission ex ante scrutiny on cases with the biggest impact on internal market whilst strengthening the Member States cooperation in State aid enforcement'.[128] The underlying idea was that 'The drive towards more efficient spending should not translate into micro control of all public expenditure but rather into *prioritisation and stronger scrutiny of the aid with a significant impact on the single market*'.[129] The Commission therefore proposed certain amendments to the enabling, block exemption and *de minimis* regulations.[130]

The second axis involved streamlining the Commission's own procedures,[131] one of the objectives being to 'enabl[e] the Commission *to set priorities for complaints handling*, in order to prioritise allegations of potential aid with a large impact on competition and trade in the internal market' (emphasis added).[132] It is this aspect of the SAM that is more relevant for the present inquiry, since it suggests that one of the reasons behind the Commission's proposal to reform the PR was to curb the excessive demands that complaints place on the Commission's enforcement resources. This is confirmed by the explanatory memorandum to the proposal at the origin of the 2013 reform, where the Commission notes (somewhat bitterly) that it 'receives on average more than 300 complaints every year, whether lodged by interested parties or not, among which many are either not motivated by genuine competition concerns or not sufficiently substantiated'.[133]

It is against this background that the Commission proposed (and the Council approved) a revision of the PR. The reform did not only affect the status of complainants in State aid procedures for it also strengthened the powers of the Commission to request market information from third parties, an issue that need not be considered here.[134] However, it was particularly significant in that regard, since it explicitly recognised for the first time the right of interested parties to

[125] SAM (n 123) para 1.
[126] ibid, para 6.
[127] ibid, para 5
[128] ibid, para 8.
[129] ibid, para 19.
[130] ibid, para 20.
[131] ibid, para 8.
[132] ibid, para 23.
[133] 'Proposal for a Council Regulation amending Regulation (EC) No 659/1999 laying down detailed rules for the application of Article 93 of the EC Treaty' COM (2012) 725 final, 4.
[134] ibid, 7–11.

'*submit a complaint* to inform the Commission of any alleged unlawful aid or any alleged misuse of aid' (emphasis added)[135] and, as a corollary, the obligation of the Commission to 'examine without undue delay any complaint submitted by any interested party'[136] and to 'send a copy of the decision on a case concerning the subject matter of the complaint to the complainant'.[137] In this way, the reform put an end to the awkward silence that the PR had kept over this issue since its adoption in 1999.

At the same time, the reform articulated a series of filters that clarify the conditions that complaints need to satisfy in order to set the procedure in motion.[138] The idea behind this aspect of the reform is that any submission that fails to pass these filters will not be registered as a complaint but rather as mere 'market information', which can—but will not necessarily—'be used at a later stage to conduct ex officio investigations'.[139] This dichotomy rests on the new wording of Article 12(1) of the codified PR (ex-Article 10(1) PR). Whereas its old wording provided in very general terms that the Commission was bound to examine 'without delay' any information in its possession pointing to possible unlawful aid, no matter its 'source',[140] the amended version specifies that 'the Commission *may* on its own initiative examine information regarding alleged unlawful aid from whatever source' and that the Commission is only under an obligation to examine 'complaint[s] submitted by any interested party in accordance with Article 24(2)' (emphasis added).

There are basically three filters. The first filter is discreetly inserted into Article 12(1) itself, which restricts the obligation of the Commission to examine complaints to those submitted by 'any interested party' (*subjective filter*). This provision empowers the Commission to ponder the relationship of the applicant with the subject matter of the complaint in order to manage the flow of submissions that it faces. This may prove to be an insurmountable obstacle for some complainants, but is unlikely to have any impact on competitors, because Article 1(h) PR explicitly mentions them among interested parties. From their perspective, then, it is the two other filters that matter.

The second filter stems from Article 24(2) of the codified PR (ex-Article 20(2) PR), which provides that interested parties 'shall duly complete a form' to be defined in the implementing regulation (*formal filter*). The rule prior to the reform was that complaints were not subject to specific formal requirements. In its endeavour to promote complaints, the Commission had included in its webpage a

[135] Article 20(2) PR.
[136] Article 10(1) PR.
[137] Article 20(2) PR.
[138] Proposal (n 133) 5.
[139] ibid.
[140] Article 10(1) PR, as originally drafted, read as follows: 'Where the Commission has in its possession information from whatever source regarding alleged unlawful aid, it shall examine that information without delay'.

user-friendly form.[141] However, the European Courts had clarified that 'use of that form is not required by any rule of European Union law and consequently cannot be set up as a condition of "admissibility" for lodging a complaint concerning State aid'.[142] By introducing such a rule, the reform provides the Commission with the legal basis that it lacked to reject *in limine* any submission that fails to make use of the form.

Article 24(2) PR also lays down a third filter, for it also requires interested parties to 'provide the mandatory information requested' in the form (*information filter*). This requirement is not novel since it was already implicit in the possibility foreseen in the old version of the regulation of informing interested parties that there were 'insufficient grounds for taking a view on the case'. The novelty lies in the fact that the reform codifies the procedure spelled out by the ECJ in *Athinaïki Techniki* for disposing of insufficiently substantiated complaints, making it extend to formally defective submissions. Indeed, the reform adds a second paragraph to Article 24(2) PR, which reads as follows:

> Where the Commission considers that the interested party does not comply with the compulsory complaint form, or that the facts and points of law put forward by the interested party do not provide sufficient grounds to show, on the basis of a prima facie examination, the existence of unlawful aid or misuse of aid, it shall inform the interested party thereof and call upon it to submit comments within a prescribed period which shall not normally exceed one month. If the interested party fails to make known its views within the prescribed period, the complaint shall be deemed to have been withdrawn. The Commission shall inform the Member State concerned when a complaint has been deemed to have been withdrawn.

The codification of this procedure implies that the Commission may only rely on the formal and information filters to avoid taking a formal decision after providing the applicant with an opportunity to revise its initial submission. When the applicant misses this opportunity, the new wording of Article 24(2) PR imports from antitrust the 'legal fiction' that the complaint is deemed to be withdrawn.[143] The reform does not clarify what happens when, on the contrary, the applicant makes use of that opportunity, but there is no reason to believe that the position of the European Courts on this point should change after the reform. Thus, everything seems to suggest that the Commission remains bound by the obligation to close the file with a decision, in accordance with *Athinaïki Techniki*, and that 'obstinate complainants' will be able to overcome the information and formal filters 'quite easily'.[144]

[141] Michael Niejahr and Tibor Scharf, 'Third Parties in State Aid Control: More Than Just a Source of Information?' in *EC State Aid Law/Le droit des aides d'État dans la CE. Liber Amicorum Francisco Santaolalla Gadea* (The Hague: Kluwer Law International, 2008) 350.

[142] Case T-442/07 *Ryanair v Commission* [2011] ECR II-333, para 33.

[143] Hans P Nehl, '2013 Reform of EU State Aid Procedures: How to Exacerbate the Imbalance between Efficiency and Individual Protection' (2014) 13 *European State Aid Law Quarterly* 235, 241.

[144] ibid, 241.

This observation raises the question of the logic of a reform that was meant to strengthen the capacity of the Commission 'to set priorities for complaints handling'.[145] The preceding analysis indicates that the reform has not brought back to the field of State aid the general rule in EU administrative law according to which the Commission has the power to refrain from investigating complaints (subject to the requirement, in certain areas, to justify this decision on the basis of the Community interest). Whether this was at all the objective of the reform is open to question.[146] In any event, it seems that the actual reform was more modest, in the sense that it simply creates new tools for the Commission to manage the flow of complaints that it receives, without releasing it from the obligation to respond (at some point) to them.

It confirms, in this sense, that the type of prioritisation that the Commission is entitled to apply in the field of State aid does not concern the selection of complaints that it investigates but only the possibility 'to give differing degrees of priority to the complaints brought before it'.[147] In other words, it confirms that there is no room for a selective policy of enforcement in the field of State aid and that the Commission can only *postpone* dealing with measures that are not top priority.[148] These are likely to be complaints as opposed to notifications,[149] given the tighter time limits that the Commission faces in relation to the latter,[150] and the rule that deems the aid authorised in case of administrative silence.[151] The upshot is that the investigation of complaints is likely to take longer than the investigation of notifications,[152] but that persistent complainants have the tools to ensure that the Commission eventually takes a decision on their claims.[153]

3. The Consolidation of Complainants Within State Aid Procedures

The preceding analysis has shown that the possibility of bringing complaints in State aid matters empowers competitors to push the Commission to investigate and take a formal decision on the merits of their claims.

[145] Proposal (n 133) 5.

[146] According to Nehl (n 143) 242, the draft of the Code of Best Practice proposed reflecting 'on the opportunity to reject State aid complaints for lack of Community interest', but this idea did not make it to the final version of the Proposal.

[147] Case T-475/04 *Bouygues SA v Commission* (2007) ECR II-2097, para 158.

[148] 'Communication from the Commission—Code of Best Practice for the conduct of State aid control procedures' (OJ C136, 16.6.2009, p 13) para 48.

[149] María J Segura Catalán and Marianne Clayton, 'State Aid Modernisation: Another Reform?' (2013) 14 *ERA Forum* 21, 29.

[150] Two months according to Article 4(5) PR.

[151] Article 4(6) PR.

[152] According to the Proposal (n 133) 4, 'As of 31 March 2012, the average duration of pending complaint cases in DG COMP was 17 months'.

[153] But see Albert Sánchez-Graells, 'Digging Itself Out of the Hole? A Critical Assessment of the European Commission's Attempt to Revitalize State Aid Enforcement After the Crisis' (2016) 2 *Journal*

The analysis has not concealed the limitations of this power. First, complainants need to accommodate to the Commission's demands in terms of form. Second, they need to substantiate their claim with a minimum amount of information, which may prove difficult in some cases. Third, the time limits faced by the Commission in the handling of complaints are not as tight as in the case of notifications, which means that they are unlikely to receive a response within a short time. Finally, and more importantly, the preliminary phase remains an exclusive dialogue between the Commission and the Member State concerned as a result of the refusal of the European Courts and legislator to provide complainants with specific information or participatory rights within that context, which means that their chances of offsetting the influence of the Member State concerned remain slim.[154]

It is important to be aware of these limitations so as not to overstate the power of complainants within State aid procedures. Still, the possibility of bringing about a decision on the merits of their allegations (with the help, if need be, of the action for failure to act)[155] represents an important asset in the toolkit of competitors because of the courses of action that it opens up. The decision may be one of two types. It may be a decision to open the formal investigation phase, in which case complainants (and competitors at large) will have the possibility to participate—see next chapter. It may also be a decision to close the file (ie, a final decision that there is no aid or that the aid is compatible), which implies a rejection of the complaint, but in that case *Cook* opens the door for complainants to invoke the serious difficulties test before the European Courts—see Chapter 6.

Conclusion

Access

Despite the difficulties raised by the strongly bilateral design of the system of State aid control, the practice of the Commission and the case law of the European Courts secured from a very early stage the possibility for competitors to have access to State aid procedures through the submission of complaints. This possibility was implicitly recognised in the original version of the PR and is now explicit after the 2013 reform.

of Antitrust Enforcement 157, who argues that the reform 'has effectively restricted (if not fundamentally excluded) the possibility for complainants to force an intervention based on a complaint'.

[154] This is the aspect of the reform that has attracted more criticism. Nehl (n 143) and Bartosch (n 92).

[155] See, eg, Case C-615/11 P *Commission v Ryanair*, ECLI:EU:C:2013:310.

Leverage

The definition of the status of complainants (and hence of their actual chances of influencing the outcome of State aid procedures) has taken longer. It seems, however, that the ECJ (in *Athinaïki Techniki*) and the legislator (in the PR, especially after the 2013 reform) have both made a choice to grant State aid complainants a power that they seldom enjoy in other fields of EU administrative law, namely the power to force the Commission to investigate and take a decision on the merits of their claims. This power is subject to important limitations, which stem for the most part from the privileged position of Member States within the State aid procedure, but it challenges the instrumental conception of competitors that is normally associated with the bilateral design of State aid procedures.

5

The Participation of Competitors in State Aid Procedures

Introduction

The previous chapter looked at the position of complainants in State aid procedures. One of the points made in that chapter was that the possibility of lodging complaints is the only door that is open to competitors in the course of the preliminary phase, which is otherwise opaque and closed to the input of third parties. This is the reason why the focus of the book now shifts to the second stage of the procedure. Thus, the aim of this chapter is to assess the significance, in terms of access as well as leverage, of the participatory opportunities available to competitors within the so-called formal investigation phase. The chapter will soon show that these participatory opportunities basically come down to the possibility of submitting comments in the course of the consultation phase provided for by Article 108(2) TFEU.

The first part of this chapter reviews the general approach that EU administrative law takes to the participation of interested parties in individual decision-making procedures, showing that there are two basic regimes (the fundamental right to a hearing and the consultation rights of third parties). The purpose of that analysis is to locate the participation of competitors in State aid procedures within that divide, but also, more importantly, to identify the criteria that determine the value of these regimes in terms of access and leverage. It is against this background that the second part of the chapter addresses the issue of access, analysing the way in which the European Courts have defined the scope of the participatory opportunity sketched out by Article 108(2) TFEU. Finally, the third part of the chapter examines the way in which the European legislator and Courts have modulated the content of this participatory opportunity, using the criteria identified in the first part of the chapter to assess its significance in terms of leverage.

I. Participation in EU Administrative Procedures

1. The Fundamental Right to a Hearing in EU Administrative Law

The standard account of the participatory opportunities available to individuals under EU administrative law distinguishes two scenarios, depending on whether or not the so-called rights of the defence are triggered.[1] The rights of the defence are basically triggered in individual decision-making procedures liable to produce an adverse effect on their addressee and their main component is the right to a hearing, which entitles its holder to make his views known on the evidence held against him by the institution in charge of the procedure. For reasons that will immediately become apparent, individuals may not rely on this right in the context of State aid procedures. It is, however, useful to analyse the operation of this right as a model of a participatory regime that seeks to maximise the chances of access and leverage provided to its holders.

The right to a hearing was recognised for the first time in the context of disciplinary action taken by the European Institutions against its officials,[2] but was soon transposed to the field of economic regulation. In *Consten and Grundig*, the ECJ held that 'the parties concerned [by a procedure for the application of current Article 101 TFEU] should be put in a position before the decision is issued to present their observations on the complaints which the Commission considers must be upheld against them'.[3] It would later be elevated to the category of a 'fundamental principle of Community law' in *Hofmann-La Roche*[4] and codified in Article 41(2)(a) of the Charter of Fundamental Rights of the EU, which recognises 'the right of every person to be heard, before any individual measure which would affect him or her adversely is taken'.

Although the case law is not always clear and consistent, the applicability of the right to a hearing is normally subject to two conditions.[5] The first condition is the 'adverse effects requirement'—the right is triggered in procedures 'which are liable to culminate in a measure adversely affecting' their addressee.[6]

[1] Paul P Craig, *EU Administrative Law*, 2nd edn (Oxford: Oxford University Press, 2012) 316 and 322; Herwig CH Hofmann, Gerard C Rowe and Alexander H Türk, *Administrative Law and Policy of the European Union* (Oxford: Oxford University Press, 2011) 380–82; Jürgen Schwarze, *European Administrative Law*, rev 1st edn (Luxembourg: Office for Official Publications of the European Communities/ Sweet & Maxwell, 2006) 1325. Note that the latter speaks, somewhat confusingly, of the 'rights of defence for third parties'.

[2] Case 32/62 *Maurice Alvis v Council* [1963] ECR 49, 55.

[3] Joined Cases 56 and 58/64 *Consten and Grundig v Commission* [1966] ECR 299.

[4] Case 85/76 *Hoffmann-La Roche & Co v Commission* [1979] ECR 461, para 9. See also: Joined Cases 46/87 and 227/88 *Hoechst AG v Commission* [1989] ECR 2859, para 14.

[5] Eric Barbier de la Serre, 'Procedural Justice in the European Community Case-Law Concerning the Rights of the Defence: Essentialist and Instrumental Trends' (2006) 12 *European Public Law* 225, 238, which is also where I borrow the labels of the requirements from.

[6] Case C-301/87 *France v Commission (Boussac)* [1990] ECR I-307, para 29. See also Joined Cases C-48 and 66/90 *Netherlands and others v Commission* [1992] ECR I-565, para 44; Case C-135/92

This requirement is not precisely defined in the case law;[7] it covers procedures where sanctions or penalties are involved,[8] but clearly goes beyond those.[9] The second condition is the 'against requirement'—the right is triggered 'in all proceedings which are initiated against a person',[10] the idea being that 'the rights of the defence are applicable only if the party is sufficiently "targeted" by the procedure'.[11] The European Courts have departed, in some instances, from this requirement,[12] but in general the right to a hearing is not available to any party other than the formal addressee of the procedure. It follows that the right to a hearing does not cover many situations in which a stakeholder may be negatively affected by the outcome of a procedure.[13] In particular, it implies that complainants are a priori excluded from the scope of application of this right.[14] It implies, more generally, that the competitors of the addressee of a favourable decision will not be protected by the rights of the defence, despite the likelihood of their being negatively affected by such a decision.[15]

The fundamental right to a hearing represents a strong participatory entitlement for at least two reasons. The first reason is linked to its fundamental nature, which implies that it must be observed by the EU institutions even in the absence of express legislative recognition (access). The European Courts have indeed repeatedly held that

> observance of the right to be heard is, in all proceedings initiated against a person which are liable to culminate in a measure adversely affecting that person, a fundamental principle of Community law which must be guaranteed *even in the absence of any rules governing the procedure in question* (emphasis added).[16]

Fiskano v Commission [1994] ECR I-2885, para 39; and Case T-450/93 *Lisretal and others v Commission* [1994] ECR II-1177.

[7] Barbier de la Serre (n 5) 238.

[8] See, eg, Case 85/76 *Hoffmann-La Roche & Co v Commission* [1979] ECR 461, para 9.

[9] Case 32/62 *Maurice Alvis v Council* [1963] ECR 49, 55. See also Joined Cases 46/87 and 227/88 *Hoechst AG v Commission* [1989] ECR 2859, para 15 (right extended to preliminary investigations leading to sanctions); and Case 17/74 *Transocean Marine Paint Association v Commission* [1974] ECR 1063, para 15 (right triggered in procedure where Commission imposes condition on exemption).

[10] Case C-301/87 *France v Commission (Boussac)* [1990] ECR I-307, para 29.

[11] Barbier de la Serre (n 5) 238.

[12] Takis Tridimas, *The General Principles of EU Law*, 2nd edn (Oxford: Oxford University Press, 2006), who refers to Case T-260/94 *Air Inter v Commission* [1997] ECR II-997 (air carriers) and Case T-450/93 *Lisretal and others v Commission* [1994] ECR II-1177 (financial assistance programmes).

[13] Barbier de la Serre (n 5) 238.

[14] Joined Cases 142/84 and 156/84 *BAT and Reynolds v Commission* [1987] ECR 4487, paras 19 and 20 ('It follows that the companies which are the object of the investigation and the companies which have submitted [a complaint under Article 3 of Regulation No 17/62], having shown that they have a legitimate interest in seeking an end to the alleged infringement, are not in the same procedural situation and the latter cannot invoke the right to a fair hearing'); Case T-65/96 *Kisch Glass v Commission* [2000] ECR II-1885, para 33.

[15] Schwarze (n 1) 1326.

[16] Case C-301/87 *France v Commission (Boussac)* [1990] ECR I-307, para 29. See also Case 142/87 *Belgium v Commission (Tubemeuse)* [1990] ECR I-959, para 46; and Case T-450/93 *Lisretal and others v Commission* [1994] ECR II-1177, para 42.

It further means that its application 'cannot be excluded or restricted by any legislative provision'.[17]

The second reason why the right to a hearing represents a strong participatory entitlement is the way in which the European Courts have modulated its content (leverage). The core of the right to a hearing is the possibility of having a say in the decision-making procedures of the EU administration, but such a participatory opportunity does not exhaust the content of the right. Indeed, the case law of the European Courts attaches to this right a series of adjunct guarantees, which can be broken down into two different bundles.

The first bundle is made up of various information rights that seek to place their holder in a position to participate in a meaningful way. The first of such rights is the rule that 'the person concerned should be informed of the commencement of the proceedings, since without such information he or she cannot submit observations'.[18] The second aspect is the right to be informed of the objections sustained by the deciding institution, so as to be able to challenge them. In the field of antitrust, compliance with this right is ensured through the statement of objections.[19] The third aspect is the right to have access to all the information gathered in the non-confidential version of the administrative file so as to be able to rebut the objections with full knowledge of their foundations. This right is now codified in Article 42(1)(b) of the Charter of Fundamental Rights, which recognises 'the right of every person to have access to his or her file, while respecting the legitimate interests of confidentiality and of professional and business secrecy'.

The second bundle of guarantees is made up of the obligations that the exercise of the right to a hearing entails on the deciding institution. There is a negative and a positive dimension to this. The right to a hearing limits the grounds on the basis of which the final decision may be taken, insofar as the administrative authority may not rely on facts, circumstances or documents other than those which the applicant has been given an opportunity to comment upon (negative dimension).[20] Although the administrative authority is not bound to respond to all the comments made by the applicant,[21] the general duty to provide reasons (combined with the duty of care) additionally entails an obligation to justify the rejection of the relevant issues raised by the applicant (positive dimension).[22]

This multi-layered regime responds to the idea of 'effective participation', according to which the right to a hearing requires that its holder 'should be placed

[17] Case T-260/94 *Air Inter v Commission* [1997] ECR II-997, para 60.

[18] Schwarze (n 1) 1335.

[19] Case T-260/94 *Air Inter v Commission* [1997] ECR II-997, para 83.

[20] Case 85/76 *Hoffmann-La Roche & Co v Commission* [1979] ECR 461, para 14.

[21] Case C-301/96 *Germany v Commission* [2003] ECR I-9919, para 140.

[22] Loïc Azoulai, *Les garanties procédurales en droit communautaire: recherches sur la procédure et le bon gouvernement* (Ph.D. Thesis) (Florence: European University Institute, 2013) 109 (footnote 505) where he acknowledges that the duty to provide reasons is independent of the rights of the defence but nevertheless claims that it represents, together with the right to a hearing and its adjunct information rights, one indivisible whole ('un ensemble logique et chronologique indissociable').

in a position in which he may *effectively* make known his views on the evidence against him' (emphasis added).[23] The Courts have thus declared, for example, that

> the purpose of access to the file is in particular to enable the addressees of a statement of objections to acquaint themselves with the evidence in the Commission's file, so that they can express their views effectively, on the basis of that information, on the conclusions reached by the Commission in its statement of objections.[24]

Thus, what the regime of the fundamental right to a hearing seems to protect is 'the right to have an effective influence on the outcome of the decision'.[25]

The strength of the fundamental right to a hearing as an instrument to exert leverage over the European Institutions should not be overstated. The information rights associated to this right are not boundless—they do not give access to the confidential aspects of the file[26] and they do not require the final decision to be 'a replica of the Commission's statement of objections' since

> the Commission must take into account the factors emerging from the administrative procedure in order either to abandon such objections as have been shown to be unfounded or to amend and supplement its arguments, both in fact and in law, in support of the objections which it maintains.[27]

More importantly, the breach of these information rights does not necessarily invalidate the final decision, because the European Courts often apply a harmless error type of reasoning to avoid this result. The examples abound in relation to the right of access to the file.[28] These limitations notwithstanding, the fundamental right to a hearing is informed by a strongly protective rationale, which is why it constitutes a good example of a participatory regime that seeks to maximise the chances of access and leverage provided to its holders.[29]

2. The Consultation Rights of Third Parties in EU Administrative Law

As noted earlier, the fundamental right to a hearing is only triggered within a limited set of administrative procedures and, within them, only in respect of certain

[23] Case T-450/93 *Lisretal and others v Commission* [1994] ECR II-1177, para 42.
[24] Case T-24/07 *ThyssenKrupp Stainless v Commission* [2009] ECR II-2309, para 247.
[25] Barbier de la Serre (n 5) 233.
[26] Case T-48/05 *Yves Franchet and Daniel Byk v Commission* [2008] ECR II-1585, para 257.
[27] Joined Cases 100 to 103/80 *SA Musique Diffusion française and others v Commission* [1983] ECR 1825, para 14.
[28] Case 142/87 *Belgium v Commission (Tubemeuse)* [1990] ECR I-959, para 48: 'For such an infringement of the right to be heard to result in an annulment it must, however, be established that, had it not been for that irregularity, the outcome of the procedure might have been different'. See also: Case 107/82 *AEG-Telefunken AG v Commission* [1983] ECR 3151, para 30; Case T-30/91 *Solvay v Commission* [1995] ECR II-1775, para 58; and Case C-301/87 *France v Commission (Boussac)* [1990] ECR I-307, para 31.
[29] This is the main argument developed by Barbier de la Serre (n 5), albeit speaking of an 'essentialist' rationale.

stakeholders. However, the participatory opportunities afforded to individuals by EU administrative law are not restricted to this right. Leaving aside the issue of participation in rulemaking procedures, EU law does indeed recognise other consultation rights that empower private parties to have a say in administrative procedures. It is on the basis of these other consultation rights that third parties may participate in certain procedures.

The recognition of these rights is done by secondary law, on a sector-specific basis.[30] The point to note is that these rights generally constitute a weaker form of participation than the fundamental right to a hearing. This is because their non-fundamental nature implies that neither their scope nor their content is constitutionally predetermined, but also—more importantly—because they are normally informed by a more instrumental conception of the function of participation.[31] This conception explains their lesser value in terms of access and of leverage.

From the perspective of access, the instrumental conception that informs these rights manifests itself in the fact that it is often for the administration to decide in which cases to consult interested parties. In the field of antitrust, for example, Article 27(3) of Regulation 1/2003 provides that '*If the Commission considers it necessary*, it may also hear other natural or legal persons' (emphasis added). In the field of merger control, Article 18(4) of Regulation 139/2004 similarly provides that '*In so far as the Commission or the competent authorities of the Member States deem it necessary*, they may also hear other natural or legal persons' (emphasis added). Both regulations reserve a special treatment to certain third parties. Indeed, the Commission is bound to grant the applications to be heard submitted by third parties with a 'sufficient interest'[32] and, in the case of Regulation 1/2003, to associate complainants 'closely with the proceedings'.[33]

Still, even when access is granted, the rights of these 'special' third parties are not comparable to the fundamental right of a hearing, because their instrumental logic also manifests itself in their content, which is meagre in terms of leverage. Because they are seen as a source of information for the Commission, the

[30] See, eg, Article 5(10) of Council Regulation (EC) No 1225/2009 of 30 November on protection against dumped imports from countries not members of the European Community (codified version) (OJ L343, 22.12.2009, p 51); Article 27(3) of Regulation (EC) No 1/2003 of 16 December 2002 on the implementation of the rules on competition laid down in Articles 81 and 82 of the Treaty (OJ L, 4.1.2003, p 1); and Article 18(4) of Regulation (EC) No 139/2004 of 20 January 2004 on the control of concentrations between undertakings (OJ L24, 29.1.2004, p 1).

[31] Hofmann, Rowe and Türk (n 1) 381; Azoulai (n 22) 273–75; Joana Mendes, *Participation in EU Rule-Making. A Rights-Based Approach* (Oxford: Oxford University Press, 2011) 188.

[32] See Article 27(3) of Regulation 1/2003, second sentence ('Applications to be heard on the part of such persons shall, where they show a sufficient interest, be granted') and Article 18(4) of Regulation 139/2004, second sentence ('Natural or legal persons showing a sufficient interest and especially members of the administrative or management bodies of the undertakings concerned or the recognised representatives of their employees shall be entitled, upon application, to be heard').

[33] Article 27(1) of Regulation 1/2003. This is developed by Article 6 of Commission Regulation (EC) No 773/2004 of 7 April 2004 relating to the conduct of proceedings by the Commission pursuant to Articles 81 and 82 of the EC Treaty (OJ L123, 27.4.2004, p 18), which recognises the right of complainants to have access to the file and, 'where appropriate', to participate in the oral hearing.

consultation rights of third parties normally lack the type of adjunct procedural guarantees that ensure a meaningful and effective type of participation under the regime of the fundamental right to a hearing. Thus, their information rights are almost non-existent: the Commission is under no obligation to notify them individually of the existence of the procedure and, once they apply to intervene, they are only entitled to be informed 'of the nature and subject matter of the procedure', without access to the file.[34] The upshot is that, in general, secondary legislation affords third parties a bare right to submit comments.[35]

Of course, the status of third parties within EU administrative procedures is also shaped by certain across-the-board principles of EU administrative law. Two of them are particularly noteworthy. The first of them is the principle of openness, which is now enshrined in several provisions of the Treaties,[36] together with its two main components: the principles of transparency and participation.[37] This is the result of the 'EU turn to openness'[38] that was initiated in the early 1990s, mostly as an attempt to cure the legitimacy deficit from which the EU administration was perceived to suffer.[39] It is not necessary to review in detail these developments, because they were mostly concerned with participation and transparency in administrative *rulemaking* and, more generally, in the political decision-making process of the EU institutions.[40] It should be noted, however, that they had some spill-over effects on the *enforcement* procedures of the Commission, most notably as a result of the recognition of a general right of access to documents, which is now enshrined in the Treaty[41] as well as in the Charter of Fundamental Rights,[42] and developed in Regulation 1049/2001.[43] This right is subject to exceptions and gives access to particular documents rather than to the whole administrative file,

[34] Article 13(1) of Regulation 773/2004 and Article 16(1) of Regulation 139/2004.

[35] The status of complainants in antitrust cases is, as noted earlier, an exception (see n 33).

[36] Article 1 TEU ('This Treaty marks a new stage in the process of creating an ever-closer union among the peoples of Europe, in which decisions are taken as openly as possible and as closely as possible to the citizen').

[37] Article 15(1) TFEU ('In order to promote good governance and ensure the participation of civil society, the Union institutions, bodies, offices and agencies shall conduct their work as openly as possible') and Article 15(3) TFEU ('Any citizen of the Union ... shall have a right of access to documents of the Union institutions, bodies, offices and agencies, whatever their medium, subject to the principles and the conditions to be defined in accordance with this paragraph').

[38] Alberto Alemanno, 'Unpacking the Principle of Openness in EU Law: Transparency, Participation and Democracy' (2014) 39 *European Law Review* 72, 85.

[39] ibid, 84. For an account of the origins and evolution of these principles, see Francesca Bignami, 'Three Generations of Participation Rights Before the European Commission' (2004) 68 *Law and Contemporary Problems* 61, 68–72, and Deirdre M Curtin and Joana Mendes, 'Transparence et participation: des principes démocratiques pour l'administration de l'Union européenne' (2011) 137 *Revue Française d'Administration Publique* 101, 102.

[40] Joana Mendes, 'Participation and the Role of Law After Lisbon: A Legal View on Article 11 TEU', (2011) 48 *Common Market Law Review*, 1849, 1850.

[41] Article 15(3) TFEU.

[42] Article 42 CFR and Article 296(2) TFEU.

[43] Regulation (EC) No 1049/2001 of the European Parliament and of the Council of 30 May 2001 regarding public access to European Parliament, Council and Commission documents (OJ L145, 31.5.2001, p 43).

but it can nevertheless supplement—in some cases at least—the otherwise weak information rights of third parties.

The second principle is the idea of good administration and, more specifically, the duty of care and the duty to provide reasons that it entails for the EU administration.[44] The previous chapter discussed the implications of these duties for the status of complainants under EU administrative law. The point to note here is that these principles are also relevant when we think, more broadly, about the position of third parties in EU administrative procedures. These principles may not be used to read into primary or secondary law new participatory rights—ie, they are not by themselves a source of access.[45] But they do provide some leverage—when access can be grounded elsewhere—insofar as they allow the European Courts to assess the diligence of the Commission in managing the information on the basis of which it makes its decisions, which includes the information produced by third parties.[46] This is the reason why the duty to provide reasons and the duty of care have been described as a 'compensation' for the weak procedural position reserved to third parties within EU administrative procedures.[47] The significance of these principles for the inquiry carried out in this book will be discussed in more depth in the last part of the next chapter.

3. Participation in State Aid Procedures

The foregoing analysis has shown that participation in EU administrative procedures may be governed by two different regimes, depending on whether it is imposed by the fundamental right to a hearing or recognised as a matter of secondary law. The analysis has also spelled out the reasons why the fundamental right to a hearing is stronger than the type of consultation rights that third parties normally derive from secondary law. The question that arises is where to locate competitors and State aid procedures within this divide.

It is perhaps obvious yet important to note that the participation of interested parties within State aid procedures cannot be grounded on the fundamental right to a hearing. This is because the European Courts have taken a formalistic approach to the bilateral character of State aid procedures, declaring time and again that they are only targeted against the concerned Member State.[48] Two consequences follow from this characterisation. The first one is that it is the Member State concerned that is protected by the fundamental right to

[44] Article 41 of the Charter of Fundamental Rights.

[45] Hofmann, Rowe and Türk (n 1) 196, who refer to the *Technische Glaswerke Ilmenau I* case, discussed at the end of this chapter.

[46] ibid, 195.

[47] Azoulai (n 22) 237 (translation mine).

[48] Joined Cases C-74 and 75/00 *Falck SpA and Acciaierie di Bolzano SpA v Commission* [2002] ECT I-7862, para 81; Case T-198/01 *Technische Glaswerke Ilmenau GmbH v Commission* [2004] ECR II-2717, para 191.

a hearing.[49] The second one is that any actor other than the granting Member State has the status of a third party to the procedure, which cuts interested parties away from the fundamental right to a hearing. This includes the 'other Member States'[50] and competitors[51] (even if they acted as complainants),[52] but also State aid beneficiaries.[53]

Some commentators have taken issue with 'the legal fiction that the administrative procedure … is a procedure between the Commission and the Member State in question, to which the recipient of the putative aid is only a third party'.[54] In the same vein, State aid beneficiaries have argued before the European Courts that their position 'differs from that of interested third parties in that, although they are not direct parties to the procedure, their existence may be threatened by a final decision ordering recovery of the aid'.[55] In general, however, the European Courts have stuck to the third-party status of State aid beneficiaries,[56] albeit with some hesitations on the part of the General Court.[57] This is certainly a 'complex and controversial' issue,[58] in which we might witness some changes in the near future. However, these developments do not affect in any way the position of competitors in State aid procedures, whose third-party status raises no doubts. Although it could be argued that 'persons whose economic activities may suffer injuries or losses as a result of an infringement of the rules regulating economic activities should [not] be treated differently from the person to whom the infringement is imputed',[59] this idea is foreign to EU administrative law.

It follows that the participation of interested parties (in general) and competitors (in particular) in State aid procedures cannot be grounded on the fundamental right to a hearing. It should be noted, however, that the participatory regime that governs their involvement is unlike any other, in that State aid procedures

49 Case 234/84 *Belgium v Commission (Meura)* [1986] ECR 2263, para 27.

50 Case 84/82 *Germany v Commission* [1984] ECR 1451, para 13.

51 Joined Cases T-371 and 394/94 *British Airways and others v Commission* [1998] ECR II-2405, para 60.

52 Case T-613/97 *Ufex and others v Commission* [2000] ECR II-4055, para 86.

53 Joined Cases C-74 and 75/00 *Falck SpA and Acciaierie di Bolzano SpA v Commission* [2002] ECR I-7862, para 83.

54 James Lever, 'The EC State Aid Regime: The Need for Reform' in Andrea Biondi, Piet Eeckhout and James Flynn (eds), *The Law of State Aid in the European Union* (Oxford: Oxford University Press, 2004) 304. See also Philip Bentley, 'State Aid, Subsidies and Complainants' (1990) 1 *European Business Law Review* 91, 94; and Themistoklis K Giannakopoulos, *Safeguarding Companies' Rights in Competition and Anti-dumping/Anti-subsidies Proceedings*, 2nd edn (Aalphen aan den Rijn: Wolters Kluwer, 2011) 500–01.

55 Case T-198/01 *Technische Glaswerke Ilmenau GmbH v Commission* [2004] ECR II-2717, para 178.

56 ibid, paras 193–95.

57 See, below, the discussion of Case T-34/02 *Le Levant 001 and others v Commission* [2006] ECR II-267.

58 Opinion of Advocate General Mengozzi in Case C-290/07 P *Commission v Scott SA* [2010] ECR I-7763, para 52. See also: Leigh Hancher, 'EU State Aid Law—Now a Truly Ugly Sister?' in Leigh Hancher, Tom Ottervanger and Pieter J Slot (eds), *EU State Aids* (London: Sweet & Maxwell, 2012) 19–20.

59 Mendes (n 31) 188.

constitute 'the rare case in which a duty to give notice to parties concerned by the possible outcome of an administrative procedure is enshrined in primary EU law'.[60] Indeed, Article 108(2) TFEU provides that

> [i]f, *after giving notice to the parties concerned to submit their comments*, the Commission finds that aid granted by a State or through State resources is not compatible with the internal market having regard to Article 107, or that such aid is being misused, it shall decide that the State concerned shall abolish or alter such aid within a period of time to be determined by the Commission (emphasis added).

Thus, whereas the consultation rights of third parties are normally defined by secondary law, the right of third parties to participate in State aid procedures is entrenched in the Treaty itself.

This is the background against which the chapter needs to investigate the value (in terms of access and leverage) of the possibility of submitting comments in the course of the State aid procedure. The next section deals with the issue of access, looking at the conditions under which the Commission is bound to go through this consultation phase and to hear the concerns raised by competitors. The last section of the chapter will then address the issue of leverage, analysing (in light of the two participatory regimes outlined above) the way in which the European Courts have modulated the content of this participatory opportunity.

II. The Participation of Competitors in State Aid Procedures

This section departs from the text of Article 108(2) TFEU and investigates the implications that it has, in terms of access, for competitors. The analysis starts with a very brief discussion of the notion of 'the parties concerned' (ie, of the *subjective* scope of the participatory opportunity foreseen in that provision) and then moves on to examine the conditions under which these parties are entitled to be consulted (ie, its *objective* scope). For the sake of clarity, it should be observed that the issue of access essentially scrutinises the conditions under which the Commission is bound to open the second phase of the procedure (ie, the so-called formal investigation phase). This is because the biphasic structure of the State aid procedure is based, precisely, on the text of Article 108(2) TFEU, which makes it possible to draw a distinction between a preliminary phase (where competitors enjoy no participatory rights whatsoever, even when they act as complainants),[61]

[60] ibid, 380. See also Koenraad Lenaerts and Jan Vanhamme, 'Procedural Rights of Private Parties in the Community Administrative Process' (1997) 3 *Common Market Law Review* 531, 533, who write (referring to current Article 108(2) TFEU) that 'Only in the field of state aid does the Treaty refer to the right to a fair hearing'.

[61] Case C-367/95 P *Commission v Sytraval and Brink's France SARL* [1998] ECR I-1719, paras 58–59.

and the formal investigation phase (which is characterised by the consultation of the parties concerned).

1. The Notion of 'the Parties Concerned' Under Article 108(2) TFEU

The consultation phase foreseen in Article 108(2) TFEU is open to 'the parties concerned'. The Court defined this concept in *Intermills*, where it held that

> the 'parties concerned' referred to in that provision are not only the undertaking or undertakings receiving the aid but equally the persons, undertakings or associations whose interests might be affected by the grant of the aid, *in particular competing undertakings* and trade associations (emphasis added).[62]

This definition is now codified in Article 1(h) of the Procedural Regulation, which refers to 'interested' rather than 'concerned' parties, the two notions being interchangeable.[63]

The status of competitors as 'parties concerned' within the meaning of Article 108(2) TFEU is not problematic, which is why this issue need not be discussed any further. The only point to note is that this status is not conditional in any way on the role played by competitors in the first phase of the procedure. The previous chapter analysed the position of complainants in State aid procedures. Should the Commission's investigation reach the second phase of the procedure, complainants may certainly grasp this opportunity to reiterate or expand the allegations made in their initial submission. Yet the opportunity to submit comments foreseen by Article 108(2) TFEU is open to competitors and interested parties at large. It may therefore be the first time in the course of the procedure that competitors come forward in order to voice their concerns about the measure under scrutiny.

2. The Asymmetrical Design of the Consultation Phase of Article 108(2) TFEU

The breadth of its subjective scope notwithstanding, a brief look at the text of the Treaty suffices to show that the consultation phase of Article 108(2) TFEU suffers from a major shortcoming from the perspective of competitors. Article 108(2) TFEU requires the Commission to collect comments from interested parties as a precondition to declaring that a measure constitutes incompatible State aid, but imposes no similar requirement for the declaration of compatibility. In other words, the Treaty only subjects to a participatory procedure the adoption of

[62] Case 323/82 *Intermills v Commission* [1984] ECR 3809, para 16.

[63] Adinda Sinnaeve and Pieter J Slot, 'The New Regulation on State Aid Procedures' (1999) 36 *Common Market Law Review* 1153, 1184.

negative decisions, which seems to imply that positive decisions may be adopted without any input from interested parties. In principle, it is therefore possible for the Commission to clear State aids without consulting competitors, despite the likelihood of their being adversely affected by such a decision.

From a procedural perspective, there is therefore a certain asymmetry between the rules that govern the clearance and blocking of State aids, the latter being subject to stricter conditions. This may seem paradoxical, given that the Commission's powers are framed by a general prohibition.[64] The incompatibility of State aids being the default rule, one could imagine that the derogation from the prohibition represented by positive decisions would be subject to harsher or, at least, equal conditions than its straightforward application. And yet the opposite is actually true: it is only when the Commission plans to block a State aid that it is bound to go through the consultation phase.

The articulation of a stricter procedure for the blocking of State aids is consistent, however, with the view of State aid procedures as a device intended to protect the granting Member State and, indirectly, State aid beneficiaries. Indeed, the asymmetrical design of the Treaty responds to the idea that it is the clash between the interests of the granting Member State (in going forward with the State aid plan) and the Commission (in impeding the implementation of the plan) that calls for a special procedure. Opening a consultation phase may then be a means of involving State aid beneficiaries in the procedure and ensuring that their voice is also heard by the Commission before the State aid plan is definitively blocked. Although State aid beneficiaries are not the only actors that may use the consultation phase to push their case, there is actually some historical evidence that the drafters of this provision were mostly thinking of them when they introduced this procedural step.[65]

From the viewpoint of competitors, however, this asymmetrical design is problematic, because it limits the scope of the participatory opportunity of Article 108(2) TFEU to those instances where they are less likely to be harmed by the outcome of the procedure—namely, to those cases where the Commission takes the preliminary view that the State aid under scrutiny is incompatible with the common market. Albeit referring to third-party Member States, Advocate General Slynn made this point in one of his opinions:

> It may be of more concern to another Member State ..., that an aid should be found compatible than that it should be found incompatible. One would therefore expect that the Member States would have been given the right to make their views known when the Commission proposed to accept an aid as being compatible.[66]

Thus, the asymmetrical design of State aid procedures is problematic because it reduces the scope of the obligation of the Commission to move beyond the

[64] Luc Gyselen, 'La transparence en matière d'aides d'État: Les droits des tiers' (1993) 3 *Cahiers de Droit Européen* 417, 420.

[65] Mendes (n 31) 383.

[66] Opinion of Advocate General Slynn in Case 84/82 *Germany v Commission* [1984] ECR 1451, p 1498.

preliminary stage of the procedure—which is opaque and closed to the input of competitors and other interested parties—and to set in motion the formal investigation phase—which is open and participatory by virtue of Article 108(2) TFEU. Were the Commission bound to go through both stages on a systematic basis, the biphasic structure of the procedure would not be a problem. It would simply mean a postponement of the participatory rights of interested parties to the closing steps of the procedure. However, the asymmetrical design of the State aid procedure empowers the Commission to authorise the implementation of State aids at the end of the preliminary phase, without informing or consulting interested parties in any way. From the perspective of competitors, this is a major pitfall in terms of access.

3. Minimising the Asymmetry: The *Cook/Matra* Case Law

The asymmetrical structure of the State aid procedure, with a closed and opaque phase that only needs to be followed by a participatory and open phase in a limited set of circumstances, makes it necessary to define the conditions that govern the opening of the latter. In the cases analysed in this section, competitors and other interested parties have challenged the discretion of the Commission to decide whether to go through the consultation phase or to content itself instead with the preliminary phase of the procedure. The receptivity of the European Courts to some of their demands has limited the circumstances in which the consultation phase may be omitted, thereby reducing the asymmetry that stems from the Treaty.

Germany v Commission[67] (which was briefly considered in the previous chapter) stands out as the first case in which the Court of Justice considered the relationship between the two phases of the State aid procedure. In that case, the Court was faced with an action of annulment brought by Germany against the decision of the Commission to raise no objections to a Belgian plan to restructure its textile and clothing industry. One of the pleas submitted by Germany was that the decision was void because the Commission 'was bound to initiate the procedure for the review of aid referred to in [Article 108(2) TFEU] and could not, as it did, confine itself to the preliminary stage of review provided for in [Article 108(3)]'.[68]

It should be noted that the object of the action of annulment brought by Germany was a positive decision. Accordingly, there had been no manifest breach of the text of current Article 108(2) TFEU, which confines itself to presenting the consultation phase as a precondition for the adoption of negative decisions. The problem was that the Commission had not approved the State aid plan as initially notified by Belgium, but had undertaken a process of negotiations so as to see it modified. It was only after Belgium agreed to introduce some changes in its

[67] Case 84/82 *Germany v Commission* [1984] ECR 1456.
[68] ibid, para 6.

design that the Commission declared it compatible, albeit without opening at any moment the second phase of the procedure.

The Commission clung itself to the wording of the Treaty to argue that this background was irrelevant, since the procedure had finally resulted in a positive decision. Its position was therefore based on the narrowest possible reading of current Article 108(2) TFEU, one that sees the consultation phase as a precondition for the adoption of negative decisions only.[69] On the contrary, the plea submitted by Germany suggested that a broader reading of the Treaty was possible. It implied that the effect of current Article 108(2) TFEU goes beyond the prohibition for the Commission to block State aids without going through the consultation phase, in that it also limits the circumstances in which the Commission is entitled to clear a State aid at the preliminary phase.

In his Opinion, Advocate General Slynn favoured the position taken by Germany and argued that 'The power of the Commission to approve a plan for aid during the preliminary period (on a prima face view) is a limited one and outside that limited area Member States have a right to be heard'.[70] He then went on to reflect on the limits of this power. He considered the possibility that it be limited to the application of the exemptions foreseen in what is now Article 107(2) TFEU as opposed to those foreseen in Article 107(3) TFEU, but he discarded this option as devoid of any basis in the Treaty.[71] It is against this background that he put forward the interpretation that would then be followed by the Court, namely, that 'if the Commission is unable to say that the plan as presented is, on a prima facie view, clearly compatible with the common market, then the Article [107(2)] procedure must be initiated'.[72] The 'serious doubts' displayed by the Commission with regard to the compatibility of the aid, as initially presented by Belgium, clearly called for the initiation of such a procedure.[73]

In its judgment, the Court of Justice endorsed the approach of its Advocate General. The Court departed from the observation that one of the main characteristics distinguishing the two phases of the State aid procedure is that 'the Commission is under no obligation at the preliminary stage to give notice to the parties concerned to submit their comments' and added that 'such a procedure, which guarantees the other Member States and the sectors concerned an opportunity to make their views known and allows the Commission to be fully informed of all the facts of the case before taking its decision, is essential whenever the Commission has serious difficulties in determining whether a plan to grant aid is compatible with the common market'.[74] On the facts of the case, and given the peculiar itinerary followed by the contested aid, the Court concluded that the Commission

[69] Opinion of Advocate General Slynn in Case 84/82 *Germany v Commission* [1984] ECR 1451, 1493.

[70] ibid, 1498.

[71] ibid.

[72] ibid.

[73] ibid.

[74] Case 84/82 *Germany v Commission* [1984] ECR 1456, para 13.

'encountered serious difficulties' and 'was therefore under an obligation to initiate the consultation procedure provided for in Article [108(2) TFEU] before taking its decision'.[75]

The judgment of the Court of Justice in *Germany v Commission* was important for two reasons. First, it implied that the decisions adopted by the Commission at the end of the preliminary procedure are subject to judicial review, an issue that would be expressly confirmed in *CIRFS*.[76] Second, and more importantly, it spelled out the 'serious difficulties test', which would thereinafter determine the legality of the closure of the file without going through the consultation procedure. The exact operation of this test will be analysed in the next chapter, which looks more closely at the review exercised by the European Courts over the decisions adopted by the Commission in this field. The point to note here is that the serious difficulties test limits the power of the Commission to decide on the progress of the procedure and therefore partially redresses its asymmetrical design. It was therefore a first step in the transformation of the consultation phase of Article 108(2) TFEU into a subjective right to participate in State aid procedures.

A further step would be taken in the *Cook* case.[77] *Germany v Commission* concerned an action for the annulment of a phase 1 decision brought by a privileged applicant (Belgium, acting as a third-party Member State), but the same test would be used in *Cook* to review the legality of a similar decision in the context of an annulment action brought by a private applicant. The Court confirmed in *Cook* that, in the face of serious difficulties, the obligation to go through the consultation phase is a procedural guarantee that protects private actors and third-party Member States alike.[78] Accordingly, it adapted the rules on standing to ensure that non-privileged actors could also enforce their right.[79] This is how the consultation phase of Article 108(2) TFEU came to be seen as an actionable subjective right to participate in every State aid procedure where the compatibility of a measure is not straightforward.

The foregoing analysis has described the two moves that have led the Court of Justice to see the consultation phase of Article 108(2) TFEU as embodying a right to participate in State aid procedures whenever the compatibility of the measure under scrutiny is not self-evident. When viewed from the perspective of competitors, this jurisprudence is important for two reasons. First, it implies a choice in favour of a wide interpretation of the circumstances that require consultation by the Commission with parties concerned, one that fits but is not necessarily imposed by the wording of the Treaty. Second, it implies a choice in favour of the construction of this participatory opportunity as an actionable subjective right.

[75] ibid, para 17.

[76] Case 313/90 *Comité International de la Rayonne et des Fibres Synthétiques (CIRFS) and others v Commission* [1993] ECR I-1125, paras 26–27.

[77] Case C-198/91 *William Cook plc v Commission* [1993] ECR I-2487.

[78] It did not do so explicitly but simply relied on *Germany v Commission*, whose reasoning was equally applicable to 'the sectors concerned' (ibid, paras 29 and 38).

[79] See next chapter.

The combined effect of these two developments is the strengthening of the right of access of competitors to the State aid procedure.

A word of caution is due. It is certainly the case that the State aid control procedure still suffers from a certain asymmetry, since none of these developments has gone as far as to eliminate the possibility for the Commission to clear certain aids without gathering comments from competitors and other parties concerned. This asymmetry is encoded into Article 107(2) TFEU, so nothing but a Treaty revision could completely redress it. And it represents without any doubt an important limitation when it comes to assessing the right of access of competitors to State aid procedures. This limitation is all the more important given some of the rules that govern the operation of the serious difficulties test—such as the rule that allocates the burden of proof to the applicant[80] or the rule according to which the legality of State aid decisions 'is to be assessed in the light of the information available to the Commission when the decision was adopted',[81] all of which tip the balance in favour of the validity of the Commission's initial decision.

Yet, important as they may be, these qualifications should not overshadow the significance of the analysis put forward in the preceding paragraphs, which reveals a clear commitment on the part of the European Courts to reduce the asymmetry of the State aid procedure to its minimum expression. The result has been the maximisation of the possibilities for access to the formal investigation phase afforded to competitors and, hence, the expansion of the scope of their right to participate in State aid procedures.

III. The Content of the Right to Participate in State Aid Procedures

The previous section of this chapter described the way in which the European Courts have shored up the right of access of competitors to State aid procedures. By constraining the power of the Commission to omit the second phase of the procedure, and by empowering competitors and other interested parties to resort to the judiciary when the Commission exceeds that power, the European Courts have secured the right of competitors to participate in State aid procedures. This section takes the analysis one step further: it addresses the issue of leverage, trying to determine the extent to which this participatory right represents an actual opportunity to influence the decision-making process of the Commission.

In order to do so, this section deconstructs the content of the right to participate in State aid procedures laid down by Article 108(2) TFEU, as developed by secondary legislation and by the case law. It does so in order to determine whether

[80] Case T-73/98 *Société chimique Prayon-Rupel v Commission* [2001] ECR II-867, para 49.
[81] Case 234/84 *Belgium v Commission (Meura)* [1986] ECR 2263, para 16.

it constitutes a bare right to submit comments or whether it encompasses any of the adjunct guarantees analysed at the beginning of this chapter in relation to the fundamental right to a hearing. The section starts with an analysis of the content of the right to submit comments itself and then considers the information rights that surround this participatory opportunity.

1. The Right to Submit Comments

The starting point of this analysis will be the content of the very right to participate in State aid procedures that the European Courts have read into Article 108(2) TFEU. This provision does not cast light on this issue: it merely states—almost in passing—that interested parties shall be given the opportunity to submit comments when the Commission considers that a measure constitutes incompatible State aid, without specifying the way in which this submission is to take place. For its part, the Procedural Regulation does not add anything in that respect, since it confines itself to restating the Treaty-based right to submit comments amongst the rights of interested parties listed in Article 20(1) PR. It is against this meagre legislative framework that the European Courts have been called to define the exact content of the right of interested parties to participate in State aid procedures.

In general, the European Courts have been reluctant to endorse the demands of private litigants pushing for an extensive interpretation of these scarcely detailed provisions. In order to expose their stance on this issue, it is necessary to resort once again to the *Sytraval* case, which was analysed in the previous chapter. As the reader probably recalls, the *Sytraval* case involved the review of a decision not to raise objections adopted by the Commission at the outset of a preliminary procedure initiated in response to a complaint. The then CFI made an extensive interpretation of the procedural rights of private parties within the preliminary investigation phase, going as far as to impose on the Commission the obligation to enter into a dialogue with the complainant, in certain cases, before taking its final decision.[82] On appeal, the Court of Justice upheld the judgment (finding that the decision was vitiated by insufficient reasoning) but rejected the existence of the 'dialogue requirement' that the CFI had read into the procedure.[83]

Granted, the controversy in *Sytraval* turned on the rights of complainants in the first phase of the State aid control procedure, an issue that falls outside the scope of this chapter. The judgment of the ECJ is relevant, however, because it grounded its rejection of the dialogue requirement on the observation that the second phase of the State aid procedure lacks a similar requirement, despite its more participatory character. After noting that 'in the context of an examination under Article [108(2) TFEU] the Commission is required merely to give notice to the parties concerned to submit their comments', the Court held that 'the imposition on the

[82] Case T-95/94 *Sytraval and Brink's France SARL v Commission* [1995] ECR-II 2651, para 78.
[83] Case C-367/95 P *Commission v Sytraval and Brink's France* [1998] ECR I-1719, paras 58–9.

Commission of an obligation requiring it to conduct an exchange of views and arguments with the complainant in the context of the initial review provided for by Article [108(3) TFEU] could lead to conflict between the procedural regime established by that provision and that laid down by Article [108(2)]'.[84]

The impossibility of founding a right to a dialogue on the right to submit comments was confirmed, more recently and explicitly, in *Falck and Acciaierie di Bolzano*.[85] The action at the origin of that case was lodged by the recipient of the controversial aid, rather than by one of its competitors. But, in dismissing the action, the Court offered a general review of the procedural rights of interested parties that is equally applicable to both types of stakeholders. Indeed, it confirmed that the only role of 'interested parties other than the Member State concerned' within the State aid procedure is to submit comments so that the Commission gathers all the information required for its future action and that 'they cannot themselves seek to engage in an adversarial debate with the Commission in the same way as is offered to the abovementioned Member State'.[86]

It is therefore settled case law that the right to participate in the second phase of State aid procedures does not include the right to enter into any type of dialogue with the Commission. Later cases have clarified that it does not encompass either any type of interaction with other participants, given the absence of a right to be sent the replies or comments submitted by other interested parties.[87] The upshot is that the right of competitors to participate in State aid procedures comes down to a one-shot, unidirectional opportunity to submit comments, without any entitlement to an adversarial debate of any type, either with the Commission or with any other participant.[88]

In some of its judgments, the General Court (GC) has attempted to provide a more general definition of the content of this right, as encompassing 'only the right to be involved in the administrative procedure to the extent appropriate in light of the circumstances of the case'.[89] In terms of precision, this formula may seem wanting, since it fails to offer a clear description of the type of participation available to interested parties. Yet it is in fact coherent with the instrumental rationale for the participation of competitors in State aid procedures, in that it prescribes a casuistic approach that modulates their degree of involvement depending on the information needs of the Commission. Seen in this light, it may be more significant than it seems. It is a manifestation of a clear choice in favour of a minimalist interpretation of the participatory right afforded to interested

[84] ibid, para 59.

[85] Joined Cases C-74/00 P and C-75/00 P *Falck SpA and Acciaierie di Bolzano SpA v Commission* [2002] ECR I-7869.

[86] ibid, para 82, read in connection with para 80.

[87] Case T-198/01 *Technische Glaswerke Ilmenau GmbH v Commission* [2004] ECR II-2717, para 197.

[88] Gyselen (n 64) 432: 'Comme dans la phase préliminaire, les intéressés n'ont donc qu'une seule occasion d'exprimer leur point de vue'.

[89] Joined Cases T-371 and 394/94 *British Airways and others v Commission* [1998] ECR II-2405, paras 59 and 60; Case T-613/97 *Ufex and others v Commission* [2000] ECR II-4055, para 89; Case T-354/99 *Kuwait Petroleum v Commission* [2006] ECR II-1475, para 80.

parties by the Treaty, one that sees them as mere 'information sources' for the Commission[90] and deprives them of any power besides the written submission of comments.

2. The Right to be Informed of the Procedure

The next object of this inquiry will be the information rights associated with the right to submit comments in the course of the second phase of the State aid procedure. The starting point here will also be the provisions laid down by primary and secondary law, which confer on interested parties two types of information rights. On the one hand, it follows from Article 108(2) TFEU that interested parties shall be given notice of the opening of the second phase of the procedure, an issue that is developed by Article 6(1) PR, which defines the content of the decision to initiate the formal investigation procedure. On the other hand, Article 20(1) PR lists amongst the rights of interested parties the right of 'any interested party which has submitted comments' to receive a copy of the final decision of the Commission. The function of this right is obviously more closely connected to the possibility of seeking judicial review of the final decision than to affecting its content, which is why it will not be discussed here.

The focus will therefore be on the right to be informed of the initiation of the formal investigation procedure. This is the first information right that competitors have in the course of the procedure, for no similar right exists in relation to the preliminary phase.[91] It should be noted, however, that this right does not encompass the right to be individually notified. The Court of Justice clarified in *Intermills* that current Article 108(2) TFEU 'does not require individual notice to be given to particular persons' and that 'the publication of a notice in the Official Journal is an appropriate means of informing all the parties concerned that a procedure has been initiated'.[92] This rule has been restated in later judgments and constitutes settled case law.[93] It is therefore not open to interested parties to challenge State aid decisions on the grounds that they were not individually asked to comment on the effects of the measure under scrutiny.[94]

From the perspective of interested parties, this rule represents an important limitation, since it increases the likelihood of their overlooking the opening of the

[90] Joined Cases T-371 and 394/94 *British Airways and others v Commission* [1998] ECR II-2405, para 59; Case T-613/97 *Ufex and others v Commission* [2000] ECR II-4055, para 89; Case T-354/99 *Kuwait Petroleum v Commission* [2006] ECR II-1475, para 89.

[91] Case T-266/94 *Skibsvaerftsforeningen and others v Commission* [1996] ECR II-1399, para 238.

[92] Case 323/82 *Intermills v Commission* [1984] ECR 3809, para 17.

[93] See, eg, Joined Cases C-74/00 P and C-75/00 P *Falck SpA and Acciaierie di Bolzano SpA v Commission* [2002] ECR I-7869, para 80; Joined Cases T-371 and 394/94 *British Airways and others v Commission* [1998] ECR II-2405, para 59; Case T-354/99 *Kuwait Petroleum v Commission* [2006] ECR II-1475, para 81; Case T-291/06 *Operator ARP v Commission* [2009] ECR II-2275, para 31.

[94] Joined Cases T-129/95 and T-2 and 97/96 *Neue Maxhütte Stahlwerke and others v Commission* [1999] ECR II-17, para 232.

formal investigation procedure, be it because they fail to notice it altogether or because they fail to realise that they are potentially affected by it.

The first problem (the risk that interested parties overlook the opening of the consultation phase) is intrinsic to the policy choice in favour of a system of general publication rather than a system of individual notification, which is in turn justified by the predominance of the instrumental rationale for the consultation of private parties in State aid procedures. Although one of the functions of the notice is to allow interested parties to exercise their participatory right,[95] the case law has repeatedly stressed the idea that its main function is to allow the Commission to gather all the information required to assess the compatibility of the aid with the common market.[96] From this perspective, the publication of a general notice in the Official Journal appears as a more effective means of announcing the opening of the consultation phase. This is because it can reach a broader range of potentially interested parties and, more importantly, because it allows potentially interested parties to identify themselves as such, which is one of the advantages of open consultation phases in situations where the underlying web of interests is complex.[97]

The second problem (the risk that interested parties fail to realise that they are potentially affected by a particular State aid procedure) has been brought to the attention of the European Courts in a considerable number of cases, with many applicants arguing that they could not infer from the text of the notice published in the Official Journal that they were liable to be affected by the outcome of the procedure. It is within this context that the European Courts have come to impose on the Commission a minimum level of specificity in the content of the notice. This requirement, which had already been hinted at in *Intermills*,[98] has been more explicitly developed by the GC in later cases, the rule being that 'The Commission must ... define sufficiently the framework of its investigation so as not to render meaningless the right of interested parties to put forward their comments'.[99] At first sight, the articulation of this rule—and the very language of the Court, referring to the 'right' of interested parties—seems to be more heavily informed by the legal protection paradigm than by the instrumental logic of this participatory opportunity.

Yet the significance of this requirement should not be overstated. First of all, the CFI itself has carefully limited the reach of the requirement, explicitly releasing

[95] Joined Cases C-74/00 P and C-75/00 P *Falck SpA and Acciaierie di Bolzano SpA v Commission* [2002] ECR I-7869, para 80; Joined Cases T-371 and 394/94 *British Airways and others v Commission* [1998] ECR II-2405, para 58.

[96] Case 70/72 *Commission v Germany* [1973] ECR 813, para 19; Case T-266/94 *Skibsvaerftsforeningen and others v Commission* [1996] ECR II-1399, para 256; Case T-354/99 *Kuwait Petroleum v Commission* [2006] ECR II-1475, para 81; Case T-291/06 *Operator ARP v Commission* [2009] ECR II-2275, para 36.

[97] Eberhard Schmidt-Assmann, *La teoría general del Derecho administrativo como sistema. Objeto y fundamentos de la construcción sistémica* (Mariano Bacigalupo et al tr, Madrid: Marcial Pons, 2003) 161.

[98] Case 323/82 *Intermills v Commission* [1984] ECR 3809, para 18.

[99] Case T-354/99 *Kuwait Petroleum v Commission* [2006] ECR II-1475, para 85; Case T-291/06 *Operator ARP v Commission* [2009] ECR II-2275, para 38.

the Commission from the obligation 'to present a complete analysis of the aid in question'[100] since its analysis at that stage is 'necessarily preliminary in nature'.[101] It has also stressed the subsidiary role that the consultation phase plays in relation to the information submitted by the granting Member State, allowing the Commission to focus on the 'essentials of the planned aid' and on 'those aspects of the [State aid plan] concerning which it still harbours doubts' after the preliminary examination procedure.[102] The resulting rule is a general and open-textured standard whose precise implications are hard to pinpoint, but the wording chosen by the CFI in its formulation suggests that it constitutes a rather lenient requirement.

This is confirmed by the fact that its application rarely results in the disapproval of the notice published by the Commission. To the best of my knowledge, *Le Levant* stands out as the only case in which the then CFI annulled a Commission decision on the ground that the notice published in the Official Journal did not meet the minimum information requirements.[103] The State aid at the origin of that case concerned a series of measures related to the building of a vessel. The action was brought by a group of investors who had been allowed to deduct the amount of their investment from their taxable income and who were affected in their capacity as State aid beneficiaries by the recovery decision adopted by the Commission. Their argument was that the notice published in the Official Journal pointed to the operator of the vessel as the only possible beneficiary, which is why they only became aware of their being targeted by the procedure after it had come to an end. The CFI upheld their claim, ruling that they had not been given proper notice of the initiation of the formal investigation phase.[104]

Le Levant constitutes an important departure from the instrumental paradigm expounded in Chapter 2,[105] but it represents the exemption rather than the rule. The ruling is based on the assumption that the Commission is obliged to identify individually the possible State aid beneficiaries whenever this is possible, a requirement that does not stem from Article 6(1) PR and which has not been restated in any other case. In any event, even if this rule is good law, it only affects State aid beneficiaries. As noted earlier, the case law of the European Courts is at odds when it comes to defining the procedural status of State aid beneficiaries, whose situation seems to trigger more intensely the principle of legal protection.[106] However,

[100] Case T-354/99 *Kuwait Petroleum v Commission* [2006] ECR II-1475, para 85.

[101] Case T-291/06 *Operator ARP v Commission* [2009] ECR II-2275, para 38.

[102] Joined Cases T-371 and 394/94 *British Airways and others v Commission* [1998] ECR II-2405, para 62.

[103] Case T-34/02 *Le Levant 001 and others v Commission* [2006] ECR II-267.

[104] ibid, para 91.

[105] Mendes (n 31) 401.

[106] Note that in *Le Levant* one of the arguments put forward by the applicant was breach of Article 6 of the European Convention on Human Rights (ECHR), an issue that the Court did not need to address since it annulled the decision. See Case T-34/02 *Le Levant 001 and others v Commission* [2006] ECR II-267, para 68.

even if the European Courts decided to go down the road initiated in *Le Levant* and to strengthen the procedural rights of State aid recipients, this would have no direct effect on the status of competitors and other interested parties. In sum, *Le Levant* can be read either as a ruling that departs from previous and subsequent case law or as a case that only concerns a particular set of interested parties with which this chapter is not concerned (namely, the beneficiaries of aid).

The preceding analysis suggests that the main information right enjoyed by competitors in State aid procedures is rather weak. On the one hand, the right to be informed of the initiation of the consultation procedure is satisfied with the publication of a general notice in the Official Journal, without it being necessary for the Commission to request comments from particular stakeholders, no matter how close their connection to the State aid at stake may be. On the other hand, the requirements imposed on the Commission with regard to the content of the notice are not very strict.

3. Access to the File and Access to Documents

This problem is compounded by the fact that the right to be informed of the initiation of the formal investigation phase is the only information right that interested parties enjoy within the State aid procedure (that is, besides the right to be sent a copy of the final decision). Indeed, the European Courts have systematically rejected the attempts made by interested parties to read a right of access to the file into the State aid procedure. The *Technische Glaswerke Ilmenau* saga illustrates their stance on this issue.

The case has its origins in the sale of various glass production lines that used to be under State control in the former German Democratic Republic (GDR). The seller (a public-law body responsible for the restructuring of undertakings of the former GDR) and the acquiring company (Technische Glaswerke Ilmenau GmbH) renegotiated the initial deal after the latter ran into cash-flow problems. The two main aspects of the new deal were a partial waiver of the price of the sale and the deferment of the date of payment. Germany notified these arrangements to the Commission under the rules on State aid, which gave rise to two different formal investigation procedures (one for each aspect of the deal). The interesting point about the case is that one of the procedures was initiated before the adoption of Regulation 1049/2001 on access to documents (and concluded within days of its entry into force), whereas the other one was initiated after that date.

The *Technische Glaswerke Ilmenau I* case concerns the first procedure, which resulted in a declaration that the payment waiver constituted incompatible State aid, because a private creditor would not have consented to it. In the course of that procedure, Technische Glaswerke Ilmenau had asked to be given access to the non-confidential version of the file in order to submit informed comments. The Commission did not satisfy the request for access and this is one of the arguments that the applicant put forward in support of the action of annulment that it brought, later, before the European Courts.[107]

Technische Glaswerke Ilmenau was the alleged State aid beneficiary, rather than one of its competitors, which is why it framed its claim against the idea (already mentioned earlier) that 'the position of aid recipients differs from that of interested third parties in that, although they are not direct parties to the procedure, their existence may be threatened by a final decision ordering recovery of the aid'.[108] Yet the Court firmly rejected this contention, making it clear that State aid beneficiaries enjoy no more procedural rights than any other third party.[109] This is the reason why the attempt of the applicant to invoke the rights of the defence in support of its claim was fruitless.[110] It is also the reason why the finding that interested parties enjoy no guarantees 'over and above the right to submit comments' and, in particular, no right of access to the non-confidential version of the file and no right to be sent the comments submitted by other parties,[111] is equally applicable to competitors.

Technische Glaswerke Ilmenau I was about the right of access to the file 'under the law of the procedure'.[112] *Technische Glaswerke Ilmenau II* tested instead the possibility of grounding this right on the general provisions on freedom of information contained in Regulation 1049/2001, which recognises the right of any natural or legal person to have access to the documents of the EU institutions,[113] unless one of the exceptions applies.[114] The regulation entered into force right before the initiation of the second investigation procedure launched by the Commission in relation to the arrangements at the origin of this dispute. Unlike in the previous procedure, Technische Glaswerke Ilmenau was thus able to rely on the regulation and to submit a formal request to have access to the documents held by the Commission in relation to its case.[115] It did so in vain, however, because the Commission invoked one of the exceptions of the regulation to reject the request—namely, the possibility of 'refus[ing] access to a document where disclosure would undermine the protection of … the purpose of inspections, investigations and audits'.[116]

[107] The applicant also challenged the merits of the decision on the ground that the Commission had misapplied the private investor test and provided an inadequate statement of reasons, but neither the CFI nor the ECJ found any mistake. See Case T-198/01 *Technische Glaswerke Ilmenau GmbH v Commission* [2004] ECR II-2717, paras 140 and 176; and Case C-404/04 P *Technische Glaswerke Ilmenau GmbH v Commission* [2007] ECR I-1, paras 99 and 127.

[108] Case T-198/01 *Technische Glaswerke Ilmenau GmbH v Commission* [2004] ECR II-2717, para 178.

[109] ibid, paras 193 and 195.

[110] ibid, para 181.

[111] ibid, paras 177 and 197.

[112] Opinion of Advocate General Kokott in Case C-139/07 P *Commission v Technische Glaswerke Ilmenau* [2010] ECR I-5885, para 2.

[113] Article 2 of Regulation 1049/2011.

[114] Article 4 of Regulation 1049/2011.

[115] Case T-237/02 *Technische Glaswerke Ilmenau GmbH v Commission* [2006] ECR II-5131, para 9.

[116] Article 4(2) of Regulation 1049/2011.

Technische Glaswerke Ilmenau challenged this refusal before the CFI, which recognised that State aid procedures can be considered an 'investigation' within the meaning of the exception invoked by the Commission,[117] but held that 'the mere fact that a document concerns an interest protected by an exception cannot justify application of that exception'.[118] After noting that the Commission had failed to undertake 'a concrete, individual assessment of the content of the documents covered by the application for access',[119] without there being any justification,[120] the CFI held that the Commission had infringed Article 4(2) of Regulation 1049/2001 and therefore annulled its decision.[121]

Insofar as it confirmed the possibility of invoking Regulation 1049/2001 within State aid procedures, and the obligation of the Commission to provide an individualised and reasoned response to that request, the ruling of the CFI in *Technische Glaswerke Ilmenau II* seemed to open the door for third parties to gain access to the file in this type of procedure. However, the ruling of the CFI was reversed on appeal by the ECJ, which held that

> the General Court should, in the judgment under appeal, have taken account of the fact that interested parties other than the Member State concerned in the procedures for reviewing State aid do not have the right to consult the documents in the administrative file, and, therefore, acknowledged the existence of a general presumption that disclosure of documents in the administrative file in principle undermines protection of the objectives of investigation activities.[122]

The reasoning followed by the ECJ to reach that conclusion is not particularly clear.[123] The ECJ explicitly acknowledged that the right of access to the file under the rules of the State aid procedure and the general right of access to documents are 'legally distinct' issues,[124] but it nevertheless held that it was necessary to take account of the scope of the former in order to interpret the latter.[125] This is how it concluded that 'the system for the review of State aid would be called into question' if interested parties could gain access to the file on the basis of Regulation 1049/2001.[126]

Its shortcomings notwithstanding, this ruling has been followed in later cases[127] and constitutes, for the time being, good law. It follows that the Commission may

[117] Case T-237/02 *Technische Glaswerke Ilmenau GmbH v Commission* [2006] ECR II-5131, para 76.
[118] ibid, para 77.
[119] ibid, para 80.
[120] ibid, paras 84–99.
[121] ibid, para 100.
[122] Case C-139/07 P *Commission v Technische Glaswerke Ilmenau* [2010] ECR I-5885, para 61.
[123] María Muñoz de Juan and José Manuel Panero Rivas, 'The ECJ's Backlash on Access to Documents in the Commission's file on State Aid Cases by Private Parties. Comment on C-139/07 P' (2010) 9 *European State Aid Law Quarterly* 871, 876.
[124] ibid, para 59.
[125] ibid, para 58.
[126] ibid.
[127] Joined Cases T-498 to 500 and 509/08 *Ryanair Ltd v Commission*, ECLI:EU:T:2010:511, paras 70–72.

rely on the general presumption that access to documents threatens its investigations in State aid cases in order to reject the requests made by interested parties under Regulation 1049/2001. Although the rule does not completely foreclose the possibility of access, it places on the applicants the burden of proving that specific documents are not covered by the presumption or that 'there is a higher public interest justifying the disclosure of the document concerned'.[128] Thus, it constitutes yet another manifestation of the resistance of the European Courts to developing the content of the right of interested parties to participate in State aid procedures.

Conclusion

Access

The participation of competitors in State aid procedures is grounded on Article 108(2) TFEU, which provides that the parties concerned shall be given notice and an opportunity to submit comments as a precondition for the declaration of incompatibility of State aids. The asymmetrical design encoded in the Treaty (which foresees participation as a precondition for the declaration of incompatibility only) has been reduced to its minimum possible expression by the European Courts, which have coined the serious difficulties test as a mechanism to discipline the decision of the Commission to omit the consultation phase. The result has been the consolidation and expansion of the right of competitors to access the second phase of the State aid procedure through the submission of comments.

Leverage

By contrast, the European Courts have been reluctant to put flesh on the right to submit comments, systematically favouring a restrictive interpretation of the faculties that it entails. They have thus rejected the attempts by certain applicants to rely on this right to enter into a dialogue with the Commission and have reduced to its minimum expression the information rights associated with it. The upshot is that the type of participation to which competitors are entitled in State aid procedures is a bare right to make their views known to the Commission, with little or no adjunct mechanisms to ensure a meaningful and effective type of participation.

[128] Case C-139/07 P *Commission v Technische Glaswerke Ilmenau* [2010] ECR I-5885, para 62.

6

Judicial Review of State Aid Decisions

Introduction

The previous two chapters have analysed the opportunities to influence the outcome of State aid procedures that are available to competitors in each of the two phases that make up these procedures. Chapter 4 looked at complaints as a means to set into motion the preliminary stage of the procedure, and Chapter 5 at the consultation phase inserted into the so-called formal investigation phase. Both chapters have therefore considered different gateways into the administrative procedure that takes place before the Commission itself.

In principle, however, the possibility of having a say in the administrative procedure does not exhaust the opportunities of competitors to exert some influence over the application of the rules on State aid. This is because, as Craig puts it, 'There are two crucial access points in any legal regime': the 'procedural rules determining who is entitled to be heard or intervene before the initial decision is made' and the 'rules of standing that determine who should be able to complain to the court that the initial decision-maker overstepped its powers'.[1] This chapter is concerned with the latter. Thus, the focus shifts here from the administrative to the judicial review procedure, the aim of this chapter being to investigate the opportunities for access and leverage that the European Courts offer to competitors in their fight against State aid.

The first part of this chapter provides an overview of the rules that govern access of individuals to the European judicature and of the way in which they have been specifically applied to competitors in the State aid context (Section I). It shows that the main hurdle faced by competitors in State aid cases is the 'individual concern requirement' of Article 263 TFEU, which is interpreted differently depending on the type of clearing decision that is challenged: a 'decision to raise no objections' adopted at the end of the preliminary phase ('phase 1 decision') or a 'positive' or 'conditional' decision adopted at the end of the formal investigation phase ('phase 2 decision').

[1] Paul P Craig, *EU Administrative Law*, 2nd edn (Oxford: Oxford University Press, 2012) 313.

This is the reason why the following two sections focus on each of these scenarios, ie, on judicial review of phase 1 decisions (Section II) and on judicial review of phase 2 decisions (Section III). In both cases, however, the analysis follows the same scheme. It starts with the issue of access, going over the operation of the rules of standing applicable in each case. It then addresses the issue of leverage, looking at the type of review that the Courts exercise over State aid decisions, which is a good indicator of the power of influence that competitors may actually exert through this route.

I. The Position of Individuals in Judicial Review of EU Administrative Action

1. General Rules on Access of Individuals to the European Courts

In order to understand the rules that govern access of individuals to judicial review of the Commission's decisions, it is necessary to depart from the observation that the jurisdictional system of the EU responds to a two-tier model, which tends to channel the judicial actions of individuals through national courts.[2] This is consistent with the decentralised model of implementation that presides over the whole system of EU law, and which implies that the implementation and application of EU law corresponds as a general rule to national authorities. It is only by way of exception that individuals are given direct access to the EU Courts, basically in those cases where the EU institutions themselves discharge the task of implementing and applying EU law. This is the reason why the possibility for individuals to resort to the EU Courts is subject to stringent conditions.

These conditions are of two sorts. There is, in the first place, the *objective* requirement to address one's challenge against an attackable act (in the case of the action of annulment) or against the failure of the Commission to discharge an obligation (in the case of the action for failure to act). There is, in the second place, the *subjective* requirement to satisfy the relevant test of standing amongst those laid down by Article 263-IV TFEU. Whereas the access of the EU institutions and Member States to the EU Courts is only subject to the objective requirement, individuals must additionally meet the subjective one. This is the reason why the former are referred to as 'privileged' and the latter as 'non-privileged' applicants.[3]

[2] Eric Stein and G Joseph Vining, 'Citizen Access to Judicial Review of Administrative Action in a Transnational and Federal Context' (1976) 70 *The American Journal of International Law* 219, 222.

[3] Trevor C Hartley, *The Foundations of European Community Law: An Introduction to the Constitutional and Administrative Law of the European Community*, 6th edn (Oxford: Oxford University Press, 2007) 342–43.

2. The Objective Condition as Applied in Judicial Review of State Aid Decisions

Several developments in the case law of the European Courts have facilitated the fulfilment of the objective requirement as a precondition to challenge State aid decisions. Albeit from a different angle, these developments have already been examined in the previous chapters, which is why they will only be briefly discussed here.

(a) State Aid Decisions as Attackable Acts

The first development is the clarification that all State aid decisions are attackable acts. This was a non-issue with regard to phase 2 decisions, but could have raised some doubts with regard to the decisions adopted by the Commission at the end of the preliminary phase. The previous chapter has already introduced the *Germany v Commission* case, where the ECJ coined a specific test for the review of this type of decision and hence implicitly settled the matter.[4] It did so explicitly a few years later in *CIRFS*, where it declared that a decision not to raise objections adopted at the end of the preliminary phase does not constitute 'a mere preparatory act' because it has 'definitive legal effects' and is therefore open to challenge.[5] Granted, certain phase 1 decisions are not open to challenge (eg, decision to open the formal investigation phase in respect of a State aid measure which has already been fully implemented),[6] but this qualification does not affect the type of decisions that competitors would normally attack—namely clearing decisions. Thus, the consideration of all (clearing) State aid decisions as attackable acts, irrespective of the stage of the procedure at which they are adopted, facilitates the fulfilment of the objective requirement for the purposes of the action of annulment.

(b) The Duty of the Commission to Adopt a Formal Decision

The second development is the imposition on the Commission of the duty to embody its views in a formal decision. This is partially the result of the Procedural Regulation, which codifies the practice of the Commission and provides that both the preliminary and the formal investigation phases shall result in formal decisions.[7] It is also the result of *Athinaïki Techniki*[8] and of the 2013 reform of the Procedural Regulation,[9] which constrain the capacity of the Commission to

[4] Case 84/82 *Germany v Commission* [1984] ECR 1451.

[5] Case 313/90 *Comité International de la Rayonne et des Fibres Synthétiques (CIRFS) and others v Commission* [1993] ECR I-1125, paras 26–27.

[6] Case T-517/12 *Alro SA v Commission*, ECLI:EU:T:2014:890, para 42; Case T-251/13 *Gemeente Nijmegen v Commission*, ECLI:EU:T:2015:142, para 37.

[7] See Articles 4 and 15 (for the preliminary phase) and Article 9 of the codified PR (for the formal investigation phase).

[8] Case C-521/06 P *Athinaïki Techniki AE v Commission* [2008] ECR I-5829, para 40.

[9] See Article 24(2) of the codified PR, analysed in Chapter 4.

escape taking a formal decision in response to complaints. The reader is referred to Chapter 4 for a longer discussion of this issue. The point to note here is that the obligation of the Commission to put an end to the procedure with a formal decision facilitates the fulfilment of the objective requirement and hence access to the judicial review phase, be it through the action of annulment (if the Commission complies with that obligation) or through the action for failure to act (should the Commission disregard it).

(c) The Construction of Dubious Acts as Decisions

The last development is the tendency of the European Courts to adopt a flexible and un-formalistic approach with regard to the actionable character of those acts whose nature is unclear. This approach is not specific to State aid,[10] but it has also manifested itself in this field with regard to acts adopted at the end of both phases of the procedure.

Deutsche Bahn[11] (in the case of the then CFI) and, again, *Athinaïki Techniki*[12] (in the case of the ECJ) are good examples of the flexible approach adopted by the European Courts with regard to the actionable character of acts adopted in the course of the preliminary phase of the procedure. The problem in *Athinaïki Techniki* was that the Commission had not adopted any formal decision on the subject matter of the complaint at the origin of the case; instead, it had contented itself with sending the complainant a letter informing it of the closure of the file. Rather than inviting the applicants to bring an action for failure to act, the ECJ declared that there can be a decision—and therefore an attackable act—even if the Commission has adopted no act under that name, has not referred to Article 4 PR and has not identified the Member State concerned; what matters is whether the Commission 'has definitely established its position ... on the measure under review and, therefore, whether it has decided that that measure constituted aid or not, that it had no doubts as regards its compatibility with the common market, or that it did have such doubts'.[13] On the facts of the case, the ECJ found that the letter sent to the complainant was a decision and could therefore form the basis of an action of annulment.

Cofaz shows that the Court has adopted an equally flexible approach with regard to the existence of an attackable act at the end of the formal investigation

[10] Anthony Arnull, 'The Action for Annulment: A Case of Double Standards?' in David O'Keeffe (ed), *Judicial Review in the European Union* (The Hague: Kluwer Law International, 2000) 180; Paul P Craig, 'Standing and Substantive Review in Community Law' (1994) 14 *Oxford Journal of Legal Studies* 507, 516. See, eg, Case 22/70 *Commission v Council* [1971] ECR 263 (where the ECJ held that the action of annulment is admissible against all acts of the institutions that are intended to have legal effects, whatever their nature or form) and Case 294/83 *Parti écologiste 'Les Verts' v European Parliament* [1986] ECR 1339 (where the annulment of an act of the European Parliament was declared admissible, although the European Parliament was not mentioned at that time amongst the institutions whose acts were liable to form the basis of this type of action).

[11] Case T-351/02 *Deutsche Bahn v Commission* [2006] ECR II-1047.

[12] Case C-521/06 P *Athinaïki Techniki AE v Commission* [2008] ECR I-5829.

[13] ibid, para 46.

procedure.[14] In that case, the Commission launched the formal investigation procedure in order to investigate the preferential tariff for the supply of natural gas granted to Dutch producers of ammonia and nitrate fertilizers by Gasunie, a company in which the Netherlands government had a 50 per cent share. The Commission had simultaneously initiated the standard infringement procedure, acting on a complaint by the French government, and had actually issued a reasoned opinion. This prompted the introduction of certain amendments in the controversial scheme, after which the Commission became satisfied that the measure raised no problems and therefore decided to bring the investigation to an end. It did so, however, without adopting a formal decision, and yet at no point did the Advocate General or the Court consider whether there was an attackable act. The absence of a formal decision addressed to the Member State did not prevent the ECJ from ruling on the merits of the application, which shows it willingness to ease access to the judicial review procedure via the action of annulment, rather than the action for failure to act.

3. The Subjective Requirement as Applied to Judicial Review of State Aid Decisions

Article 263-IV TFEU lays down the rules that govern the *locus standi* of non-privileged applicants in the exercise of the action of annulment. It provides that 'Any natural or legal person may … institute proceedings against an act addressed to that person or which is of direct and individual concern to them, and against a regulatory act which is of direct concern to them and does not entail implementing measures'. Three different situations and three different rules are thus distinguished.

(a) Article 263-IV imposes no special subjective requirements *when the action is brought by the addressee of the act that is challenged*, but this is never the case within the context of the State aid control procedure. This is because State aid decisions are always formally addressed to the granting Member State—and never to the beneficiary or to complainants. After some hesitations,[15] the ECJ dispelled any possible doubts in that regard in *Sytraval*. The Court did not follow the Opinion of Advocate General Lenz, who had argued that the 'most natural solution' for the Commission was to address the decision to the complainant.[16] It followed instead the theory of Advocate General Tesauro in *Cook*[17] and held that 'decisions adopted by the Commission in the field of

[14] Case 169/84 *Compagnie francaise de l'azote (Cofaz) SA v Commission* [1986] ECR 391.
[15] Joined Cases 166 and 220/86 *Irish Cement v Commission* [1988] ECR 6473, para 11.
[16] Opinion of Advocate General Lenz in Case C-367/95 P *Commission v Sytraval and Brink's France SARL* [1998] ECR I-1719, para 47.
[17] Opinion of Advocate General Tesauro in Case C-198/91 *William Cook plc v Commission* [1993] ECR I-2487, para 32: 'under the Article [108(3) TFEU] procedure, in contrast to procedures for the

State aid must be held to be addressed to the Member States concerned'.[18] It follows that the standing of competitors in State aid cases is not governed by this rule.

(b) Article 263-IV imposes the 'direct concern' requirement *when the action is brought against a regulatory act, provided it does not entail implementing measures*. The main novelty introduced by the Treaty of Lisbon is the elimination of the 'individual concern' requirement in this type of situation. Were the guidelines adopted by the Commission to be considered as regulatory acts, this amendment may ease the *locus standi* of competitors and other third parties to challenge State aid decisions on the ground that they were grounded on an invalid soft-law rule.[19] But, in general, the standing of competitors to challenge State aid decisions is not affected by this rule.[20]

(c) When the action is *brought by a non-privileged applicant against an act addressed 'to another person'*—as Article 230 EC used to state—the applicant needs to fulfil the 'direct and individual concern requirement'. Since State aid decisions are always addressed to the Member State concerned, this is the subjective requirement that private applicants have to meet in order to challenge State aid decisions.

Article 265-III TFEU, on the other hand, lays down the rule that governs the exercise by non-privileged applicants of the action for failure to act. Article 265-III only empowers them to 'complain to the Court that an institution, body, office or agency of the Union has failed to address *to [them]* any act other than a recommendation or an opinion' (emphasis added). The case law has made clear, however, that the action for failure to act can also be exercised when a European institution or body has failed to adopt a decision addressed to another person, provided the 'direct and individual concern' requirement is met.[21] Since the interpretation of the requirement is the same in both situations—and since the interpretation of the objective requirement made by the Courts favours the action of annulment as a channel to review—the following discussion will mostly focus on the latter.

Application of Articles [101 and 102 TFEU], the only decision which the Commission is empowered to take is a decision on the compatibility of the aid. There is no place, on the other hand, for an independent and separate decision rejecting a complaint submitted by a competitor of the undertaking in receipt of aid'.

[18] Case C-367/95 P *Commission v Sytraval and Brink's France SARL* [1998] ECR I-1719, para 44. See also Case T-189/97 *Comité d'Entreprise de la Société Française de Production and others v Commission* [1998], para 31.

[19] Henrik Peytz and Thomas Mygind, 'Direct Action in State Aid Cases—Tightropes and Legal Protection? A Review of Recent Jurisprudence on Direct and Individual Concern and Reviewable Acts. Part One' (2010) 9 *European State Aid Law Quarterly* 331, 332.

[20] Hans P Nehl, 'Direct Actions and Judicial Review before the Union Courts' in Herwig CH Hofmann and Claire Micheau, *State Aid Law of the European Union* (Oxford: Oxford University Press, 2016) 429.

[21] Case C-107/91 *ENU v Commission* [1993] ECR I-599, para 18.

(a) The Direct Concern Requirement

In general terms, the direct concern requirement has been given two different meanings by the European Courts. In its initial case law, the ECJ construed this requirement as meaning that a direct causal link had to be established between the contested measure and the prejudice on the basis of which the applicant grounds its standing. Thus, it was not met in cases where the contested act required national measures of implementation before being effective.[22] Later cases have eased the fulfilment of the requirement, holding that the need to adopt implementing measures did not prevent the requirement from being met when the implementing authority enjoys no discretion or when the non-implementation of the act is only an unrealistic possibility.[23] The rule is therefore that for a decision to be of direct concern to the applicant 'it must directly affect the applicant's legal situation and its implementation must be purely automatic and result from Community rules alone without the application of other intermediate rules'.[24]

It should be noted, however, that the analysis of the European Courts is not usually very probing with regard to this requirement, which has a 'lower profile' and a 'much less decisive' role than the individual concern requirement.[25] This is also true in the field of State aid, where the European Courts tend to devote little or no attention at all to the direct concern requirement in the assessment of the standing of non-privileged applicants—and to invariably find, when they do address the issue, that the requirement is met.[26] The upshot is that the direct concern requirement does not stand out as a significant barrier to competitors challenging State aid decisions.[27]

(b) The Individual Concern Requirement

Consequently, the main hurdle faced by competitors in their endeavour to challenge State aid decisions is the individual concern requirement. The meaning of this requirement was defined in *Plaumann*, where the ECJ held that persons others

[22] Case 69/69 *SA Alcan Aluminium Raeren and others v Commission* [1970] ECR 385, para 8.

[23] Case 62/70 *Bock v Commission* [1971] ECR 897, paras 6–8; Case 11/82 *Piraiki-Patraiki and Others v Commission* [1985] ECR 207, paras 8–10, and Case C-386/96 P *Dreyfus v Commission* [1998] ECR I-2309, para 44.

[24] Case C-386/96 P *Dreyfus v Commission* [1998] ECR I-2309, para 43, and Case T-69/99 *DSTV v Commission* [2000] ECR II-4039, para 24.

[25] Albertina Albors-Llorens, 'The Standing of Private Parties to Challenge Community Measures: Has the European Court Missed the Boat?' (2003) 62 *Cambridge Law Journal* 72, 72.

[26] See, eg, Case T-9/98 *Mitteldeutsche Erdöl-Raffinerie GmbH v Commission* [2001] ECR II-3367, para 52; Case T-287/11 *Heitkamp BauHolding GmbH v Commission*, ECLI:EU:T:2016:60, para 58 (actions brought by the beneficiary).

[27] Johannes A Winter, 'The Rights of Complainants in State Aid Cases: Judicial Review of Commission Decisions Adopted under Article 88 (Ex 93)' (1999) 36 *Common Market Law Review* 521, 526. But see Viktor Kreuschitz, 'Some Thoughts on the Jurisprudence of European Courts Concerning the Admissibility of Actions against State Aid Decisions' in *EC State Aid Law/Le droit des aides d'etat dans la CE. Liber Amicorum Francisco Santaolalla Gadea* (The Hague: Kluwer Law International, 2008) 373–74, who argues that the application of the direct concern requirement should be stricter.

than those to whom a decision is addressed are individually concerned if that decision affects them by reason of certain attributes which are peculiar to them or by reason of circumstances that differentiate them from all other persons and thus distinguish them individually just as in the case of the addressee.[28] On the facts of the case, the ECJ found that the contested regulation only affected the applicant in its condition of importer of mandarins (the goods subject to antidumping duties), which was insufficient to meet the individual concern requirement.

The exact meaning of the individual concern requirement has been extensively discussed in the literature, which still strives to define the precise scope of the formula defined in *Plaumann*.[29] Yet this discussion is of limited relevance for the inquiry carried out in this book since there is no doubt that competitors fall outside the *Plaumann* formula, in the sense that the existence of a competitive relationship between the applicant and the addressee (or beneficiary) is not a sufficient individualising factor within the meaning of *Plaumann*. Indeed, the ECJ held in *Eridania* that

> [t]he mere fact that a measure may exercise an influence on the competitive relationships existing on the market in question cannot suffice to allow any trader in any competitive relationship whatever with the addressee of the measure to be regarded as directly and individually concerned by that measure.[30]

Eridania does not rule out the possibility that competitors meet the individual concern requirement, but it makes this result conditional on their pointing to some additional 'specific circumstances'.[31]

It is against this background that the European Courts have articulated the principles that govern the standing of competitors in the fields of antidumping and antitrust—and only later, by extension, in the field of State aid—generally showing a 'more liberal attitude' than in other fields.[32] In *Metro I* (antitrust), the Commission cleared a selective distribution system following a complaint by a

[28] Case 25/62 *Plaumann v Commission* [1961] ECR 409.

[29] To cite but a few examples, see Ami Barav, 'Direct and Individual Concern: An Almost Insurmountable Barrier to the Admissibility of Individual Appeal to the EEC Court' (1974) 11 *Common Market Law Review* 191; Hjalte Rasmussen, 'Why Is Article 173 Interpreted against Private Plaintiffs?' (1980) 5 *European Law Review* 112; Anthony Arnull, 'Private Applicants and the Action for Annulment under Article 173 of the EC Treaty' (1995) 32 *Common Market Law Review* 7; Angela Ward, *Judicial Review and the Rights of Private Parties in EC Law* (Oxford: Oxford University Press, 2000); Anthony Arnull, 'Private Applicants and the Action for Annulment since Codorniu' (2001) 38 *Common Market Law Review* 7; Angela Ward, 'Locus Standi under Article 230(4) of the EC Treaty: Crafting a Coherent Test for a "Wobbly Polity"' (2003) 22 *Yearbook of European Law* 45; John A Usher, 'Direct and Individual Concern: An Effective Remedy or a Conventional Solution?' (2003) 28 *European Law Review* 575; Stefan Enchelmaier, 'No-One Slips through the Net? Latest Developments, and Non-Developments, in the European Court of Justice's Jurisprudence on Art. 230(4) EC' (2005) 24 *Yearbook of European Law* 173; Takis Tridimas and Sara Poli, 'Locus Standi of Individuals under Article 230(4): The Return of Euridice?' in *Continuity and Change in EU Law: Essays in Honour of Sir Francis Jacobs* (Oxford: Oxford University Press, 2008).

[30] Joined Cases 10 and 18/68 *Eridania Zuccherifici and others v Commission* [1969] ECR 459, para 7.

[31] ibid.

[32] Hartley (n 3) 362; Albertina Albors-Llorens, *Private Parties in EC Law* (Oxford: Oxford University Press, 2006) 43.

competitor that had been excluded from it. The ECJ held that the action of annulment brought by the latter was admissible because 'the contested decision was adopted in particular as a result of a complaint submitted by the [applicant]' and because it related to a distribution system from which the applicant had been excluded.[33] The ECJ added that

> [i]t is in the interests of a satisfactory administration of justice and of the proper application of Articles [101] and [102] that natural or legal persons who are entitled [to bring complaints] should be able, if their request is not complied with, either wholly or in part, to institute proceedings in order to protect their legitimate interests.

In *Timex* (antidumping), the ECJ reached the same result with regard to an action for the annulment of an antidumping regulation brought by a producer of watches, whereby it challenged as insufficient the antidumping duties imposed on a competitor. Several factors led the ECJ to conclude that the applicant met the individual concern requirement, but it gave special weight to the observation that the investigation owed its origin to complaints made by the applicant[34] and that the contested regulation took account of its specific market situation in the calculation of the antidumping duties.[35] The judgment also referred to the facts that the applicant was the leading manufacturer of the type of goods affected by the regulation and that 'the conduct of the investigation was largely determined by [its] observations'.[36]

It is on the basis of *Timex* that the ECJ came to define the conditions that govern the standing of competitors to challenge State aid decisions. Indeed, the ECJ held in *Cofaz* that the individualising factors considered in *Timex* could also be applied to applicants that have played a similar role in the State aid procedure, 'provided, however, that their position on the market is significantly affected by the aid which is the subject of the contested decision'.[37] Despite the elusive language used by the Court in the judgment, *Cofaz* would soon become the main reference on the standing of competitors in State aid cases. In order to meet the individual concern requirement, they would thus need to satisfy two cumulative conditions: the condition to have somehow participated in the previous administrative procedure (participation requirement) and the condition to show harm (significant effect requirement). More on this later.

Cofaz involved a State aid decision adopted at the end of the formal investigation phase (ie, a phase 2 decision). As the reader already knows, the Court faced the same problem in *Cook*,[38] albeit in relation to a decision adopted at the end of the preliminary phase. Cook had lodged a complaint challenging the compatibility

[33] Case 26/76 *Metro SB v Commission* [1977] ECR 1875, para 13.
[34] Case 264/82 *Timex Corporation v Commission* [1985] ECR 849, para 14.
[35] ibid, para 15.
[36] ibid.
[37] Case 169/84 *Compagnie francaise de l'azote (Cofaz) SA v Commission* [1986] ECR 391, paras 24–25.
[38] Case C-198/91 *William Cook plc v Commission* [1993] ECR I-2487.

of several aids granted to a competitor by different Spanish authorities and it then challenged the decision of the Commission to raise no objections. It is not clear whether the standing of Cook could have been established on the basis of the conditions defined in *Cofaz*,[39] but the Advocate General argued that these conditions should not apply as such in the context of phase 1 decisions.[40] The first requirement should not apply because the applicant normally has little information concerning the aid during the preliminary procedure; he should therefore not be expected to formulate 'precise submissions regarding the size and the effect of the aid'.[41] The second requirement should not apply either because 'the participation of a third party in the preliminary procedure—a procedure of which that party is normally unaware—cannot constitute a condition *sine qua non* for bringing an action against a decision "not to raise objections"', since third parties are only invited to participate at the second stage of the procedure.[42] Advocate General Tesauro was therefore inviting the Court to formulate a new rule of standing, one according to which '*any* competitor of the undertaking must be deemed to have standing to institute proceedings against (a decision not to raise objections), *regardless of whether he has previously participated in the administrative procedure*' (emphasis added).[43]

The Court accepted the invitation and formulated a wider rule of standing than the one resulting from *Cofaz*. However, it did so without following the reasoning of its Advocate General. Indeed, the Court relied instead on the need to recognise standing to the parties concerned that are protected by the consultation phase of Article 108(2) TFEU, the crux of the argument being that 'the persons intended to benefit from those procedural guarantees may secure compliance therewith only if they are able to challenge that decision by the Commission before the Court'.[44] Thus, the rule of standing elaborated in *Cook* provides that competitors—and any other party concerned within the meaning of Article 108(2) TFEU—shall be individually concerned for the purposes of Article 256-IV TFEU whenever they challenge a positive decision adopted by the Commission without opening the formal investigation phase.

The foregoing discussion has shown that the access of individuals to the EU Courts is generally subject to two types of requirement—an objective and a subjective one. In the field of State aid, the main hurdle faced by competitors is the subjective requirement, which is interpreted differently in actions for the annulment of phase 1 and phase 2 decisions. Whereas in the former case it suffices to be in a competitive relationship with the beneficiary of the aid (and hence to be a

[39] Spain and the Commission disputed the 'substantial' dimension of the effect of the aid on the applicant's competitive position. See Opinion of Advocate General Tesauro in Case C-198/91 *William Cook plc v Commission* [1993] ECR I-2487, para 25.

[40] ibid, para 44.

[41] ibid, para 41.

[42] ibid, para 43.

[43] ibid, para 44.

[44] Case C-198/91 *William Cook plc v Commission* [1993] ECR I-2487, para 23.

party concerned for the purposes of Article 108(2) TFEU), in the latter case it is necessary to meet the participation and significant effect requirements. The next two sections analyse in more depth the operation of these filters (access) and the type of review to which they each lead (leverage).

II. Judicial Review of 'Phase 1 Decisions'

1. The Refinement of the *Cook/Matra* Rule of Standing[45]

The general rule of standing that governs the challenge of phase 1 decisions was articulated in *Cook*, where the ECJ held that the conditions laid down in *Cofaz* do not apply when the action is addressed against a positive decision adopted at the end of the preliminary phase.[46] When this is the case, the only condition that the applicant needs to meet is to have the status of 'party concerned' within the meaning of current Article 108(2) TFEU. The rule was confirmed shortly after in *Matra*.[47] Cook had participated as a complainant in the administrative procedure leading to the contested decision, and so had Matra. Yet the Court did not assign any weight to this factor, which means that participation is not a requirement to rely on the rule of standing articulated in these cases.[48]

The breadth of the rule is not exempted from difficulties. It fits uneasily with the *Eridania* principle according to which the existence of a competitive relationship between the applicant and the addressee of an act is not a stand-alone individualising factor within the meaning of *Plaumann*. More generally, it is difficult to reconcile with Article 263-IV TFEU itself, which clearly calls for a certain degree of restrictiveness in the conditions that govern the access of non-privileged applicants to the European Courts.[49] It is probably as a result of these difficulties that the European Courts have been called—and willing—to reconsider the scope of the rule in later cases.

In the *Danish Shipyards* case, the CFI held that the *Cook/Matra* rule of standing is only applicable where the applicant bases its action of annulment on the ground that the Commission was in breach of the obligation to initiate the formal

[45] I have published part of the analysis that follows in Fernando Pastor-Merchante, 'On the Rules of Standing to Challenge State Aid Decisions Adopted at the End of the Preliminary Phase' (2012) 11 *European State Aid Law Quarterly* 601.

[46] Case C-198/91 *William Cook plc v Commission* [1993] ECR I-2487, para 23.

[47] Case C-225/91 *Matra SA v Commission* [1993] ECR I-3203, paras 16–20.

[48] Sara Poli, 'The Legal Standing of Private Parties in the Area of State Aids After the Appeal in *Commission v. Kronoply/Kronotex*' (2012) 39 *Legal Issues of Economic Integration* 357, 360–61.

[49] Enchelmaier (n 29) 184. See also Opinion of Advocate General Jacobs in Case C-78/03 P *Commission v Aktionsgemeinschaft Recht un Eigentum (ARE)* [2005] ECR I-10737, paras 138–41, and Opinion of Advocate General Mengozzi in Case 487/06 P *British Aggregates Association v Commission* [2008] ECR I-10515, para 48.

investigation procedure or on the ground that the procedural safeguards provided for by current Article 108(2) TFEU were infringed—which after all comes down to calling into question the premature closure of the file. Otherwise, 'the mere fact that the applicants may be considered to be parties "concerned" within the meaning of Article [108(2) TFEU] cannot be sufficient to render the application admissible'.[50]

This qualification does not stem from the rulings of the Court in *Cook* and *Matra*, which did not discuss the nature of the pleas put forward by the applicants. However, it was endorsed by the ECJ in *ARE*, where the rule of standing that governs the challenge of phase 1 decisions was rephrased in the following terms:

> [T]he Court declares to be admissible an action for the annulment of [a phase 1 decision] brought by a person who is concerned within the meaning of Article [108(2) TFEU] *where he seeks, by instituting proceedings, to safeguard the procedural rights available to him under the latter provision* (emphasis added).[51]

The ECJ further added that this is only deemed to be the purpose of an action when the application contains 'a plea expressly alleging breach by the Commission of its obligation to initiate the formal investigation procedure'[52]—laying down the *explicit plea requirement* and, as a corollary, the '*ban on reinterpretation*'.[53]

Consequently, the case law of the European Courts has come to draw a distinction between 'two scenarios'—to use the words of Advocate General Jacobs in *ARE*.[54] The first scenario covers all actions brought by private applicants *on the ground that the Commission should have proceeded to the formal investigation phase*; the status of party concerned within the meaning of Article 108(2) TFEU then suffices to have standing. The second scenario concerns any action that attacks the *merits* of the contested decision; the standing of the applicant to bring proceedings depends, in that case, on the fulfilment of the stricter conditions established in *Cofaz*, as interpreted by the subsequent case law. This means that the admissibility bar is considerably higher in the second scenario, for it is anything but easy to meet these conditions, as will be discussed below.

Several Advocates General have taken issue with this distinction, which is generally perceived to be excessively complex and formalistic.[55] These critiques have

[50] Case T-266/94 *Skibsvaerftsforeningen and others v Commission* [1996] ECR II-1399, para 45.

[51] Case C-78/03 P *Commission v Aktionsgemeinschaft Recht und Eigentum (ARE)* [2005] ECR I-10737, para 35.

[52] ibid, para 44.

[53] Henrik Peytz and Thomas Mygind, 'Direct Action in State Aid Cases—Tightropes and Legal Protection? A Review of Recent Jurisprudence on Direct and Individual Concern and Reviewable Acts. Part Two' (2010) 9 *European State Aid Law Quarterly* 617, 627.

[54] Opinion of Advocate General Jacobs in Case C-78/03 P *Commission v Aktionsgemeinschaft Recht und Eigentum (ARE)* [2005] ECR I-10737, para 106.

[55] Opinion of Advocate General Jacobs in Case C-78/03 P *Commission v Aktionsgemeinschaft Recht und Eigentum (ARE)* [2005] ECR I-10737, paras 101–02; Opinion of Advocate General Bot in Joined Cases C-75 and 80/05 P *Germany and others v Kronofrance* [2008] ECR I-6619, paras 101–13; Opinion

also been echoed by many commentators.[56] This is probably the reason why the European Courts have been very flexible in the application of the two-scenario doctrine. Indeed, they have clarified that the inclusion of a plea that attacks the merits of the contested decision, alongside a strictly procedural plea, does not necessarily bring an application within the second scenario.[57] Furthermore, they have accepted that the ban on reinterpretation does not 'prevent [them] from examining arguments which the applicant has put forward regarding the substance, in order to ascertain whether strands of those arguments additionally support a plea, also raised by the applicant, which expressly alleges the existence of serious difficulties'.[58] Finally, they have loosened the explicit plea requirement, holding that an application could be admissible on the basis of *Cook* even if 'it [did] not contain a particularly clear statement of the applicants' plea, and, specifically, a plea which is distinctly identifiable as seeking to safeguard [their] procedural rights'.[59]

These developments notwithstanding, the European Courts have firmly adhered to the two-scenario theory itself—in other words, to the idea that there can be two types of challenges addressed against phase 1 decisions, each of which is governed by a different rule of standing.[60] What this theory suggests is that each scenario gives access to a different type of judicial review, for it would otherwise make no sense to impose a different test of standing in each case. More precisely, the underlying assumption is that the review exercised by the Courts is more probing in the second scenario (where the action attacks the merits of the decision) than in the first one (where the action attacks the procedural regularity of the decision). This in turn suggests that competitors may exert different degrees of leverage through the challenge of phase 1 decisions; they may enforce their procedural rights (first scenario), but they may also ask the Courts to reverse the substantive findings made by the Commission (second scenario).

It is in order to verify this hypothesis—and to gauge the power of leverage that competitors may exert through this route—that the next two sections compare the type of review exercised by the Courts in each scenario.

of Advocate General Mengozzi in Case C-487/06 P *British Aggregates Association v Commission* [2008] ECR I-10515, para 71–6; Opinion of Advocate General Sharpston in Case C-319/07 P *3F v Commission* [2009] I-5963, paras 36–49; Opinion of Advocate General Jääskinen in Case C-83/09 P *Commission v Kronoply and Kronotex* [2011] ECR I-4441, paras 27–40.

[56] Poli (n 48) 364; Küllike Jürimäe, 'Standing in State Aid Cases: What's the State of Play?' (2010) 9 *European State Aid Law Quarterly* 303, 315.

[57] Case C-319/07 P *3F v Commission* [2009] I-5963, para 35.

[58] Case C-83/09 P *Commission v Kronoply and Kronotex* [2011] ECR I-4441, para 56, in connection to 58. This 'pick and choose approach' (Poli (n 48) 367) is very common in the case law of the GC. See, eg, Case T-158/99 *Thermenhotel Stoiser Franz Gesellschaft and others v Commission* [2004] ECR II-1.

[59] See Case C-148/09 P *Belgium v Deutsche Post and DHL International* [2011] ECR I-8573, para 62, in connection to paras 59–60 and my discussion in Pastor-Merchante (n 45) 606–08.

[60] See, more recently, Case T-118/13 *Whirlpool Europe BV v Commission*, ECLI:EU:T:2016:365, para 44.

2. Judicial Review of Phase 1 Decisions in the First Scenario

The first scenario is that in which an applicant challenges a phase 1 decision 'on the ground that the Commission was in breach of the obligation to initiate the procedure provided for in Article [108(2) TFEU] or on the ground that the procedural safeguards provided for by Article [108(2) TFEU] were infringed'.[61] Although this formula suggests that both grounds are alternative, they basically come down to challenging the premature closure of the file.

As noted in the previous chapter, the standard that determines the legality of the closure of the procedure at the end of the preliminary phase is the serious difficulty test, which was formulated by the ECJ in *Germany v Commission*:

> [The opening of the second phase of the procedure] is essential whenever the Commission has *serious difficulties* in determining whether a plan to grant aid is compatible with the common market. It follows that the Commission may restrict itself to the preliminary examination under Article [108(3) TFEU] when taking a decision in favour of a plan to grant aid only if it is convinced after the preliminary examination that the plan is compatible with the Treaty. If, on the other hand, the initial examination leads the commission to the opposite conclusion or if it does not enable it to overcome all the difficulties involved in determining whether the plan is compatible with the common market, the Commission is under a duty to obtain all the requisite opinions and for that purpose to initiate the procedure provided for in Article [108(2) TFEU].[62]

Cook made it clear that the test would apply irrespective of the privileged or non-privileged status of the applicant.[63] Later cases have further clarified that this is an 'exclusive criterion', which means that the Commission may not 'decline to initiate the formal investigation procedure in reliance upon other circumstances, such as third party interests, considerations of economy of procedure or any other ground of administrative convenience'.[64] The upshot is that the serious difficulties test is the only standard of legality that the EU Courts apply in the first scenario, yet they may do so using one of two methods: the reviewing Court either looks at the circumstances surrounding the adoption of the decision (as it did in *Germany v Commission*) or it looks at the grounds of the decision (as it did in *Cook*).[65] Both methods are analysed in the following.

[61] Case T-266/94 *Skibsvaerftsforeningen and others v Commission* [1996] ECR II-1399, para 45.

[62] Case 84/82 *Germany v Commission* [1984] ECR 1451, para 13.

[63] Case C-198/91 *William Cook plc v Commission* [1993] ECR I-2487, para 22.

[64] Case T-73/98 *Société chimique Prayon-Rupel v Commission* [2011] ECR II-867, para 44; Case T-375/04 *Scheucher-Fleisch and others v Commission* [2009] ECR II-4155, para 72; Case T-79/14 *Secop GmbH v Commission*, ECLI:EU:T:2016:118, para 25.

[65] See the Opinion of Advocate General Trestnjak in Case C-431/07 P *Bouygues SA and Bouygues Télécom SA v Commission* [2009] ECR I-2665, paras 209–14, where she identifies three 'types of signs' of serious difficulties: '[a] first type of sign may emerge from the discussions between the Commission and the Member State concerned'; '[a] second type of sign may be given by the length of time which has elapsed during the preliminary investigation stage'; '[a] third type of sign of serious difficulties is the assessments upon which the Commission has relied'. Arguably, the two first signs can be seen as the same method.

(a) *First Method: Analysis of the Circumstances Surrounding the Adoption of the Contested Decision*

The first method is the one originally followed by the ECJ in *Germany v Commission*. It consists in looking at the way in which the Commission has conducted the preliminary procedure or, as the Court of Justice put it, at the 'circumstances in which the contested measure was adopted'.[66]

In *Germany v Commission*, the ECJ reached the conclusion that the Commission had encountered serious difficulties in assessing the compatibility of the Belgian aid plan on the basis of three factors. First, the Commission was not satisfied with the State aid plan as notified by the Belgian government, which is why they both entered into 'extensive bilateral negotiations' so as to amend it and make it compatible with the common market.[67] Secondly, 16 months elapsed between the moment when the aid was notified and that at which it was approved.[68] Finally, the Commission itself acknowledged in its own decision that all the difficulties raised by the case had not been resolved by declaring that 'it remain[ed] very concerned about the effects which the application of the plan may have on competition within the Community'.[69]

Similar factors have been considered in later cases,[70] while in others the GC has declared that it may also weigh in factors such as the existence of complaints[71] or objections by a high number of third parties[72] in order to ascertain whether the circumstances surrounding a case reveal the existence of serious difficulties.

Under the first method, then, the GC considers a myriad of factors related to the way in which the procedure leading to the adoption of the contested decision unfolded: the length of the procedure, the negotiations between the Commission and the Member State, the complaints and objections raised by third parties, etc. None of these factors is in and of itself sufficient to conclude that the assessment of the contested measure raises serious difficulties. Indeed, the GC is supposed to carry out an overall assessment of the circumstances of the case, so that certain factors such as an abnormally long period of examination 'can only constitute an indication of the existence of serious difficulties if it is supported by other factors'.[73] More importantly, this method should not be seen as a box-ticking exercise in which it suffices to verify the occurrence of certain external factors to conclude

[66] Case C-148/09 P *Belgium v Deutsche Post and DHL International* [2011] ECR I-8573, para 79.

[67] Case 84/82 *Germany v Commission* [1984] ECR 1451, para 14.

[68] ibid, para 15.

[69] ibid, para 16.

[70] See, eg, Case T-46/97 *Sociedade Independente de Comunicaçao (SIC) v Commission* [2000] ECR II-2125, paras 89–102; Case T-73/98 *Société chimique Prayon-Rupel v Commission* [2001] ECR II-867, para 107.

[71] Case T-140/13 *Netherlands Maritime Technology Association v Commission*, ECLI:EU:T:2014:1029, para 58, upheld in Case C-100/15 P *Netherlands Maritime Technology Association v Commission*, ECLI:EU:C:2016:254.

[72] Case T-57/11 *Castelnou Energía SL v Commission*, ECLI:EU:T:2014:1021, para 83.

[73] ibid, para 66.

that the Commission should have opened the second phase of the procedure. Indeed, the GC often insists that what matters is the *content* of the objections raised by third parties[74] and of the discussions between the Commission and the Member State,[75] rather than their mere *existence*.

(b) *Second Method: Analysis of the Assessments Relied Upon By the Commission in Order to Adopt the Contested Decision*

The second method is the one followed in *Cook*, where the ECJ did not look at the circumstances surrounding the adoption of the decision, but rather at 'the assessments on which the Commission relied'.[76] Thus, in order to ascertain whether the Commission had wrongfully failed to open the formal investigation procedure, the ECJ looked at the grounds on which the decision had been taken, namely, the absence of overcapacity in the relevant market. After noting that the applicant had provided the ECJ with 'consistent documents' disputing this fact, the ECJ identified the statistics upon which the Commission based its claim.[77] The ECJ then added:

> The figures set out in [the statistics upon which the Commission based its claim] are only partial, in that they relate only to production, the value of such production and the number of persons employed. They do not make it possible to ascertain production capacity and to compare it with production and demand on the market. The absence or the existence of overcapacity of production cannot therefore be inferred from those figures with any degree of certainty.[78]

Since 'such a finding would have necessitated a complex analysis of the sub-sector in question and further investigations into the undertakings in that sub-sector',[79] the ECJ concluded that the Commission should have initiated the formal investigation procedure 'in order to ascertain, after obtaining all the requisite opinions, whether its assessment—which gave rise to serious difficulties—was correct'.[80] The contested decision was therefore annulled.

A similar approach was followed by the CFI in *Kronofrance*.[81] The Commission had approved the investment project notified by Germany because it was intended to promote the development of a region eligible under Article 107(3)(a) TFEU. The CFI annulled the Commission's decision because it had failed to ascertain

[74] Case T-140/13 *Netherlands Maritime Technology Association v Commission*, ECLI:EU:T:2014:1029, para 60; Case T-57/11 *Castelnou Energía SL v Commission*, ECLI:EU:T:2014:1021, para 84.
[75] Case T-140/13 *Netherlands Maritime Technology Association v Commission*, ECLI:EU:T:2014:1029, para 74.
[76] Case C-198/91 *William Cook plc v Commission* [1993] ECR I-2487, para 31.
[77] ibid, para 34.
[78] ibid, para 35.
[79] ibid, para 37.
[80] ibid, para 38.
[81] Case T-27/02 *Kronofrance SA v Commission* [2004] ECR II-4177.

whether the proposed aid was for a declining market, a condition required by the multisectoral framework on regional aid for large investment projects. The judgment of the CFI was then confirmed, on appeal, by the ECJ.[82] The approach of the CFI is similar to the one followed by the ECJ in *Cook*, in that it infers the existence of serious difficulties from the fact that the analysis of the Commission can be deemed to be incomplete ('there ha[d] been no assessment … of the compatibility of the notified aid on the basis of *all* the applicable criteria' (emphasis added)).[83] In this case, however, the need for a more elaborate analysis was imposed by a piece of soft law. A similar approach has been followed in later cases.[84]

The method followed by the European Courts in these cases differs from the one analysed earlier, in that the circumstances surrounding the adoption of the contested decision are not considered. Instead, the Commission looks at the grounds on which the Commission based its finding that the aid is compatible, in order to ascertain whether they reveal any serious difficulty. It concludes that they do when they are insufficient to ground the conclusion reached by the Commission. In other words, it is a two-stage method that involves, first, identifying the grounds upon which the Commission relied in order to adopt a favourable decision and, secondly, ascertaining whether these grounds are sufficient and adequate to justify the finding the aid is compatible or, as the GC has recently put it, whether the evidence relied on by the Commission is 'complete and reliable'.[85]

(c) The Two Methods Compared

The review carried out under this method is not strictly procedural, because the Court does not rely on procedural signs such as the length of the procedure, the statements made by the Commission, or the intensity and content of the negotiations carried out with the granting Member State. Overall, however, the review remains procedural, in that it assesses the lawfulness of the premature closure of the file. This affects the possible outcomes of the process of judicial review: should the action be successful, the annulment of the decision will result in a referral of the case back to the preliminary stage of the administrative procedure[86] or, directly, to the formal investigation phase[87]—the general rule being that the

[82] Joined Cases C-75 and 80/05 P *Germany and others v Kronofrance SA* [2008] ECR I-6619.

[83] ibid, para 110.

[84] Case T-375/04 *Scheucher-Fleisch and others v Commission* [2009] ECR II-4155 (infringement of a substantive provision contained in the applicable soft-law instrument).

[85] Case T-388/02 *Kronoply and Kronotex v Commission* [2008] ECR II-305, para 115.

[86] Case T-27/02 *Kronofrance SA v Commission* [2004] ECR II-4177, para 111: 'In complying with the present judgment, it will be for the Commission, in the light of the data relating to the apparent consumption of the relevant products during the reference period, to assess the compatibility of the notified aid and, in so far as it encounters serious difficulties in that regard, to initiate the formal examination procedure provided for in Article 88(2) EC'.

[87] Case C-198/91 *William Cook plc v Commission* [1993] ECR I-2487, para 38 (the Commission 'should have initiated the [formal investigation procedure]').

Commission may not 'pick up the procedure again at a stage earlier than the exact point at which the illegality found had occurred'.[88] These are, precisely, the same outcomes that the first method may produce.[89]

The upshot is that both methods differ in the indicators that they use but not in the result to which they are conducive. This is because, whichever method is followed, the only outcome that the applicants may expect from a first-scenario type of challenge (limited standing, procedural plea) is the referral of the case back to the Commission, so that it resumes its assessment at the stage determined by the Court. In terms of leverage, this means that the influence that competitors may exert through this channel is limited. In case of success, the ruling must not prejudge the compatibility of the State aid under scrutiny; all it may afford them is a second shot at the administrative procedure. The question that arises, then, is whether the opportunities for leverage afforded to competitors under the second scenario are greater. This question is considered next.

3. Judicial Review of Phase 1 Decisions in the Second Scenario

The second scenario is defined by the case law as a default category: any action seeking to challenge a phase 1 decision *on any ground other than* the breach by the Commission of its obligation to open the second phase of the procedure falls within this scenario. It therefore encompasses very different situations, which makes it impossible to identify the grounds on which the applications falling within this scenario may be based, unless one resorts to the general formulation of the grounds of review laid down by Article 263-II TFEU: lack of competence, infringement of an essential procedural requirement (other than the failure by the Commission to open the formal investigation procedure), infringement of the Treaties or of any rule of law relating to their application, and misuse of powers.

The fact that a stricter test of standing is imposed in this scenario (and that this scenario is often considered a challenge of the 'merits' of the decision)[90] suggests that the 'full *locus standi*'[91] of the applicants gives access to an unrestricted type of judicial review, ie, one that is not restricted to the lawfulness of the closure of the file but goes instead to the substantive findings made by the Commission with regard to the existence or compatibility of the measure at stake. Not in vain, the first phase of the procedure can result in a decision that there is no aid as well as

[88] Case C-362/09 P *Athinaïki Techniki AE v Commission* [2010] ECR I-13275, para 70.

[89] See, eg, Case T-46/97 *Sociedade Independente de Comunicaçao (SIC) v Commission* [2000] ECR II-2125, para 108: 'the Commission was under a duty to initiate the procedure under Article [108(2) TFEU] so that, having obtained all the necessary views, it could check the validity of its assessment'.

[90] See, eg, Case C-287/12 *Ryanair v Commission*, ECLI:EU:C:2013:395, para 56.

[91] I borrow the phrase from Michael Honoré, 'The Standing of Third Parties in State Aid Cases. The Lessons to be drawn from the Judgment Case C-78/03 P, Aktionsgemeinschaft Recht Und Eigentum V. Commission' (2006) 5 *European State Aid Law Quarterly* 269.

in a decision to raise no objections, which presupposes the existence of aid but sees no concerns in its implementation. In *DHL and Deutsche Post*, the CFI stated that in the *Cook* type of scenario 'it is not for the Court of First Instance to rule at that stage of the Commission's procedure for the examination of aid on whether aid exists or whether it is compatible with the common market'.[92] *A contrario*, it is possible to expect the now GC to rule on the existence and compatibility of the aid when it reviews the legality of a phase 1 decision in the second scenario.

(a) Some Examples

As noted earlier, the origin of the two-scenario distinction is the *Danish Shipyards* ruling, which can also be considered the first 'second scenario case', given that the applicants were found to meet the *Cofaz* test of standing.[93] The analysis of this ruling, however, can provide little insight into the outcome of the review exercised by the Courts in the second scenario, because all the pleas put forward by the applicants were eventually dismissed by the Court. This is the reason why my analysis will focus on second-scenario cases where the action of annulment was successful.

In the *British Aggregates Association II* case,[94] the CFI was called to review the legality of the decision not to raise objections to the special relief scheme from the British aggregates levy established for Northern Ireland. The standing of the applicant was not explicitly analysed by the CFI, because the Commission withdrew its objection of inadmissibility in the course of the procedure. It did so, however, as a result of the *British Aggregates Association I* judgment,[95] which was issued in the meantime, and where the ECJ declared that the British Aggregates Association satisfied the conditions laid down in *Cofaz* and was therefore entitled to challenge the approval of the aggregates levy.[96] Since this case involved the same applicant and the same general measure, it is possible to assume that the procedural status of the applicant was the same in *BAA II*, and that the case therefore fell within the second scenario.

Two of the pleas put forward by the applicant clearly attacked the merits of the decision: the first plea alleged infringement of current Articles 28 and 30 TFEU or Article 110 TFEU; the second one alleged infringement of the Community Guidelines on State aid for environmental protection. And yet the CFI decided to focus on the third plea, alleging that the Commission had infringed its obligation to open the formal investigation procedure, and to consider the other pleas

[92] Case T-388/03 *Deutsche Post AG and DHL International v Commission* [2009] ECR II-199, para 66.
[93] Case T-266/94 *Skibsvaertftsvaerft and others v Commission* [1996] ECR II-1399, paras 47–48.
[94] Case T-359/04 *British Aggregates Association and others v Commission* [2010] ECR II-427. The analysis that follows builds on my annotation to the case published as Fernando Pastor-Merchante, 'State Aids and Environmental Taxes: The Northern Ireland Exemption to the UK Aggregates Levy' (2011) 2 *European Journal of Risk Regulation* 125–8.
[95] Case C-487/06 P *British Aggregates Association v Commission* [2008] ECR I-10505, issued on appeal against Case T-210/02 *British Aggregates Association v Commission* [2006] ECR II-2780.
[96] ibid, para 36.

only insofar as they provided evidence of the existence of serious difficulties which should have led the Commission to open the formal investigation procedure.[97] It is on the basis of this approach that the CFI concluded that the failure by the Commission to consider the alleged discriminatory character of the contested measure was indicative of the existence of serious difficulties, and that the Commission was therefore not entitled to adopt the contested decision without opening the formal investigation procedure.[98]

A similar approach was followed in *Prayon-Rupel*.[99] *Prayon-Rupel* is a difficult case, in that the procedural status of the applicant (and, hence, the scenario under which it falls) was not discussed. The fact that some of its pleas attacked the merits of the contested decision, combined with the fact that the Commission did not object to their admissibility, suggests that the applicants had full *locus standi*, but some commentators have expressed the opposite view.[100] It should therefore be treated with caution. Although the first plea clearly attacked the merits of the contested decision, alleging that it was vitiated by factual inaccuracies and manifest errors of assessment and that it infringed the relevant Guidelines, the CFI decided to start its analysis with the second plea, which called into question the failure of the Commission to open the second phase of the procedure, and to do it 'in the light of the arguments and evidence put forward to prove the manifest errors of assessment and factual inaccuracies alleged in the first plea'.[101] Again, the application of the serious difficulties test led the CFI to annul the contested decision, without analysing any of the other pleas.[102]

This approach is reminiscent of the approach taken by the ECJ itself in cases involving privileged applicants. The *French wines and eaux de vie* case provides a good example thereof.[103] This is certainly a case falling outside the scope of this chapter, since it involves a challenge of a phase 1 decision promoted by a privileged applicant. Nevertheless, it provides some insight into the way in which the Court carries out the review of this type of decisions in cases where the procedural capacity of the applicant is not limited. Given the privileged status of Portugal and the fact that it challenged both the failure of the Commission to open the formal investigation phase and the merits of the decision,[104] this case can be assimilated to a case falling within the second scenario. And yet, again, the ECJ restricted its analysis to the plea alleging breach of the obligation to open the formal investigation procedure, something which it was not obliged to do by the procedural status of the applicant. It found that the contested decision could be annulled on this ground alone, which made it unnecessary to consider the merits of the plea

[97] Case T-359/04 *British Aggregates Association and others v Commission* [2010] ECR II-427, para 59.
[98] ibid, para 102.
[99] Case T-73/98 *Société chimique Prayon-Rupel v Commission* [2011] ECR II-867, para 44.
[100] Honoré (n 91) 283.
[101] Case T-73/98 *Société chimique Prayon-Rupel v Commission* [2011] ECR II-867, para 29.
[102] ibid, para 108.
[103] Case C-204/97 *Portugal v Commission* [2001] ECR I-3175.
[104] ibid, paras 20–21.

alleging breach of the criteria governing the application of the derogations of current Article 107(3) TFEU.[105]

(b) *The Serious Difficulties Test as the Standard of Review in the Second Scenario*

The preceding analysis suggests that the European Courts tend to restrict their review of phase 1 decisions to the application of the serious difficulties test, even in those cases that fall within the second scenario (full standing, substantive challenge). One could be tempted to resort to the principle of judicial economy to explain this result: the finding that one of the pleas suffices to annul the contested decision makes it unnecessary to carry the analysis any further. However, the principle of judicial economy operates where the different pleas submitted by the applicants are equivalent, in that their endorsement by the Court would lead to the same outcome. When this is not the case, the Court is expected to consider the different pleas or, at least, not to restrict itself to considering the least restrictive plea—that is, *restrictive* from the perspective of the leeway that the endorsement of the plea would leave in the hands of the original decision-making institution (in this case, the Commission).

The Court hinted at this idea in the *Belgian Textiles* case, another case involving a privileged applicant.[106] Germany put forward two pleas in support of its action for the annulment of the decision approving the Belgian aid plan for its textile industry; the first one alleged breach of the obligation to open the formal investigation procedure but the second one challenged the finding that the aid granted by Belgium was compatible with the common market. After concluding that the first plea was well founded, the ECJ went on to analyse the substantive plea. It did so with full awareness that the second plea 'was made in view of the possibility that the Court might declare the contested decision … void for infringement of procedural rules *without ruling on the submission that the Belgian restructuring plan is incompatible with the common market*' (emphasis added).[107] 'Since that is precisely what has happened—the Court added—it is necessary to give a ruling on that claim in spite of the declaration that the contested decision is void'.[108] The plea was eventually dismissed,[109] but the willingness of the Court to consider it was premised on the assumption that both pleas could lead to different results: the imposition of a procedural obligation to the Commission (in the first case), an assessment of the compatibility of aid (in the second one).

If this analysis is correct, the reluctance of the European Courts to go beyond the serious difficulties test in the second scenario is quite striking, for the two-scenario

105 ibid, para 52.
106 Case 84/82 *Germany v Commission* [1984] ECR 1451.
107 ibid, para 20.
108 ibid.
109 ibid, para 23.

distinction presupposes that two types of review are possible with regard to phase 1 decisions: the *procedural* review of the first scenario (which only assesses the lawfulness of the closure of the file and can only result in the referral of the case back to the Commission) and the *substantive* review of the second scenario (which additionally assesses the findings made by the Commission with regard to the existence or compatibility of the aid). Thus, the European judicature seems to be very strict in diverting certain applicants through an alternative, more demanding route, despite the fact that all routes lead to the same place—namely to judicial review of the *procedural* regularity of phase 1 decisions.

This has two implications. The first implication is that the two-scenario distinction and the dichotomy between their respective rules of standing may not be justified, for it is hard to see the rationale of having two different tests of standing if they both give access to the same type of review. The second implication is that the types of rulings that applicants may secure are identical in both scenarios, which means, in turn, that the considerations applied earlier in relation to the first scenario can therefore be extended to this one. The upshot is that, no matter which scenario their application falls under, all that competitors can get through the challenge of phase 1 decisions is a second shot at the administrative procedure.

III. Judicial Review of 'Phase 2 Decisions'

1. The Refinement of the *Cofaz* Rule of Standing

As a general rule, the standing of competitors to challenge State aid decisions adopted at the end of the formal investigation phase is subject to the two-prong test adopted by the ECJ in *Cofaz*, which requires applicants to show that they participated in the previous administrative procedure and that their position on the market was significantly affected by the contested State aid. Under this test, then, it is the combination of both conditions (participation and significant effect) that individualises non-privileged applicants, in general, and competitors, in particular, for the purposes of Article 263-IV TFEU.

The real novelty of *Cofaz* lay in the second condition, which was not present in the line of antitrust and antidumping cases within which the Court explicitly embedded its decision.[110] The reference to the 'significant' effect of the contested State aid on the applicant echoes the words of Advocate General Verloren Van Themaat, who wrote:

> I would remind the Court that, in my view, on the basis of the principal criterion for the application of Article [107(1) TFEU—namely, the distortion of competition element of the definition of State aid], an undertaking in receipt of aid and an undertaking adversely

[110] Case 169/84 *Compagnie française de l'azote (Cofaz) v Commission* [1986] ECR 391, para 24.

> affected thereby are in principle both to the same degree directly and individually concerned by a decision concerning such aid. However, by analogy to some extent with the case-law of the Court concerning Article [101(1) TFEU] (which applies only to restrictions of competition affecting a significant part of the market), I consider it legitimate to restrict the admissibility of actions by competitors to undertakings *which have established that a substantial proportion of their sales are in direct competition with a substantial proportion of the sales of undertakings which, according to the application, are favoured by the measure to which the Commission's contested decision relates* (emphasis added).[111]

Thus, in the Advocate General's view, the function of this requirement was to narrow down the circle of competitors who would have access to judicial review of State aid decisions, leaving out those whose competitive relationship with the beneficiary was so negligible that they were unlikely to sustain any damage as a result of the aid. The only thing that applicants would need to show, in order to pass muster, is that a significant part of their output is in competition with a significant part of the beneficiary's own products. On the facts of the case, both the Advocate General and the Court concluded that the applicants had done so to the requisite legal standard, by pointing to the market shares that both the beneficiaries and themselves had on the French market.[112]

It is thus difficult to escape the conclusion that neither the Advocate General nor the Court intended to set the admissibility bar very high, at least not for competitors who had participated in the administrative procedure.[113] This is confirmed by the clarification introduced by the Court immediately after the analysis of the arguments submitted by the applicants in connection with their competitive relationship with the beneficiaries:

> It is not for the Court, at this stage of the procedure, when it is considering whether the application is admissible, to make a definitive finding on the competitive relationship between the applicants and the [beneficiaries]. It is sufficient to note that the applicants have adduced pertinent reasons to show that the Commission's decision may adversely affect their legitimate interests by seriously jeopardizing their position on the market in question.[114]

The upshot is that *Cofaz* left the door wide open for competitors to have access to judicial review of State aid decisions. Granted, the interpretation of the rules of standing embraced by the Court left out some interested parties. However, it seemed rather generous with regard to *competitors* themselves: they would only have to show that they participated in the administrative procedure and that their competitive relationship with the beneficiary affected a non-negligible part of their output. In sum, *Cofaz* did not set the admissibility bar very high for the *actual* competitors of the State aid beneficiaries.

[111] Opinion of Advocate General Verloren Van Themaat in Case 169/84 *Compagnie française de l'azote (Cofaz) v Commission* [1986] ECR 391, pp 405–06.

[112] ibid, p 406; Case 169/84 *Compagnie française de l'azote (Cofaz) SA v Commission* [1986] ECR 391, para 28.

[113] Case 169/84 *Compagnie française de l'azote (Cofaz) SA v Commission* [1986] ECR 391, para 25.

[114] ibid, para 28.

This competitor-friendly reading of *Cofaz* might come as a surprise for any reader familiar with modern State aid litigation, given the controversy that surrounds the strict standing requirements faced by competitors.[115] The point to note is that the origin of this problem is not so much in *Cofaz* as in the three following jurisprudential developments that occurred afterwards.

(a) The Abandonment of the Participation Requirement

The first development is the abandonment of the participation requirement as the main condition qualifying competitors to have standing before the European Courts.

This departure from the participation requirement was initiated by the CFI, with its holding in *ASPEC* that *Cofaz* 'does not preclude the possibility that an undertaking may be in a position to demonstrate by other means, by reference to specific circumstances distinguishing it individually as in the case of the addressee, that it is individually concerned'.[116] The ECJ explicitly endorsed this non-exclusive reading of *Cofaz* in the *Sniace* judgment, where it held that

> it does not follow from the case-law of the Court that [participation in the administrative procedure] is a necessary condition for the finding that a decision is of individual concern to an undertaking within the meaning of [Article 263-IV TFEU], precluding the possibility of the undertaking putting forward other specific circumstances which distinguish it individually in a way that is similar to the case of the person addressed by that decision.[117]

Sniace clearly indicates that one of the two prongs of *Cofaz* is an essential condition (significant effect), whereas the other is not (participation).

The disentanglement of the rules of standing to challenge State aid decisions from the position adopted by the applicant in the previous administrative procedure has been criticised on the ground that it discourages participation by interested parties in the formal investigation procedure and, hence, runs counter to the rationale of the consultation phase, which is to gather as much information as possible in order to get a complete picture of the likely effects of State aids.[118] This criticism is based on the observation that *Sniace* implies

[115] J Battista, 'Is Participation in the Commission's Administrative Procedure a Necessary Condition for Legal Standing? Commentary on Case C-265/05 P, Sniace v. Commission' (2008) 7 *European State Aid Law Quarterly* 317, 325, and Gerrit Schohe, 'Le statut du plaignant', in Mariana Dony and Catherine Smits (eds), *Aides d'État* (Brussels: Éditions de l'Université de Bruxelles, 2005) 219, who considers the admissibility of annulment actions against positive decisions a 'game of chance' ('jeu de hasard'). But see Marc Barennes, 'The Standing of the Competitors of the Aid Recipients in State Aid Cases', in Heikki Kanninen, Nina Korjus and Allan Rosas (eds), *EU Competition Law in Context: Essays in Honour of Virpi Tiili* (Oxford: Hart Publishing, 2009) 321.

[116] Case T-435/93 *ASPEC v Commission* [1995] ECR II-1281, para 64. See also Case T-11/95 *BP Chemicals v Commission* [1998] ECR II-3225, para 76, and Case T-358/02 *Deutsche Post AG and DHL v Commission* [2004] ECR II-1565, para 36.

[117] Case C-260/05 P *Sniace SA v Commission* [2007] ECR I-10005, para 57.

[118] Barbara Jankovec and Vincent Kronenberger, 'Third Parties in State Aid Litigation: Locus Standi and Procedural Guarantees' in Michael Sánchez Rydelski (ed), *The EC State Aid Regime—Distortive Effects of State Aid on Competition and Trade* (London: Cameron May, 2006) 753.

> that even very active complainants will not have standing if their market position has not been substantially affected, while those competitors who are individually concerned by the aid, do not need to do more efforts than what is in their interests during the administrative procedure, to ensure the possibility to defend their rights in Court, should a decision being of prejudice to them be adopted.[119]

A possible response to this criticism is that the disentanglement of participation and judicial review is 'more apparent than real',[120] because playing an active role in the administrative procedure 'lower[s] the evidential bar in relation to demonstrating that there will be competitive/commercial harm'.[121] This is probably the reason why *ASPEC* remains one of the rare cases in which standing was established on the basis of the effects-based requirement alone. In *Sniace*—as well as in the other cases where the CFI embraced the non-exclusive reading of *Cofaz*—the actions were eventually dismissed as inadmissible for lack of standing.[122]

Be that as it may, there is no doubt that the significant effect requirement has taken centre stage in the admissibility analysis of the European judicature: it is no longer a merely complementary condition but rather the main hurdle that interested parties have to overcome in order to have standing. Not surprisingly, this shift has also had an impact on the meaning of the significant effect requirement, which has become a much more exacting condition for competitors.

(b) The Hardening of the Significant Effect Requirement

Indeed, the shift in the centre of gravity of the admissibility test from the participation to the significant effect requirement has resulted in a hardening of the latter. This is because the European Courts seem to have abandoned the idea that the admissibility of this type of action should not be conditional upon a searching analysis of the competitive relationship between the applicants and the beneficiaries.[123]

In *Cofaz*, the Court focused its analysis on the competitive relationship between the applicants and the beneficiaries and concluded that their position on the market was significantly affected by the contested State aid because they

[119] Jasmin Battista, 'Is Participation in the Commission's Administrative Procedure a Necessary Condition for Legal Standing? Commentary on Case C-265/05 P, Sniace v. Commission' (2008) 7 *European State Aid Law Quarterly* 317, 324, who is not critical on this point.

[120] Winter (n 27) 529.

[121] ibid. See also Leo Flynn, 'Remedies in the European Courts', in Andrea Biondi, Piet Eeckhout and James Flynn (eds), *The Law of State Aid in the European Union* (Oxford: Oxford University Press, 2004) 295. See, eg, Case T-358/02 *Deutsche Post AG and DHL International v Commission* [2004] ECR II-1565, para 41.

[122] Case C-260/05 P *Sniace SA v Commission* [2007] ECR I-10005, para 61; Case T-11/95 *BP Chemicals v Commission* [1998] ECR II-3225, para 83 (partial inadmissibility); and Case T-358/02 *Deutsche Post AG and DHL v Commission* [2004] ECR II-1565, para 49. The appeal against the latter judgment was dismissed as inadmissible in Case C-367/04 P *Deutsche Post and DHL Express v Commission* [2006] ECR I-26.

[123] Case 169/84 *Compagnie française de l'azote (Cofaz) SA v Commission* [1986] ECR 391, para 28.

were in direct competition with each other on the French market.[124] In order to reach this conclusion, the Court did not engage in a meticulous analysis of their respective market shares, which is why it is not possible to infer from that judgment any threshold below which the competitive relationship between two companies shall be deemed insufficient. The point to note, however, is that the Court did not discuss either the way in which the contested State aid was supposed to harm the applicants. Instead, the Court accepted as a proxy for harm the existence of a significant competitive relationship between the applicants and the beneficiaries, concluding on this basis alone that 'the Commission's decision may adversely affect their legitimate interests by seriously jeopardizing their position on the market in question'.[125]

This broad-brush approach to the significant effect requirement has changed in subsequent cases. First, the bulk of the analysis has shifted from the proxy—the relative position on the market of the applicant and the beneficiary—to the harm itself—ie, the injury sustained or likely to be sustained by the applicant. Granted, the European Courts have defined in broad terms the types of harm that competitors may allege, which include actual damage (*damnum emergens*) and loss of opportunity (*lucrum cessans*).[126] They have also made it clear that competitors need not show a decline in their 'commercial or financial performance' in order to pass this test,[127] for 'it cannot be ruled out that an undertaking will succeed in avoiding or at least limiting such a decline in some circumstances, for example, by making savings or by expanding in more profitable markets'.[128] However, the approach of the European Courts has become much more searching, in that they are no longer willing to establish standing on the sole ground of the competitive relationship between the applicant and the beneficiary. They additionally expect applicants to produce a theory of harm to explain the way in which the contested State aid specifically affects them.[129]

Secondly, the most recent case law seems to be informed by the idea that the standing of competitors cannot be based on merely speculative conjectures. The subtle way in which the European Courts have rephrased one of the formulae of *Cofaz* is quite telling in that regard: rather than showing that 'the Commission's decision *may* adversely affect their legitimate interests',[130] they must now show it is 'likely' to do so.[131] Needless to say, the admissibility analysis of the European Courts is not driven by any precise standard of probability, but there is little doubt

[124] ibid, para 27.

[125] ibid, para 28.

[126] Case C-525/04 P *Spain v Lenzing* [2007] ECR I-9947, paras 34, 35; Case C-487/06 P *British Aggregates Association v Commission* [2008] ECR I-10515, para 53.

[127] ibid.

[128] Case C-525/04 P *Spain v Lenzing* [2007] ECR I-9947, para 36.

[129] See, eg, Case T-118/13 *Whirlpool Europe BV v Commission*, ECLI:EU:T:2016:365, para 51.

[130] Case 169/84 *Compagnie française de l'azote (Cofaz) SA v Commission* [1986] ECR 391, para 28.

[131] Case T-358/02 *Deutsche Post AG and DHL v Commission* [2004] ECR II-1565, para 44; Case T-362/10 *Vtesse Networks Ltd v Commission*, ECLI:EU:T:2014:928, para, 57.

that they have become more demanding in that regard.[132] In this sense, they have equally become more demanding on the causality front, when the allegations made by the applicants are not prospective but based on an injury that has already occurred—which is often the case when unlawfully implemented measures are at stake.[133]

Finally, the European Courts now insist on the idea that the harm alleged by the applicants must be 'significant'[134] or 'substantial'.[135] Thus, they do not restrict their analysis to the likelihood of the State aid having an adverse effect on the applicant, but also consider 'the seriousness of such an effect'.[136] Again, this idea was already present in *Cofaz*, where the Court referred to the adverse effect that the contested measure had on the applicants 'by seriously jeopardizing their position on the market'.[137] Yet, as already noted, this substantial adverse effect was simply inferred from the proxy used by the Court to assess the admissibility of the action. Things have now changed and the Courts devote increasing attention to the magnitude of the adverse effects of the contested State aid on the applicants.[138] Applicants are thus expected to prove that they would have *significantly* increased their sales had it not been for the restructuring aid granted to their competitor[139] or that the loss of a call for tenders for the deployment of broadband networks *seriously* compromises their position on the market.[140]

(c) *The Transformation of the Significant Effect Requirement into a Comparative Standard*

Finally, the case law of the European Courts has added to the significant effect requirement a comparative element which was completely absent in its original inception. Indeed, *Cofaz* restricted access to judicial review of State aid decisions to applicants capable of showing that there was a significant competitive relationship between themselves and the beneficiaries. Nothing in the judgment of the Court—or in the opinion of the Advocate General—suggested that the existence of other market actors in a similar position would deprive applicants of the right of standing to which they were otherwise entitled. The idea seemed to be, as the

[132] See, eg, Case T-118/13 *Whirlpool Europe BV v Commission*, ECLI:EU:T:2016:365, para 51: 'it cannot simply be presumed that the applicant would have significantly increased its sales in the event of disappearance from the market of the undertaking benefiting from the measures at issue'.

[133] Case C-33/14 P *Mory and others v Commission*, ECLI:EU:C:2015:609, para 110.

[134] Case T-358/02 *Deutsche Post AG and DHL v Commission* [2004] ECR II-1565, para 43.

[135] Case T-118/13 *Whirlpool Europe BV v Commission*, para 53; Case T-182/10 *AISCAT v Commission*, ECLI:EU:T:2013:9, para 68.

[136] Case C-487/06 P *British Aggregates Association v Commission* [2008] ECR I-10505, para 53.

[137] Case 169/84 *Compagnie française de l'azote (Cofaz) SA v Commission* [1986] ECR 391, para 28.

[138] See, eg, Case T-182/10 *AISCAT v Commission*, ECLI:EU:T:2013:9, para 68: 'In a market covering a total of 5500 km of toll motorways, if the award without a call for tenders of the concession for a section of motorway of a lengthy of approximately 32 km may have a certain effect on competition … it cannot be considered in itself as having a *substantial* effect' (emphasis added).

[139] Case T-118/13 *Whirlpool Europe BV v Commission*, ECLI:EU:T:2016:365.

[140] Case T-362/10 *Vtesse Networks Ltd v Commission*, ECLI:EU:T:2014:928, para 57.

Court itself put it in the more recent *British Aggregates* case, that 'the fact that an undefined number of other competitors may, in appropriate circumstances, allege that they have suffered similar harm does not constitute an obstacle to the admissibility of the action brought by the appellant undertaking'.[141]

Yet, in many cases, the European Courts have embraced exactly the opposite idea, dismissing as inadmissible actions brought by competitors who had failed to 'demonstrate that [their] competitive position is substantially affected *in comparison with other undertakings competing in the same market at issue*' (emphasis added).[142] This idea surfaced, for instance, in the Italian and Belgian postal cases, where Deutsche Post's subsidiaries saw their actions fail despite their being mentioned by the Commission, in the contested decision itself, as competitors of the beneficiary incumbents—Poste Italiane and La Poste.[143] The fact that 'there were several other operators on the market, some of which had higher market shares' proved to be an insurmountable obstacle.[144] The European Courts have also relied on this theory to deny standing to a competitor of the recipient of restructuring aid, on the ground that that 'there is no way of determining that the applicant would have been more capable than an average competitor of capturing the demand resulting from the disappearance of [the beneficiary]', which would have likely exited the market had it not been for the aid.[145] Finally, the same theory has been used in cases concerning State aid measures granted through competitive tendering procedures, where excluded bidders have been denied standing on the ground that there were other companies involved in the tender process.[146]

This comparative benchmark sometimes adopts a slightly different form, with the European Courts phrasing it as an obligation for applicants to show that their circumstances distinguish them 'in a similar way to the undertaking in receipt of the aid'.[147] It is difficult to understand the exact meaning of this elusive formula. For one thing, State aid beneficiaries are not the addressees of the decisions

[141] Case C-487/06 P *British Aggregates Association v Commission* [2008] ECR I-10505, para 56.

[142] Case T-118/13 *Whirlpool Europe BV v Commission*, ECLI:EU:T:2016:365, para 47. See also: Case T-358/02 *Deutsche Post AG and DHL v Commission* [2004] ECR II-1565, para 41; Case T-388/03 *Deutsche Post AG and DHL International v Commission* [2009] ECR II-199, para 51; Case T-362/10 *Vtesse Networks Ltd v Commission*, ECLI:EU:T:2014:928, para 55; Case T-182/10 *AISCAT v Commission*, ECLI:EU:T:2013:9, para 68; Case C-287/12 P *Ryanair v Commission*, ECLI:EU:C:2013:395, para 113.

[143] Case T-358/02 *Deutsche Post AG and DHL v Commission* [2004] ECR II-1565, para 39; Case T-388/03 *Deutsche Post AG and DHL International v Commission* [2009] ECR II-199, para 49.

[144] Case T-358/02 *Deutsche Post AG and DHL v Commission* [2004] ECR II-1565, para 41; Case T-388/03 *Deutsche Post AG and DHL International v Commission* [2009] ECR II-199, para 51.

[145] Case T-118/13 *Whirlpool Europe BV v Commission*, ECLI:EU:T:2016:365, para 52. See also Case T-58/10 *Phoenix-Reisen GmbH and others v Commission*, ECLI:EU:T:2012:3, para 49.

[146] Case T-362/10 *Vtesse Networks Ltd v Commission*, ECLI:EU:T:2014:928, para 55; Case T-182/10 *AISCAT v Commission*, ECLI:EU:T:2013:9, para 68.

[147] Case T-362/10 *Vtesse Networks Ltd v Commission*, ECLI:EU:T:2014:928, para 39. See also, eg, Case C-106/98 P *Comité d'entreprise de la Société française de production and others v Commission* [2000] ECR I-3659, para 41; Case C-487/06 P *British Aggregates Association v Commission* [2008] ECR I-10515, para 48; Case T-601/11 *Dansk Automat Brancheforening v Commission*, ECLI:EU:T:2014:839, para 41.

adopted by the Commission in this area, which is why this may not be the best way of transposing into the realm of State aid the logic of *Plaumann*—the idea that 'persons other than those to whom a decision is addressed' may only challenge that decision if they show that their circumstances distinguish them individually, 'just as in the case of the person addressed'.[148]

In any event, it is not possible to infer from the case law the type of factors that may assimilate the position of State aid recipients and their competitors. One could argue—like Advocate General Verloren Van Themaat in *Cofaz*—that State aid decisions affect in the same way beneficiaries and competitors, for 'the disadvantages for the latter are the counterpart of the advantages conferred on the former'.[149] However, this idea is clearly foreign to the philosophy that informs the case law concerning access to judicial review of State aid decisions, which is much more generous with regard to beneficiaries than to competitors. How, then, are competitors supposed to overcome this asymmetry? That this is no easy task is well illustrated by the cases concerning competitive tenders involving some form of State aid (eg, public procurement procedures). In this type of zero-sum game, it is difficult to escape the conclusion that the successful bidder and the other tenderers are in an almost identical situation insofar as they all sought the exact same regulatory benefit. Yet in this type of scenario the case law also offers examples of actions which did not pass the admissibility test because the applicants failed to establish the individuality of their situation.[150]

The preceding analysis shows that the case law developed over the last 30 years has provided the significant effect requirement with a comparative element that was absent in its origins. Thus, it is no longer sufficient to show that the contested State aid is likely to have a significant effect on the market position of the applicant—it is also necessary to show that the State aid is likely to have a *more* significant effect on the applicant than on other market actors. This is clearly one of the developments that has contributed to tightening the rules of standing to challenge State aid decisions, because it has resulted 'in a threshold of "comparatively more adverse substantive negative impact" that is almost impossible to discharge'.[151]

More generally, the analysis of the way in which the case law has refined the rules of standing defined in *Cofaz* reveals a shift from a relatively competitor-friendly standard to a very demanding one, where competitors need to invest a lot of argumentative effort at the admissibility stage in order to establish the risk of harm that the contested State aid entails for them. It may of course be wondered whether it makes sense to screen the admissibility of cases on the basis of such complex rules. In any event, the evolution of the case law on the standing of competitors to challenge phase 2 decisions has progressively raised the admissibility bar. From

[148] Case 25/62 *Plaumann v Commission* [1961] ECR 409.

[149] Opinion of Advocate General Verloren Van Themaat in Case 169/84 *Compagnie française de l'azote (Cofaz) v Commission* [1986] ECR 391, p 403.

[150] Case T-362/10 *Vtesse Networks Ltd v Commission*, ECLI:EU:T:2014:928, para 55; Case T-182/10 *AISCAT v Commission*, ECLI:EU:T:2013:9, para 69.

[151] Albert Sánchez-Graells, 'Another state aid decision by GC follows restrictive approach to standing of interested parties' at www.howtocrackanut.com.

the perspective of *access*, this is obviously an important limitation, for it deprives many competitors of the opportunity to bring to the judicial arena their fight against the allegedly distortionary effects of State aid measures.

2. Type of Judicial Review Exercised Over Phase 2 Decisions

The analysis of the type of judicial review exercised by the European Courts in relation to phase 2 decisions needs to depart from the distinction (already discussed in Chapter 1) between the objective character of the definition of State aid laid down by Article 107(1) TFEU and the discretionary character of the exemptions listed in Article 107(3) TFEU. This dichotomy suggests that the review exercised by the European Courts should be fundamentally different in relation to the findings of the Commission that relate to the *existence* and to the *compatibility* of State aid: whereas in relation to the existence of State aid the review should be 'comprehensive',[152] in relation to its compatibility it should be restricted 'to checking that the rules on procedure and the statement of reasons have been complied with, that the facts relied on in making the contested choice are materially accurate, and that there has been no manifest error of assessment and no misuse of powers'.[153] The truth is, however, that the review actually exercised by the European Courts with regard to State aid decisions does not lend itself easily to this type of general sketch—their review is neither so comprehensive (in the first case) nor so limited (in the latter case) as the previous account suggests.

The objective character of the definition of State aid means that the Commission enjoys no discretion in its application[154]—in other words, that the Commission is bound to declare that a measure constitutes State aid *if and only if* it meets the four conditions laid down by that provision (State resources, selective advantage, distortion of competition, effect on trade between Member States). In theory, this characterisation implies that interested parties—beneficiaries and competitors alike—may use the judicial review procedure to enforce this provision in case of disagreement with the initial determination made by the Commission with regard to the existence or non-existence of State aid. This possibility is tempered, however, by the complexity of the economic analysis required to reach that determination, which justifies some degree of judicial deference vis-à-vis the findings of the Commission.[155] Although the operation of Article 107(1) TFEU is framed by the rule that the Commission enjoys no discretion, the European Courts are thus likely to defer to its economic appraisals when it comes to reviewing the application of standards such as the private investor test.[156]

[152] Case C-487/06 P *British Aggregates Association v Commission* [2008] ECR I-10515, para 111.
[153] ibid, para 108.
[154] Case T-67/94 *Ladbroke Racing Ltd v Commission* [1998] ECR II-1, para 52.
[155] ibid.
[156] Case C-56/93 *Belgium v Commission* [1996] ECR I-723, paras 10–11.

When it comes to reviewing the application of Article 107(3) TFEU, the starting point is exactly the opposite. This is because the application of this provision is framed by the recognition of a broad margin of discretion in favour of the Commission.[157] Indeed, the administration of the exemptions foreseen in Article 107(3) TFEU is a textbook example of 'classic discretion',[158] where the Treaty defines a series of conditions that empower but do not oblige the Commission to adopt a certain course of action—in this case, the declaration that a State aid is compatible with the common market. The intrinsically discretionary nature of the decision to exempt State aids from the general prohibition of Article 107(1) TFEU has different implications for potential beneficiaries and for their competitors.

The 'classic discretion' that the Commission enjoys in the administration of the exemptions represents an important limitation from the perspective of State aid beneficiaries. This is because the general prohibition of Article 107(1) TFEU operates as a default rule, from which it is only possible to depart where the Commission agrees to resort to Article 107(3) TFEU. What this means is that State aid beneficiaries are not entitled to any of the exemptions, no matter how precisely their case matches their scope. In practice, however, the significance of this limitation is mitigated by the 'soft-law approach' of the Commission,[159] which normally formalises its criteria in guidelines and other soft-law instruments. The European Courts have recognised that these instruments can be binding on the Commission, provided they do not depart from the Treaty.[160] They can therefore be relied on by interested parties in order to claim that the administration of the exemptions conforms to the rules set therein.[161]

Article 107(3) TFEU also represents an important limitation from the perspective of competitors. This is not so much because of the classic type of discretion that it embodies: the prohibition of aids being the default rule, it is possible for competitors to challenge positive decisions on the grounds that they fail to meet the conditions that empower the Commission to issue exemptions. Rather, it is the deferential approach that the European Courts take to the complex economic appraisals involved in the administration of the exemptions that limits the power of influence that competitors may exert through the Courts—in the terminology of Craig, the 'jurisdictional discretion'[162] recognised to the Commission as a result of the open-textured nature of the conditions that determine the applicability of the exemptions.[163]

[157] Case 730/79 *Philip Morris Holland BV v Commission* [1980] ECR 2671, para 17: 'Article [107(3) TFEU], unlike Article [107(2) TFEU], gives the Commission a discretion by providing that the aid which it specifies "may" be considered to be compatible with the common market'.

[158] Craig (n 1) 430.

[159] Michelle Cini, 'The Soft Law Approach: Commission Rule-Making in the EU's State Aid Regime' (2001) 8 *Journal of European Public Policy* 192.

[160] Case C-351/98 *Spain v Commission* [2002] ECR I-8031, para 53.

[161] Case T-176/01 *Ferriere Nord SpA v Italy* [2002] ECR II-3931, para 134 (upheld in Case C-49/05 P *Ferriere Nord SpA v Commission* [2008] ECR I-68).

[162] Craig (n 1) 404.

[163] Marc Schweda, 'Compatibility of State Aid Pursuant to Article 87(3) EC' in Martin Heidenhain (ed), *European State Aid Law* (Munich: Verlag CH Beck, 2010) 153.

The upshot is that the review carried out by the European Courts is unlikely to be very probing with regard to some of the most crucial aspects of State aid decisions—the findings concerning the existence of aid that depend on the private investor test and those concerning the administration of the exemptions. This a priori restrained approach represents a major obstacle from the perspective of the influence that competitors may exert through the process of judicial review. It means that their chances of shaping the outcome of State aid procedures through this channel are slim, especially when it comes to challenging the prospective assessment of the effects of State aids on which clearing decisions are based.

It should be noted, however, that the literature on State aids has documented two moves in the jurisprudence of the European Courts, the effect of which has been to intensify the type of review exercised over the discretionary findings of the Commission.[164]

The first move is the expansion of the type of determinations that are reviewed by the European Courts, so as to include the cogency of the applied economic theory followed by the Commission in its decisions.[165] This phenomenon was first described in the field of merger control and then in antitrust, with the CFI closely scrutinising the economic reasoning of the Commission and eventually quashing some important decisions.[166] It represents a certain departure from the previous stance of the Courts on this issue, which was to defer to the determinations made by the Commission where they were based on complex economic assessments.[167]

The same move has been identified in the field of State aid control as a result of the *Lenzing* judgment.[168] The action at the origin of this case was brought by Lenzing, a cellulose producer which sought to challenge the State aid allegedly received by one of its competitors (Sniace). It was partially upheld by the CFI on the ground that the Commission had based its finding that the contested measure constituted no aid on a wrong application of the private investor test.[169] On appeal, the ECJ validated the approach of the CFI,[170] restating the principle that it had previously enunciated in *Tetralaval*: 'whilst the Court recognises that the Commission has a margin of discretion with regard to economic matters, that does not mean that the Community judicature must refrain from reviewing the

[164] Herwig CH Hofmann and Alessandro Morini, 'Judicial Review of Commission Decisions in State Aid' in Erika Szyszczack (ed), *Research Handbook on European State Aid Law* (Cheltenham: Edward Elgar, 2011) 371, whose analysis I follow.

[165] ibid.

[166] Case T-342/99 *Airtours plc v Commission* [2002] ECR II-2585 and Case T-5/02 *Tetra Laval BV v Commission* [2002] ECR II-4381, upheld in Case C-12/03 P *Commission v Tetra Laval BV* [2005] ECR I-987.

[167] The same move has been documented in relation to technically complex determinations—see Case T-13/99 *Pfizer Animal Health SA v Council* [2002] ECR II-3305, and the discussion in Craig (n 1) 446–74.

[168] Hofmann and Morini (n 164) 372; Joana Mendes, 'Discretion, Care and Public Interests in the EU Administration: Probing the Limits of Law' (2016) 53 *Common Market Law Review* 419, 428.

[169] Case T-36/99 *Lenzing AG v Commission* [2004] ECR II-3597, paras 154–60.

[170] Case C-525/04 P *Spain v Lenzing AG* [2007] ECR I-9947, para 60.

Commission's interpretation of information of an economic nature'.[171] The same idea has been restated in later cases.[172]

The second move is the 'approach of reviewing administrative activity including discretionary activity through information-related general principles of law such as the duty of care'.[173] The duty of care is a device articulated by the European Courts to discipline the exercise by the Commission of its discretionary powers. It plays an important role in relation to complaints—as explained in Chapter 4—but its function is broader, in that it embodies a standard of diligence that is applicable to the collection and analysis of information at all stages of the procedure. This approach basically allows the European Courts to check the information basis relied on by the Commission—both quantity- and quality-wise[174]—so as to ensure that its discretionary decisions have been taken under the best possible conditions.

In the context of State aid control, the European Courts have had recourse to the duty of care in two types of situations. The first situation involves State aid procedures initiated in response to complaints, an issue that was considered at length in Chapter 4. *Sytraval* stands out as the seminal case in that regard, with the ECJ declaring that the Commission is under a duty to 'to conduct a diligent and impartial examination of the complaint, which may make it necessary for it to examine matters not expressly raised by the complainant'.[175] Although the *Sytraval* Court pushed back on the most innovative aspects of the CFI ruling, it did eventually dismiss the appeal (and hence confirmed the annulment of the contested decision ordered by the CFI) on the ground that the reasoning of the Commission was insufficient with regard to certain objections raised by the complainant.[176] This came down, in essence, to censuring the Commission for failing to abide by its duty of careful examination of complaints.

The second situation involves the conduct of the consultation phase that the Treaty inserts into the second stage of the State aid procedure, as exemplified by the *British Airways* case.[177] *British Airways* turned on the compatibility of a plan for the restructuring of Air France, which included several capital injections from the French government. The plan had been duly notified to the Commission, which had gone through both phases of the procedure before concluding that it could be authorised subject to certain conditions. The action of annulment brought by British Airways and other competitors against that decision was upheld by the CFI on the ground that the Commission had not adequately responded to some of the objections raised by the applicants in the course of the consultation phase

[171] ibid, para 56. See Case C-12/03 P *Commission v Tetra Laval* [2005] ECR I-987, para 39.
[172] Case T-1/08 *Buczek Automotive v Commission* [2011] ECR II-2107, para 83; Case C-73/11 P *Frucona Kosice v Commission*, ECLI:EU:C:2013:32, para 76.
[173] Hofmann and Morini (n 164) 371.
[174] ibid.
[175] Case C-367/95 P *Commission v Sytraval and Brink's France* [1998] ECR I-1719, para 62.
[176] ibid, paras 73–78.
[177] Joined Cases T-371 and 394/94 *British Airways and others v Commission* [1998] ECR II-2405.

carried out in the context of the formal investigation phase. Some of the objections concerned (as in *Lenzing*) the application of the private investor test,[178] while others concerned the assessment of the effects of the plan on competition and trade.[179] The point to note, however, is that the CFI used the duty of care to frame its inquiry. It thus held that 'the Commission's discretion carries with it a duty to examine carefully and impartially all relevant aspects of the individual case' and that 'review of that obligation requires a sufficiently precise statement of reasons in order to enable the Court to be satisfied that it has been complied with'.[180]

It seems, in light of the foregoing, that the duty of care performs two basic functions in judicial review of State aid decisions. First, it disciplines the information-gathering task of the Commission, ensuring that the information that it collects is sufficient—quantity- and quality-wise—to substantiate its conclusions. Hence the obligation imposed on the Commission to go beyond the matters raised by complainants when this is necessary to have an accurate view of the case.[181] The duty of care mitigates, in this sense, the rule according to which the legality of the determinations made by the Commission is to be assessed in light of the information at its disposal at the time it took its decision[182]—for it implies that the Commission cannot simply sit back and expect to rely on its own passivity to justify the legality of a decision taken on the basis of incomplete information.

Secondly, the duty of care embodies a standard that can be used to discipline the way in which the Commission manages the information at its disposal. In other words, it operates as a standard of seriousness in the way in which the Commission takes account of the information available in the administrative file, which includes the submissions made by third parties—be it through complaints (as in *Sytraval*) or through comments (as in *British Airways*). The review of the conformity with this aspect of the duty of care is done through the analysis of the reasons proffered by the Commission, but its ultimate purpose is to verify that the Commission pays heed to all the possibly relevant arguments pressed upon it.

In reviewing the Commission's conformance to the duty of care, the Courts may thus assess whether the information basis relied on by the Commission was complete and whether, assuming its completeness, the Commission analysed it with the due level of diligence. The opportunities that this type of review opens up from the perspective of competitors are further explored in the next section.

3. Competitors, Participation and Judicial Review

The preceding analysis suggests that interested parties face two obstacles in their endeavour to affect the content of phase 2 decisions through the process of judicial

[178] ibid, paras 84–120.
[179] ibid, paras 238–80.
[180] ibid, para 95.
[181] Case C-367/95 P *Commission v Sytraval and Brink's France* [1998] ECR I-1719, para 62.
[182] Case 234/84 *Belgium v Commission (Meura)* [1986] ECR 2263, para 16.

review. Not only must they satisfy the rules of standing that restrict access by individuals to the European Courts—and demonstrate, in accordance with *Cofaz*, that the contested State aid inflicted harm on them—they also need to overcome a second hurdle, namely the generally deferential attitude of Courts vis-à-vis the determinations made by the Commission in this field. Indeed, the broad margin of discretion recognised to the Commission reduces the likelihood of success of the actions for the annulment of State aid decisions brought by competitors—and hence their actual chances of influencing the outcome of State aid procedures. The previous section has also highlighted, however, a series of moves made by the European Courts to intensify the type of review that they carry out in relation to State aid decisions—their willingness to test the cogency of the economic reasoning of the Commission and to verify its compliance with the duty of care. The aim of this section is to explore the repercussions that these moves have for the power of leverage of competitors in State aid procedures.

In order to grasp their implications, it is necessary to analyse in more detail the type of review exercised by the Courts when they follow either of these approaches. At first sight, the review of the economic reasoning of the Commission and that of its compliance with the duty of care seem fundamentally different—the former pointing to the substance of the decision and the latter to the formal obligations imposed upon the Commission. Yet they are in fact quite similar from the perspective of the technique of review that each entails, which tests in both cases the consistency of the decision, looking at the reasons proffered by the Commission.

Indeed, where the Courts review the economic reasoning followed by the Commission, their scrutiny tends to confine itself to looking for inconsistencies. In defining the role of the CFI in reviewing State aid decisions, the ECJ declared in *Lenzing* that the Court is not supposed to 'substitute its own economic assessment for that of the Commission' but to check whether there are any 'obvious contradictions, apparent from the text of the contested decision itself' and whether there is enough 'evidence to substantiate the Commission's conclusions'.[183] The point to note is that both functions—the search for contradictions in the contested decision and the review of the evidence that supports the Commission's conclusions—actually come down to testing the consistency of the Commission's decision. The only difference lies in the benchmark that is used in each case, which is limited to the text of the decision itself in one case[184] and extends to the whole administrative file in the other.[185] What the Court does in both cases, however, is to verify that the findings of the Commission are supported and not contradicted by the information emanating from these sources.

183 Case C-525/04 P *Spain v Lenzing AG* [2007] ECR I-9947, para 60.

184 Case T-36/99 *Lenzing AG v Commission* [2004] ECR II-3597, paras 156 and 160. See also Case T-67/94 *Ladbroke Racing Ltd v Commission* [1998] ECR II-1, para 58.

185 Case T-36/99 *Lenzing AG v Commission* [2004] ECR II-3597, paras 158 and 160. See also Case T-67/94 *Ladbroke Racing Ltd v Commission* [1998] ECR II-1, para 59.

Similarly, it is also the consistency of the Commission's decisions that the Courts actually scrutinise when they review their conformity with the duty of care. *British Airways* provides a good example thereof. The decision of the Commission was annulled as a result of two different defects in reasoning.[186] The gist of the problem, in both cases, was that the Commission had not adequately responded to the concerns raised by the comments submitted in the course of the consultation phase in relation to the possibility that the beneficiary would use the State aid to renew its fleet and to the effects that the aid would have in competition and trade. The default in the reasoning of the Commission exposed an infringement of the duty of care—it implied that the Commission had failed to assess with the requisite seriousness part of the information available to it. But it amounted, essentially, to an inconsistency between the conclusion raised by the Commission (compatibility of the aid) and the information basis on which it was grounded—again, between the decision and the evidence available on the administrative file.

The preceding analysis suggests that the type of review that the European Courts exert over phase 2 decisions generally consists in an assessment of its consistency. This assessment uses as a benchmark the text of the reviewed decision itself but also the content of the administrative file compiled by the Commission. It is the willingness of the European Courts to have recourse to the latter benchmark that is more significant for the purposes of this chapter, since it indirectly empowers competitors to influence the outcome of State aid procedures. This is because the right of competitors to participate in State aid procedures recognised by Article 107(2) TFEU means that they can affect the content of the information basis at the disposal of the Commission and hence the administrative file that the Courts use as a benchmark to review the consistency of its decisions.

The ruling of the CFI in *British Airways* is probably the best example of the opportunity for leverage represented by the combination of the right to participate with the review of State aid decisions based on their administrative file. As noted earlier, the decision to clear the restructuring plan of Air France was considered invalid as a result of two reasoning defects—the first one relating to the fact that the plan permitted Air France to review its fleet, despite this being an operational cost for which State aid is normally prohibited; the second one relating to the failure of the Commission to consider the effects that the plan would have on airlines competing with Air France on extra-European routes.[187]

In reaching its conclusion, the CFI placed great weight on the fact that both issues had been raised by the parties that participated in the consultation phase of the previous administrative procedure. Indeed, the CFI took note of the fact that these parties had 'insisted' on the unacceptable nature of the permission to acquire

[186] Joined Cases T-371 and 394/94 *British Airways and others v Commission* [1998] ECR II-2405, paras 84–120 and 238–80.

[187] ibid, para 280.

new fleet[188] and that they had 'stressed' that the Commission should assess the effects of the aid on the international airlines that competed with Air France.[189] More importantly, the CFI explicitly framed its inquiry against their objections. Thus, it set itself the task of 'ascertain[ing] whether the statement of reasons in the contested decision indicates clearly and unequivocally the Commission's reasoning, *particularly in view of the essential complaints concerning the assessment of the contested aid plan put to the Commission during the administrative procedure*' (emphasis added).[190]

The CFI was satisfied with some of the reasons proffered by the Commission.[191] However, it eventually found that the failure of the Commission to respond to some of the objections raised by the parties that participated in the administrative procedure could not be justified. It found that the 'The Commission was thus under an obligation to reply to [the contention that permitting the renewal of the fleet would amount to a breach of the principle of proportionality] in the grounds of the contested decision'.[192] It also found that

> bearing in mind the observations which the parties concerned made in that connection, the Commission was obliged to set out its views on the problem of non-EEA air routes served by Air France, the beneficiary of the authorised aid, in competition with other companies within the EEA.[193]

The failure of the Commission to tackle both issues was considered an infringement of the duty to provide reasons of current Article 296 TFEU,[194] which led to the annulment of the contested decision.[195]

British Airways provides a useful illustration of the main mechanism through which competitors may affect the outcome of State aid procedures. The previous chapter considered the issue of leverage in relation to the possibility of participating in the consultation phase of State aid procedures, focusing on the adjunct rights associated with this participatory opportunity. It found that these rights are scarce, which makes it harder for competitors to effectively defend their case before the Commission. This chapter casts new light on the significance of the possibility of participating in State aid procedures. It suggests that its force may proceed from the possibility of affecting the content of the administrative file and, hence, the benchmark used by the European Courts to review the cogency of the determinations made by the Commission in its State aid decisions.

Although participation in the administrative phase of State aid procedures is not an essential requirement to have access to the process of judicial review, this

[188] ibid, para 97.
[189] ibid, paras 261–62.
[190] ibid, para 96. See also ibid, para 260.
[191] ibid, paras 102 and 267.
[192] ibid, para 96.
[193] ibid, para 273.
[194] ibid, paras 120 and 280.
[195] ibid, para 454.

analysis suggests that exercising the right to submit comments may be the most effective strategy to maximise the chances of affecting the final outcome. This is not so much because of the easier test of standing that the applicant will then have to satisfy, but because it is the power to incorporate one's arguments into the administrative file that increases the chances of their being considered by the Courts—if not by the Commission itself. In fact, the case law developed in relation to State aid beneficiaries clearly suggests that the Commission is not to be reproved for its failure to consider arguments that were not pressed upon it in the course of the formal investigation procedure.[196] Thus, participation may have lost its pride of place amongst the conditions of standing, but there seems to be a sort of rule of estoppel in the making—one which prevents a party from raising before the Courts arguments not raised before the Commission and which thus encourages participation.

A final word of caution is due. The power of leverage represented by the possibility of seeking judicial review of the consistency of State aid decisions with their administrative file should not be exaggerated. It presents, indeed, two important limitations. The first limitation is the rule that the Commission is not bound to respond to all the comments submitted by interested parties in the course of the formal investigation procedure, but only to those that are relevant and important.[197] The Commission is not hereby given carte blanche to decide which comments it considers and which ones it ignores, but this rule certainly mitigates the pressure that competitors may exert through their comments. The second limitation stems from the technique of judicial review employed by the Court, which is ultimately based on the verification of the Commission's compliance with the duty to provide reasons. This affects the type of constraint that successful actions can generate, insofar as nothing prevents the Commission from curing the reasoning defect censored by the Court and from taking a new decision with the same content.[198]

[196] See, eg, the orders of the GC in Case T-231/00 *Adriatica di Navigazione Spa and Comitato 'Venezia vuole vivere' v Commission*, ECLI:EU:T:2012:667, paras 45–46; Case T-260/00 *Cooperative San marco fra Lavoratori della Piccola Pesca and others v Commission*, ECLI:EU:T:2012:669, paras 44–45; and Case T-261/00 *Sacaim SpA and others v Commission*, ECLI:EU:T:2012:670, para 39. See also Fernando Pastor-Merchante, 'The Follow-up of Hotel Ciprianni / Comitato "Venezia Vuole Vivere"' (2014) 13 *European State Aid Law Quarterly* 132.

[197] Case C-301/96 *Germany v Commission* [2003] ECR I-9919, para 140.

[198] See Flynn (n 121) 301, who refers to Joined Cases C-278, 279 and 280/92 *Spain v Commission* [1994] ECR I-4103 and to their sequel, Case C-415/96 *Spain v Commission* [1998] ECR I-6993, to illustrate the point that 'where the Court identified insufficient reasoning in a decision that Spain had given illegal aid to a textile firm the Commission was able to adopt a fresh decision, in which it condemned the aid on the basis of the information originally used and without reopening the formal investigation procedure'. On the duty to provide reasons, see, eg, Fernand Schockweiler, 'La motivation des décisions individuelles en droit communautaire et en droit national' (1989) 25 *Cahiers de Droit Européen* 3; Martin Shapiro, 'The Giving Reasons Requirement' (1992) *University of Chicago Legal Forum* 179.

Conclusion

Access

Article 263-IV TFEU conditions the access of competitors to judicial review of State aid decisions on the fulfilment of the 'direct and individual concern' requirement. The fulfilment of the first condition represents no challenge for them. The individual concern requirement is therefore the main obstacle that they face. The case law of the European Courts treats differently the challenges addressed against phase 1 and phase 2 decisions. The test of standing elaborated in *Cook* eases the conditions for challenging phase 1 decisions to the point that it eliminates the requirement to show any other individualising factor besides the existence of a competitive relationship between the applicant and the alleged beneficiary of the aid—at least when the application challenges the procedural regularity of the contested decision. However, the challenge of phase 2 decisions is governed by *Cofaz*, which requires competitors to satisfy two conditions: the participation requirement and the significant effect requirement. Whereas the first requirement can be dispensed with, the latter is essential. The case law has not squarely defined the indicators that can be relied on to prove that the contested State aid is liable to produce a significant effect on the applicant. However, it has clearly raised the admissibility bar, making standing conditional upon the demonstration of a likely, substantial and distinctive risk of harm for the applicant. In so doing, the Court has transformed this stage into the most difficult access point for competitors into the system of State aid control.

Leverage

The analysis of the issue of leverage carried out in this chapter has been based on the type of review exercised by the Courts over State aid decisions, the idea being that there is a correlation between the intensity of review that the Courts are willing to exercise and the actual chances of influencing the outcome of procedures that the process of judicial review represents.

The analysis of the review exercised over phase 1 decisions has shown that the Courts tend to restrict their scrutiny to the application of the serious difficulties test, even in those cases where the applicants are recognised standing to challenge the merits of the decision. In fact, the serious difficulties test looks at the merits of the decision (insofar as it calls for a preliminary but substantive assessment of the conclusion reached by the Commission), but it can only result in the imposition of a procedural constraint on the Commission: either to resume the preliminary assessment of the contested State aid or to launch the formal investigation phase. The upshot is that, in both cases, the only redress that competitors may obtain through the challenge of phase 1 decisions is a second shot at defending their case before the Commission.

The analysis of the review exercised over phase 2 has departed from the broad margin of discretion recognised to the Commission in the administration of State aid rules. This implies that the Courts are likely to be deferential vis-à-vis the determinations made by the Commission in its State aid decisions, which a priori reduces the chances of competitors of affecting the outcome of State aid procedures. However, the analysis has also shown that competitors can benefit from two moves made by the European Courts, namely their willingness to review the economic reasoning of the Commission's decisions and their conformity with the duty of care. They can do so by participating in the administrative phase of State aid procedure and, thus, affecting the content of the administrative file. This finding casts new light on the importance of participation (as defined in the previous chapter) as a source of leverage.

Conclusion

The starting point of this book was the narrative woven by Smith and other political scientists interested in the strategy followed by the Commission to shore up its control over the State aid policy of Member States. This narrative claims that one of the tactics used by the Commission was the mobilisation of private firms and their association with the task of enforcing the rules on State aid. The same narrative also claims, however, that this strategy was not without cost, because private firms came to place increasing demands on the Commission and, eventually, to threaten its autonomy. This book was born out of the observation of a certain mismatch between this appreciation and the standard discourse in legal scholarship, which tends to stress the 'bilateral' design of State aid procedures and the feeble role assigned to private firms within that framework.

It is against this background that this book set out to test the capacity of private firms to act as a constraint on the Commission in the enforcement of State aid law, by looking more specifically at the competitors of the beneficiaries of State aid. The problem would thus be to assess the capacity of competitors to affect the application of the rules on State aid in order to shield their market position against the potentially harmful effects of subsidies and other forms of State financial assistance to firms. This endeavour raised two challenges. The first challenge was to identify the procedural vehicles that competitors have at their disposal to have a say in the administration of the rules on State aid (the *issue of access*). The second challenge was to gauge the power of influence that competitors may exert through each of these vehicles (the *issue of leverage*).

In order to frame the inquiry, the first part of the book reflected on the role assigned to competitors by the basic substantive and institutional rules that support the system of State aid control. The first claim developed in the book is that the rules laid down by Articles 107 to 109 TFEU are not primarily concerned with the protection of the market position of competitors against the distortive effects of State aids. This claim was based on a theoretical analysis of the economic rationale of the European system of State aid control, as well as on a more empirical observation of the way in which its rules are applied in practice.

As the book went on to demonstrate, this observation does not imply that competitors should have no say in the administration of the rules on State aid. Their involvement in the administration of these provisions can indeed be grounded on two alternative theories, each of which assigns a different role (and, hence, a different procedural status) to competitors: the instrumental paradigm (which sees competitors as the Commission's allies in the fight against State aid and demands that they be given access but no leverage) and the legal protection paradigm (which recognises the need to afford competitors some protection against the distortionary effects of irregular State aids and demands that they be given access but also leverage).

In this sense, the second claim developed in the book is that the role assigned to competitors by the original design of the system of State aid control responds to the instrumental paradigm. This paradigm informs the 'bilateral' model that presides over the *public enforcement* side of the system of State aid control, which is inspired by the elite model that is so typical of EU administrative law. It also informs the *private enforcement* side of the system of State aid control, given its reliance on the direct effect of the standstill clause of Article 108(3) TFEU rather than on the substantive prohibition of Article 107(1) TFEU. This peculiar arrangement implies that, a priori, the private enforcement of State aid law is only a means to ensure that national State aid plans go through the hands of the Commission—in other words, that the private enforcement of State aid law triggered by competitors before national courts is subservient to the public enforcement assured by the Commission.

The book has acknowledged that this subservience has been attenuated as a result of the case law of the European Courts and of the decentralisation process fostered by the Commission and the EU legislator. Yet it has also shown that this process has not altered the Commission's central position as the main bulwark against State aid, for it remains the only institution that may declare the incompatibility with the internal market of national State aid plans. This is the reason why the third claim propounded in the first part of the book was that the prominent position occupied by the Commission in this field limits the possibilities offered to competitors by private enforcement.

It is also the reason why the inquiry carried out in the second part of the book has focused on the opportunities of access and leverage available to competitors in the context of the Commission's public enforcement procedures. The main conclusions reached in those chapters are drawn together in the two following sections.

Access

As noted earlier, the issue of access seeks to identify the procedural windows through which competitors may have a say in the administration of the rules on State aid. The book has surveyed the three phases that make up the State aid procedure (the preliminary phase, the formal investigation phase and the judicial review phase) and observed that each of them affords competitors with a distinctive opportunity to bring their input to the system of State aid control: the possibility of lodging complaints as a prelude to the preliminary phase, the possibility of submitting comments in the course of the formal investigation phase, and the possibility of resorting to the action of annulment or to the action for failure to act in order to set into motion the judicial review phase.

The book has identified a very competitor-friendly trend in the approach adopted by the case law with regard to the scope of the participatory opportunities offered to competitors in the course of the administrative procedure. Indeed, Chapter 4 described the way in which the case law has paved the way for the emergence and development of the right to submit complaints in State aid matters. On the other hand, Chapter 5 set forth the jurisprudential moves that have come to constrain the power of the Commission to omit the consultation phase of Article 108(2) TFEU. These developments indicate that the European Courts have gone out of their way to secure and, in some cases, expand the a priori limited opportunities for voice reserved to competitors within a system of governance to which they are, in principle, alien.

However, their approach to the conditions that govern the standing of competitors before the European Courts has not been so generous. While facilitating the possibility of challenging the procedural regularity of decisions adopted at the end of the preliminary phase (phase 1 decisions), they have progressively raised the admissibility bar of actions addressed against positive decisions adopted at the end of the formal investigation phase (phase 2 decisions). They have done so through an increasingly demanding interpretation of the individual concern requirement, as interpreted in *Plaumann* and *Cofaz*. The upshot is that access to the judicial arena remains difficult for competitors when it comes to questioning the substantive determinations made by the Commission in its final decisions.

Leverage

The issue of leverage seeks to gauge the power of influence that competitors may exert over the outcome of State aid procedures. In order to do so, the book has had to articulate a different standard for each of the opportunities for access identified above. In the case of complaints, the benchmark has been their impact on the autonomy of the Commission to follow its own enforcement priorities, hence the attention devoted to the obligation to investigate and respond to the merits of the allegations made by complainants. The assessment of the possibility of submitting comments in the course of the formal investigation phase has used as a benchmark the participatory regime embodied by the fundamental right to a hearing, which includes a set of information rights designed to optimise its effectiveness as a lever. Finally, the significance in terms of leverage of the possibility of resorting to the European judicature has used as a benchmark the intensity of judicial review exercised over State aid decisions.

The European Courts, backed by the EU legislator, have been very generous in the definition of the status of complainants in State aid procedures, to the point that they have handed out to them a right to a response that is unheard of in other fields of EU administrative law. On the contrary, they have resisted the demands to add flesh to the right to submit comments in the course of the formal investigation phase and to 'thicken' it with the type of information rights that could turn it into a meaningful and effective form of participation. Finally, they have found some ways to review the determinations made by the Commission in its State aid decisions and to make some inroads into its broad margin of discretion in this field, yet their approach remains quite deferential.

The time has come to draw these observations together and try to assess their significance as a whole. This is all the more necessary given that the different participatory opportunities considered in this book are not mutually exclusive, which means that it is open to competitors to make use of several of them in the course of a single procedure. It follows that the leverage of competitors in State aid procedures ultimately depends on the force that they derive from the combined effect of the three tools analysed here.

The Power to Trigger an Investigation and Force a Decision on the Merits of Complaints

The analysis carried out in Chapter 4 demonstrates that the power that competitors may exert through complaints is more than a gentle nudge. Indeed, the recognition that complaints trigger the State aid procedure in the same way as a notification implies that complainants may push the Commission to adopt a formal decision on the merits of their case. Granted, the Commission may escape this result when it deems that the information submitted by an applicant is insufficient, in which case it may register the application as mere 'market information' and avoid the effects associated with 'complaints'. It may only do so, however, after providing the applicant with an opportunity to complete its initial submission, which means that tenacious complainants have the tools to overcome the Commission's initial reluctance to investigate their allegations. This is further facilitated by the case law of the European Courts, which prevents the Commission from abusing this information alibi in order to leave complainants in a judicial limbo, from which they can only escape with an actionable act.

The dispute between Ryanair and the Commission over the transfer of 100 employees of Alitalia to Air One and Meridiana provides a good illustration of this power. Following a complaint by Ryanair in which it alleged that this transfer could constitute State aid, the Commission responded with a request for more information. Ryanair replied that it had no more specific information regarding a measure that had come to its attention through the press, but this was not followed by any type of action or communication by the Commission for more than a year. After formally calling on the Commission to act, Ryanair brought an action for failure to act that was successful, since both the GC and the ECJ confirmed the *Athinaïki Techniki* doctrine in accordance with which complaints trigger 'the preliminary examination stage, which ultimately obliges the Commission to take a position'.[1]

The Power to Trigger the Consultation Phase (ie, the Formal Investigation Stage)

The preliminary investigation that follows the submission of complaints remains an exclusive dialogue between the Commission and the Member concerned because the European Courts and legislator have refused to give complainants any type of information or participation rights at this stage of the procedure. This obviously reduces their chances of affecting the outcome of a preliminary examination that may result, despite its 'preliminary' character, in a *definitive* clearing decision.

Important as they may be, these limitations should not overshadow the significance of the power of complainants to bring about a formal decision at the first stage of the procedure. This is because, once they have such a decision, competitors have the tools to continue propelling the procedure. They may then rely on the generous rule of standing articulated in *Cook* and hold the Commission accountable for its clearing decision before the European Courts. Granted, the judicial review that the European Courts exercise in this type of situation is necessarily limited, in the sense that—more often than not—it only checks the validity of the Commission's decision to omit the consultation with interested parties in light of the serious difficulties test. Still, the possibility of triggering this type of review equips competitors with a tool to force the opening of the formal investigation phase.

The *Athinaïki Techniki* saga illustrates this point. Chapter 4 analysed the first ruling issued by the ECJ in relation to the sale by the Greek authorities of the Casino Mont Parnès to the Hyatt consortium, where the ECJ censured the decision of the Commission to close the file on the complaint lodged by a competitor through an informal letter. The same controversy would come back to the Court a few months later following the decision of the Commission to withdraw the contested letter and to request further information from the complainant.[2] The point to note is that, in spite of its initial reluctance, the Commission eventually decided

[1] Case C-615/11 P *Commission v Ryanair*, ECLI:EU:C:2013:310, para 31.

[2] The GC held that there was no need to adjudicate on its Order in Case T-94/05 *Athinaïki Techniki AE v Commission* [2006] ECR II-73. This Order was also set aside by the Court of Justice in its judgment in Case C-362/09 P *Athinaïki Techniki AE v Commission* [2010] ECR I-13275, where it held, at para 70, that 'the Commission cannot, after [it withdraws an illegal decision to take no further action on a complaint] pick up the procedure again at a stage earlier than the exact point at which the illegality found had occurred'.

to open the formal investigation phase and to invite interested parties to submit comments,[3] without even awaiting the ruling of the ECJ. Thus, 'the persistence of the complainant in contesting the acts of the Commission in the *Athinaïki Techniki* case, endorsed by the ECJ on "procedural grounds", led to the practical result of the opening by the Commission of the "phase 2" examination'.[4] Granted, the formal investigation phase only served to confirm the first impression of the Commission, since it resulted in a decision that there was no aid.[5] The next paragraphs show, however, that this does not always mean that the battle is lost.

The Power to Shape the Administrative File and Hence the Main Benchmark Used by the Court to Assess the Legality of State Aid Decisions

While wholeheartedly embracing the characterisation of the consultation phase of Article 108(2) TFEU as an 'essential procedural guarantee' that can only be omitted when a case is really straightforward, the European Courts and legislator have systematically refused to 'thicken' the content of that right. Indeed, Chapter 5 has shown that they have been very generous in the definition of the scope of the right of competitors to participate in the second phase of the procedure (access), but very strict in the determination of its content, which suggests that this is unlikely to be a very effective instrument to affect the views of the Commission (leverage). The analysis carried out in Chapter 6 suggests, however, that the value of this right lies elsewhere—namely in the fact that it empowers competitors to shape the content of the administrative file and, in so doing, to affect the main benchmark that the European Courts use to review the validity of State aid decisions.

This may seem a very remote possibility, but cases like *British Airways* show that there are instances where competitors manage to have their way and to overturn the decisions taken by the Commission in the field of State aid.[6] It will be recalled that in that case the CFI quashed the decision of the Commission to clear the restructuring plan of Air France as a result of two reasoning defects, which were

[3] Commission Decision C 15/10 (ex NN 21/10)—Greece. Privatisation of Casino Mont Parnès. Invitation to submit comments pursuant to Article 108(2) of the Treaty on the Functioning of the European Union (2010/C 233/06).

[4] Edoardo Gambaro and Francesco Mazzocchi, 'Case C-521/06 P, Athinaïki Techniki v. Commission, Judgment of the Court of Justice (Fourth Chamber) of 17 July 2008, [2008] ECR I-5829; Case C-322/09 P, NDSHT v. Commission, Judgment of the Court of Justice (Third Chamber) of 18 November 2010, nyr; Case C-362/09 P, Athinaïki Techniki v. Commission, Judgment of the Court of Justice (Third Chamber) of 16 December 2010, nyr' (2011) 48 *Common Market Law Review* 2083, 2101.

[5] Commission Decision of 24 May 2011 on partial privatisation measure C 15/10 (ex NN 21/10) implemented by Greece for Mont Parnès casino (OJ L258/74).

[6] Joined Cases T-371 and 394/94 *British Airways and others v Commission* [1998] ECR II-2405.

linked to the response given by the Commission to the allegations made by British Airways and other interested parties in the course of the consultation phase. This possibility suffers from the limitations associated with judicial review based on the duty to provide reasons, which does not prevent the Commission from curing the invalidating reasoning defect and taking a substantially identical decision. Still, the existence of this threat may be a sufficient incentive (ex ante) for the Commission to consider the case laid out by competitors in the course of the formal investigation phase.

The analysis carried out in the book challenges the purely bilateral characterisation of State aid procedures as a matter for the Commission and Member States, where individuals (in general) and competitors (in particular) have nothing to say. This is not to say that the case law or the EU legislator have embraced a purely protective paradigm, where the administration of the rules on State aid is carried out at the request and in the interest of competitors. But the observation that competitors have the power to fight the Commission's inaction and to affect its enforcement agenda means that it may be misleading to keep thinking of them as mere information sources.

The book has not downplayed the limitations of the power of competitors to affect the outcome of State aid procedures, which requires persistence—and hence time, and hence means. It has not hidden either the main flaw that the system has from the perspective of competitors, which is the stringency of the conditions that govern access to judicial review of the merits of State aid decisions. While acknowledging these limitations, the book has uncovered the legal tools that turn competitors into a potential constraint on the Commission, which cannot simply ignore their mobilisation against specific measures, unless it is willing to face a cascade of challenges that may result in judicial defeat.

BIBLIOGRAPHY

Ahlborn C and Berg C, 'Can State Aid Control Learn from Antitrust? The Need for a Greater Role for Competition Analysis under the State Aid Rules' in Biondi A, Eeckhout P and Flynn J (eds), *The Law of State Aid in the European Union* (Oxford: Oxford University Press, 2004), 41–66.

Albors-Llorens A, 'The Standing of Private Parties to Challenge Community Measures: Has the European Court Missed the Boat?' (2003) 62 *Cambridge Law Journal* 72.

—— *Private Parties in EC Law* (Oxford: Oxford University Press, 2006).

Alemanno A, 'Unpacking the Principle of Openness in EU Law: Transparency, Participation and Democracy' (2014) 39 *European Law Review* 72.

Angeli M, 'The European Commission's "New Policy" on State Aid Control: Some Reflections on Public and Private Enforcement of Recovery of Illegal Aid' (2009) 30 *European Competition Law Review* 533.

Arnstein SR, 'A Ladder of Citizen Participation' (1969) 35 *Journal of American Institute of Planners* 216.

Arnull A, 'Private Applicants and the Action for Annulment under Article 173 of the EC Treaty' (1995) 32 *Common Market Law Review* 7.

—— 'Private Applicants and the Action for Annulment Since Codorniu' (2001) 38 *Common Market Law Review* 7.

—— 'The Action for Annulment: a Case of Double Standards?' in O'Keeffe D (ed), *Judicial Review in the European Union* (The Hague: Kluwer Law International, 2001).

Association Europénne des Avocats (ed), *Un rôle pour la défense dans les procédures communautaires de concurrence: congrès organisé les 25 et 26 novembre 1996—A Role for the Defence in Community Competition Procedures: Congress Organized on 25 and 26 November 1996—Die Rolle der Verteidigung in europäischen Wettbewerbsverfahren* (Brussels: Bruylant, 1997).

Azizi J, 'The Tension between Member States' Autonomy and Commission Control in State Aid Matters: Selected Aspects' in Kanninen H, Korjus N and Rosas A (eds), *EU Competition Law in Context: Essays in Honour of Virpi Tiili* (Oxford: Hart Publishing, 2009).

Azoulai L, *Les garanties procédurales en droit communautaire: recherches sur la procédure et le bon gouvernement* (Florence: European University Institute, 2000).

—— 'Le principe de bonne administration' in Auby JB and Dutheil de la Rochère J (eds), *Droit administratif européen* (Brussels: Bruylant, 2007).

Bacon K, *European Community Law of State Aid* (Oxford: Oxford University Press, 2009).

Bandt P, 'Lufthansa: A New Era for State Aid Enforcement?' (2014) 5 *Journal of European Competition Law & Practice* 206.

Barav A, 'Direct and Individual Concern: An Almost Insurmountable Barrier to the Admissibility of Individual Appeal to the EEC Court' (1974) 11 *Common Market Law Review* 191.

Barbier de la Serre, E, 'Procedural Justice in the European Community Case-law concerning the Rights of the Defence: Essentialist and Instrumental Trends' (2006) 12 *European Public Law* 225.

Barennes M, 'The Standing of the Competitors of the Aid Recipient in State Aid Cases' in Kanninen H, Korjus N and Rosas A (eds), *EU Competition Law in Context: Essays in Honour of Virpi Tiili* (Oxford: Hart Publishing, 2009).

Barnard C, *The Substantive Law of the EU. The Four Freedoms*, 3rd edn (Oxford: Oxford University Press, 2010).

Bartosch A, 'The Procedural Regulation in State Aid Matters. A Case for Profound Reform' (2007) 6 *European State Aid Law Quarterly* 474.

—— 'Editorial. The End of Procedural Reform: the Commission, the Member States and Third Parties = the Teams that Lose' (2008) 7 *European State Aid Law Quarterly* 1.

Battista J, 'Is Participation in the Commission's Administrative Procedure a Necessary Condition for Legal Standing? Commentary on Case C-265/05 P, Sniace v. Commission' (2008) 7 *European State Aid Law Quarterly* 317.

Baumol WJ and Ordover JA, 'Use of Antitrust to Subvert Competition' (1985) 28 *Journal of Law and Economics* 247.

Bellis JF, 'Le critère de distorsion de la concurrence et de l'effet sur le commerce interétatique' in Dony M and Smits C (eds), *Aides d'État* (Brussels: Éditions de l'Université de Bruxelles, 2005) 97–106.

Bentley P, 'State Aid, Subsidies and Complainants' (1990) 1 *European Business Law Review* 91.

Berghofer M, 'The New De Minimis Regulation: Enlarging the Sword of Damocles?' (2007) 6 *European State Aid Law Quarterly* 11.

—— 'The General Block Exemption Regulation: A Giant on Feet of Clay' (2009) 8 *European State Aid Law Quarterly* 323.

Besley T and Seabright P, 'The Effects and Policy Implications of State Aids to Industry' (1999) 14 *Economic Policy* 13.

Bieber R and Maiani F, 'Enhancing Centralized Enforcement of EU Law: Pandora's Toolbox?' (2014) 51 *Common Market Law Review* 1057.

Bignami F, 'Three Generations of Participation Rights Before the European Commission' (2004) 68 *Law and Contemporary Problems* 61.

Biondi A and Eeckhout P, 'State Aid and Obstacles to Trade' in Biondi A, Eeckhout P and Flynn J (eds), *The Law of State Aid in the European Union* (Oxford: Oxford University Press, 2004).

Blauberger M, 'Of "Good" and "Bad" Subsidies: European State aid Control through Soft and Hard Law' (2009) 32 *West European Politics* 719.

Bonnor PG, 'The Right to Good Administration' (2006) 182 *Dokumentation zum 12. Deutsch-Französischen Verwaltungskolloquium* 71.

Brander JA, 'Rationales for Strategic Trade and Industrial Policy' in Paul K. Krugman (ed), *Strategic Trade Policy and the New International Economics* (Boston, MA: MIT Press, 1986).

—— and Spencer BJ, 'Tariff Protection and Imperfect Competition' in Kierzkowski H (ed), *Monopolistic Competition and International Trade* (Oxford: Oxford University Press, 1984).

—— and —— 'Export Subsidies and International Market Share Rivalry' (1985) 18 *Journal of International Economics* 83.

Brandtner B, Beranger T and Lessenich C, 'Private State Aid Enforcement' (2010) 9 *European State Aid Law Quarterly* 23.

Brodley JF, 'Antitrust Standing in Private Merger Cases: Reconciling Private Incentives and Public Enforcement Goals' (1995) 94 *Michigan Law Review* 1.
Buendía Sierra JL and Smulders B, 'The Limited Role of the "Refined Economic Approach" in Achieving the Objectives of State Aid Control: Time for Some Realism' in *EC State Aid Law—Le droit des aides d'État dans la CE: Liber Amicorum Francisco Santaolalla* (Alphen aan den Rijn: Kluwer, 2008).
Camilleri E, 'A Decade of EU Antitrust Private Enforcement: Chronicle of a Failure Foretold?' (2013) 34 *European Competition Law Review* 531.
Chari RS and Cavotorta F, 'Economic Actors' Political Activity in "Overlap Issues": Privatisation and EU State Aid Control' (2002) 25 *West European Politics* 119.
Cini M, 'The Soft Law Approach: Commission Rule-making in the EU's State Aid Regime' (2001) 8 *Journal of European Public Policy* 192.
—— and McGowan L, *Competition Policy in the European Union* (Basingstoke: Macmillan, 2008).
Coppi L, 'The Role of Economics in State Aid Analysis and the Balancing Test' in Szyszczack E (ed), *Research Handbook on European State Aid Law* (Cheltenham: Edward Elgar, 2011).
Craig PP, 'Once upon a Time in the West: Direct Effect and the Federalization of EEC Law' (1992) 12 *Oxford Journal of Legal Studies* 453.
—— 'Standing and Substantive Review in Community Law' (1994) 14 *Oxford Journal of Legal Studies* 507.
—— *EU Administrative Law*, 2nd edn (Oxford: Oxford University Press, 2012).
Crocioni P, 'Can State Aid Policy Become more Economic Friendly?' (2006) 29 *World Competition* 89.
Curtin DM and Mendes J, 'Transparence et participation: des principes démocratiques pour l'administration de l'Union européenne' (2011) 137 *Revue Française d'Administration Publique* 101.
Dashwood A, 'Control of State Aids in the EEC: Prevention and Cure under Article 93' (1975) 12 *Common Market Law Review* 43.
de Cecco F, 'The Many Meanings of "Competition" in EC State Aid Law' (2006) 9 *Cambridge Yearbook of European Legal Studies* 111.
—— *State Aid and the European Economic Constitution* (Oxford: Hart Publishing, 2013).
de Witte B, 'Direct Effect, Primacy and the Nature of the Legal Order' in Craig PP and de Búrca G (eds), *The Evolution of EU Law* (Oxford: Oxford University Press, 2011).
Deiberova K and Nyssens H, 'The New General Block Exemption Regulation (GBER): What Changed?' (2009) 8 *European State Aid Law Quarterly* 27.
Derenne J and Kaczmarek C (2009), 'La récupération des aides illégales: le rôle du juge national dans le "private enforcement" du droit des aides d'État' (2009) 10 *ERA Forum* 251.
Dewatripont M and Seabright P, '"Wasteful" Public Spending and State Aid Control' (2006) 4 *Journal of the European Economic Association* 513.
Ehlermann CD, 'State Aid Control in the European Union: Success or Failure?' (1994) 18 *Fordham International Law Journal* 1212.
—— 'State Aids Under European Community Competition Law' (1994) 18 *Fordham International Law Journal* 410.
Enchelmaier S, 'No-One Slips Through the Net? Latest Developments, and Non-Developments in the European Court of Justice's Jurisprudence on Art. 230(4) EC' (2005) 24 *Yearbook of European Law* 173.
Evans AC, 'The Enforcement Procedure of Article 169 EEC: Commission Discretion' (1979) 4 *European Law Review* 442.

Flynn J, 'The Role of National Courts' in Biondi A, Eeckhout P and Flynn J (eds), *The Law of State Aid in the European Union* (Oxford: Oxford University Press, 2004).

Flynn L, 'Remedies in the European Courts' in Biondi A, Eeckhout P and Flynn J (eds), *The Law of State Aid in the European Union* (Oxford: Oxford University Press, 2004).

Fox EM, 'State Aids Control and the Distortion of Competition—Unbundling "Distortion"' in Hawk BE (ed), *Annual Proceedings of the Fordham Corporate Law Institute. International Antitrust Law and Policy* (Irvington-on-Hudson, NY: Juris Publishing, 2002).

—— 'What is Harm to Competition? Antitrust, Exclusionary Practices and the Elusive Notion of Anticompetitive Effect' in Drexl J (ed), *The Future of Transnational Antitrust—From Comparative to Common Competition Law* (Berne: Staempfli/Kluwer Law International, 2003).

Frazer T and Holmes P, 'Self-restraint: Cars, Complaints and the Commission' (1995) 1 *European Public Law* 85.

Freeman J, 'The Private Role in Public Governance' (2000) 75 *New York University Law Review* 543.

Friederiszick HW, Röller LH and Verouden V, 'EC State Aid Control: An Economic Perspective' in Sánchez Rydelski M (ed), *The EC State Aid Regime—Distortive Effects of State Aid on Competition and Trade* (London: Cameron May, 2006).

—— 'European State Aid Control: an Economic Framework' in Buccirossi P (ed), *Handbook of Antitrust Economics* (Boston, MA: MIT Press, 2007).

Fruithof E, 'Procedural Anomalies in State Aid Cases' (1994) 10 *European Business Law Review* 227.

Gambaro E and Mazzocchi F, 'Case C-521/06 P, Athinaïki Techniki v. Commission, Judgment of the Court of Justice (Fourth Chamber) of 17 July 2008, [2008] ECR I-5829; Case C-322/09 P, NDSHT v. Commission, Judgment of the Court of Justice (Third Chamber) of 18 November 2010, nyr; Case C-362/09 P, Athinaïki Techniki v. Commission, Judgment of the Court of Justice (Third Chamber) of 16 December 2010, nyr.' (2011) 48 *Common Market Law Review* 2083.

Gamble R, 'Whether Neap or Spring, the Tide Turns for Private Enforcement: the EU Proposal for a Directive on Damages Examined' (2013) 34 *European Competition Law Review* 611.

Garcia JA and Neven D, 'State Aid and Distortion of Competition, a Benchmark Model' (2005) 6 *HEI Working Paper*.

Geradin D 'Competition between Rules and Rules of Competition: A Legal and Economic Analysis of the Proposed Modernization of the Enforcement of EC Competition Law' (2003) 9 *Columbia Journal of European Law* 1.

Giannakopoulos TK, *Safeguarding Companies' Rights in Competition and Anti-dumping/Anti-subsidies Proceedings*, 2nd edn (Aalphen aan den Rijn: Wolters Kluwer, 2011).

Gil Ibáñez AJ, *The Administrative Supervision and Enforcement of EC Law: Powers, Procedures and Limits* (Oxford: Hart Publishing, 1999).

—— 'Exceptions to Article 226: Alternative Administrative Procedures and the Pursuit of Member States' (2000) 6 *European Law Journal* 148.

Gilmour DR, 'The Enforcement of Community Law by the Commission in the Context of State Aids: The Relationship between Article 93 and 169 and the Choice of Remedies' (1981) 18 *Common Market Law Review* 63.

Grespan D, 'The Procedure Before the Commission' in Mederer W et al (eds), *EU Competition Law*, IV (Leuven: Claeys & Casteels, 2008).

Gyselen L, 'La transparence en matière d'aides d'état: les droits des tiers' (1993) 4 *Cahiers de Droit Européen* 417.

Hancher L, 'State Aids and Judicial Control in the European Community' (1994) 15 *European Competition Law Review* 134.
—— 'EU State Aid Law—Now a Truly Ugly Sister?' in Hancher L, Ottervanger T and Slot PJ (eds), *EU State Aids* (London: Sweet & Maxwell, 2012).
Harden I, 'What Future for the Centralized Enforcement of Community Law?' (2002) 55 *Current Legal Problems* 495.
Harlow C, 'Citizen Access to Political Power in the European Union' (1999) 2 *EUI—Robert Schuman Centre for Advanced Studies Working Paper*.
—— 'Three Phases in the Evolution of EU Administrative Law' in Craig PP and De Búrca G (eds), *The Evolution of EU Law* (Oxford: Oxford University Press, 2011).
—— and Rawlings R, 'Accountability and Law Enforcement: The Centralised EU Infringement Procedure' (2006) 31 *European Law Review* 447.
—— with —— *Law and Administration*, 3rd edn (Cambridge: Cambridge University Press, 2009).
Hartley TC, *The Foundations of European Community Law: An Introduction to the Constitutional and Administrative Law of the European Community*, 6th edn (Oxford: Oxford University Press, 2007).
Hofmann H, Rowe GC and Türk AH, *Administrative Law and Policy of the European Union* (Oxford: Oxford University Press, 2011).
Hofmann HCH, 'Private Participation in the Control of Public Spending—The Multi-Level Subsidy Regimes' (2003) *III Discussion Paper N°12*.
—— 'Administrative Governance in State Aid Policy' in Hofmann HCH and Türk AH (eds), *EU Administrative Governance* (Cheltenham: Edward Elgar, 2006).
—— 'State Aid Review in a Multi-level System' in Hofmann HCH and Micheau C (eds), *State Aid Law of the European Union* (Oxford: Oxford University Press, 2016).
—— and Morini A, 'Judicial Review of Commission Decisions in State Aid' in Szyszczack E (ed), *Research Handbook on European State Aid Law* (Cheltenham: Edward Elgar, 2011).
Honoré M, 'The Standing of Third Parties in State Aid Cases. The Lessons To Be Drawn from the Judgment Case C-78/03 P, Aktionsgemeinschaft Recht und Eigentum v. Commission' (2006) 5 *European State Aid Law Quarterly* 269.
Jacobs FG and Deisenhofer T, 'Procedural Aspects of the Effective Private Antitrust Enforcement of EC Competition Rules: A Community Perspective' in Ehlermann CD and Atanasiu I (eds), *European Competition Law Annual 2001: Effective Private Enforcement of EC Antitrust Law* (Oxford: Hart Publishing, 2003).
Jaeger T, 'The Inquisition Retakes Brussels' (2013) 12 *European State Aid Law Quarterly* 1.
Jankovec B and Kronenberger V, 'Third Parties in State Aid Litigation: Locus Standi and Procedural Guarantees' in Sánchez Rydelski M (ed), *The EC State Aid Regime—Distortive Effects of State Aid on Competition and Trade* (London: Cameron May, 2006).
Jürimäe K, 'Standing in State Aid Cases: What's the State of Play?' (2010) 9 *European State Aid Law Quarterly* 303.
Kagan R, 'On Regulatory Inspectorates and Police' in Hawkins K and Thomas JM (eds), *Enforcing Regulation* (Boston, MA: Kluwer/Nijhoff Publishing, 1984).
Kaupa C, 'The More Economic Approach—A Reform Based on Ideology' (2009) 8 *European State Aid Law Quarterly* 311.
Kelemen RD, 'Adversarial Legalism and Administrative Law in the European Union' in Rose-Ackerman S and Lindseth PL (eds), *Comparative Administrative Law* (Cheltenham: Edward Elgar, 2010).

Kepenne JP and Gross K, 'Quelques considérations sur le rôle du juge national dans le contrôle des aides d'État' in *EC State Aid Law/Le droit des aides d'Etat dans la CE. Liber Amicorum Francisco Santaolalla Gadea* (The Hague: Kluwer Law International, 2008).

Köhler M, 'Private Enforcement of State Aid Law—Problems of Guaranteeing EU Rights by means of National (Procedural) Law' (2012) 11 *European State Aid Law Quarterly* 369.

Komninos AP, *EC Private Antitrust Enforcement: Decentralised Application of EC Competition Law by National Courts* (Oxford: Hart Publishing, 2008).

—— 'The Road to the Commission's White Paper for Damage Actions: Where We Came From' (2008) 4 *Competition Policy International* 81.

Kornai J, 'The Soft Budget Constraint' (1986) 39 *Kyklos* 3.

Köster T, 'Recovery of Unlawful State Aid' in Sánchez Rydelski M (ed), *The EC State Aid Regime: Distortive Effects of State Aid on Competition and Trade* (London: Cameron May, 2006).

Krämer L, 'The Environmental Complaint in EU Law' (2009) 6 *Journal for European Environmental & Planning Law* 13.

Kreuschitz V, 'Some Thoughts on the Jurisprudence of European Courts Concerning the Admissibility of Actions against State Aid Decisions' in *EC State Aid Law/Le droit des aides d'Etat dans la CE. Liber Amicorum Francisco Santaolalla Gadea* (The Hague: Kluwer Law International, 2008).

Kroes N, 'Keynote Speech' in Jacques Derenne and Massimo Merola (eds), *Economic Analysis of State Aid Rules. Contributions and Limits* (Berlin: GCLC-Lexxion, 2007).

Laprévote F-C, 'A Missed Opportunity?: State Aid Modernization and Effective Third Parties Rights in State Aid Proceedings' (2014) 12 *European State Aid Law Quarterly* 426.

Lenaerts K and Vanhamme J, 'Procedural Rights of Private Parties in the Community Administrative Process' (1997) 3 *Common Market Law Review* 531.

Lever J, 'The EC State Aid Regime: The Need for Reform' in Biondi A, Eeckhout P and Flynn J (eds), *The Law of State Aid in the European Union* (Oxford: Oxford University Press, 2004).

Lübbig T and Morgan T, 'State Aid, National Courts and the Separation of Powers: Should Judges be Bound to the European Commission's Unfinished State Aid Business?' (2014) 5 *Journal of European Competition Law & Practice* 256.

Majone G, 'The Credibility Crisis of Community Regulation' (2000) 38 *Journal of Common Market Studies* 273.

Mariñas N, 'Enforcement of State Aid Recovery Decisions' (2005) *Competition Policy Newsletter* 17.

Martin S and Evans AC, 'Socially Acceptable Distortion of Competition: Community Policy on State Aid' (1991) 16 *European Law Review* 79.

—— and Strasse C, 'La politique communautaire des aides d'État est-elle une politique de concurrence?' (2005) 3 *Concurrences* 52.

—— and Valbonesi P, 'The State Aid Game' (2006) 24 Working Paper, Department of Economics, University of Padova.

Maselis I and Gilliams HM, 'Rights of Complainants in Community Law' (1997) 22 *European Law Review* 103.

Mastroianni R, 'The Enforcement Procedure under Article 169 of the EC Treaty and the Powers of the European Commission: Quis Custodiet Custodes?' (1995) 1 *European Public Law* 535.

Mattera Ricigliano A, 'La procédure de manquement et la protection des droits des citoyens et des opérateurs lésés' (1995) 3 *Revue du Marché Unique Européen* 123.

Mederer W, 'Evolution of State Aid Control' in Mederer W et al (eds), *EU Competition Law*, IV (Leuven: Claeys & Casteels, 2008).
Mendelson NA, 'Guidance Documents and Regulatory Beneficiaries' (2006) 31 *Administrative and Regulatory Law News* 8.
—— 'Regulatory Beneficiaries and Informal Agency Policymaking' (2007) 92 *Cornell Law Review* 397.
Mendes J, *Participation in EU Rule-Making. A Rights-based Approach* (Oxford: Oxford University Press, 2011).
—— 'Participation and the Role of Law After Lisbon: A Legal View on Article 11 TEU' (2011) 48 *Common Market Law Review* 1849.
—— 'Discretion, Care and Public Interests in the EU Administration: Probing the Limits of Law' (2016) 53 *Common Market Law Review* 419.
Merola M and Armati L, 'Complainants' Rights in State Aid Matters. Lost in Modernisation?' in Govaere I and Hanf D (eds), *Scrutinizing Internal and External Dimensions of European Law. Liber Amicorum Paul Demaret* (Brussels: Peter Lang, 2013).
Monti G, *EC Competition Law* (Cambridge: Cambridge University Press, 2007).
Morgan BM, 'The Economization of Politics: Meta-Regulation as a Form of Nonjudicial Legality' (2003) 12 *Social and Legal Studies* 489.
Morgan de Rivery E, Thibault-Liger S, and Derenne J, 'Procedure' in Derenne J and Merola M (eds), *Economic Analysis of State Aid Rules. Contributions and Limits* (Berlin: GCLC-Lexxion, 2007).
Mortelmans K, 'The Compensatory Justification Criterion in the Practice of the Commission in Decisions on State Aids' (1984) 21 *Common Market Law Review* 405.
Müller-Ibold T, 'The AEA Proposal for a Regulation on State Aid Procedure' (1996) 22 *Europäische Zeitschrift für Wirtschaftsrecht* 677.
Muñoz de Juan M and Panero Rivas JM, 'The ECJ's Backlash on Access to Documents in the Commission's file on State Aid Cases by Private Parties. Comment on C-139/07 P' (2010) 9 *European State Aid Law Quarterly* 871.
Muñoz R, 'The Monitoring of the Application of Community Law: the Need to Improve the Current Tools and an Obligation to Innovate' (2006) 4 *Jean Monnet Working Paper Series*.
Nazzini R and Nikpay A, 'Private Actions in EC Competition Law' (2008) 4 *Competition Policy International* 107.
Nehl HP, *Principles of Administrative Procedure in EC Law* (Oxford: Hart Publishing, 1999).
—— 'The Imperfect Procedural Status of Beneficiaries of Aid in EC State Aid Proceedings. Note on Case C-276/03 P, Scott SA v. Commission' (2005) 4 *European State Aid Law Quarterly* 57.
—— 'Good Administration as Procedural Right and/or General Principle?' in Hofmann HCH and Türk AH (eds), *Legal Challenges in EU Administrative Law. Towards an Integrated Administration* (Cheltenham: Edward Elgar, 2009).
—— 'Judicial Protection of Complainants in EC State Aid Law: A Silent Revolution?' (2009) 8 *European State Aid Law Quarterly* 401.
—— '2013 Reform of EU State Aid Procedures: How to Exacerbate the Imbalance between Efficiency and Individual Protection' (2014) 13 *European State Aid Law Quarterly* 235.
—— 'Direct Actions and Judicial Review before the Union Courts' in Herwig CH Hofmann and Claire Micheau (eds), *State Aid Law of the European Union* (Oxford: Oxford University Press, 2016) 429.
Nicolaides P, 'Decentralised State Aid Control in an Enlarged European Union: Feasible, Necessary or Both?' (2003) 26 *World Competition* 263.

——, Kekelis M and Kleis M, *State Aid Policy in the European Community: Principles and Practice* (Alphen aan den Rijn: Kluwer Law International, 2008).
—— and Rusu IE, 'The Binary Nature of the Economics of State Aid' (2010) 37 *Legal Issues of Economic Integration* 25.
Niejahr M and Scharf T, 'Third Parties in State Aid Control: More Than Just a Source of Information?' in *EC State Aid Law/Le droit des aides d'Etat dans la CE. Liber Amicorum Francisco Santaolalla Gadea* (The Hague: Kluwer Law International, 2008).
Nolin M, 'Les droits des plaignants dans le secteur des aides d'État' in Association Europénne des Avocats (ed), *Un rôle pour la défense dans les procédures communautaires de concurrence: congrès organisé les 25 et 26 novembre 1996—A Role for the Defence in Community Competition Procedures: Congress Organized on 25 and 26 November 1996—Die Rolle der Verteidigung in europäischen Wettbewerbsverfahren* (Brussels: Bruylant, 1997).
Nordberg C, 'Judicial Remedies for Private Parties under the State Aid Procedure' (1997) 24 *Legal Issues of Economic Integration* 35.
Nowak C, 'Judicial Protection of Complainants in the Scope of EC State Aid Law: New Developments and Question Marks' (2006) 5 *European State Aid Law Quarterly* 621.
Ortiz Blanco L (ed), *EC Competition Procedure*, 2nd edn (Oxford: Oxford University Press, 2006).
Papandropoulos P, Massimo Merola, Jacques Derenne, Rainer Nitsche, Bernard van de Walle de Ghelcke, Denis Waelbroeck, Frédéric Louis, Pablo Ibáñez Colomo, Julien De Beys and Julie Bousin, 'Selectivity, Economic Advantage, Distortion of Competition and Effect on Trade' in Derenne J and Merola M (eds), *Economic Analysis of State Aid Rules. Contributions and Limits* (Berlin: GCLC-Lexxion, 2007).
Pastor-Merchante F, 'State Aids and Environmental Taxes: The Northern Ireland Exemption to the UK Aggregates Levy' (2011) 1 *European Journal of Risk Regulation* 125.
—— 'On the Rules of Standing to Challenge State Aid Decisions Adopted at the End of the Preliminary Phase' (2012) 11 *European State Aid Law Quarterly* 601.
—— 'The Follow-up of Hotel Cipriani/Comitato "Venezia Vuole Vivere"' (2014) 13 *European State Aid Law Quarterly* 132.
—— 'La aplicación privada de la normativa sobre ayudas de Estado' (2015) 55 *Revista española de derecho europeo* 13.
Peytz H and Mygind T, 'Direct Action in State Aid Cases—Tightropes and Legal Protection? A Review of Recent Jurisprudence on Direct and Individual Concern and Reviewable Acts. Part One' (2010) 9 *European State Aid Law Quarterly* 331.
—— and —— 'Direct Action in State Aid Cases—Tightropes and Legal Protection? A Review of Recent Jurisprudence on Direct and Individual Concern and Reviewable Acts. Part Two' (2010) 9 *European State Aid Law Quarterly* 617.
Piernas López JJ, *The Concept of State Aid under EU Law: From Internal Market to Competition and Beyond* (Oxford: Oxford University Press, 2015).
Pijnacker Hordijk EH, 'Judicial Protection of Private Interests under the EEC Competition Rules relating to State Aids' (1985) 12 *Legal Issues of European Integration* 67.
Poli S, 'The Legal Standing of Private Parties in the Area of State Aids After the Appeal in *Commission v. Kronoply/Kronotex*' (2012) 39 *Legal Issues of Economic Integration* 357.
Prete L and Smulders B, 'The Coming of Age of Infringement Proceedings' (2010) *Common Market Law Review* 9.
Price ZS, 'Enforcement Discretion and Executive Duty' (2014) 67 *Vanderbilt Law Review* 671.

Quigley C, *European State Aid Law and Policy*, 3rd edn (Oxford: Hart Publishing, 2015).
—— 'The European Commission's Programme for State Aid Modernization' (2013) 20 *Maastricht Journal of European and Comparative Law* 35.
Rasmussen H, 'Why is Article 173 Interpreted Against Private Plaintiffs?' (1980) 5 *European Law Review* 112.
Rawlings R, 'Engaged Elites: Citizen Action and Institutional Attitudes in Commission Enforcement' (2000) 6 *European Law Journal* 4.
Rawlinson F, 'The Role of Policy Frameworks, Codes, and Guidelines in the Control of State Aid' in Harden I (ed), *State Aid: Community Law and Policy* (Cologne: Bundesanzeiger Verlagsgesellschaft, 1993).
Reich N, '"System der subjectiven öffentlichen Rechte" in the Union: a European Constitution for Citizens of Bits and Pieces', *Collected courses of the Academy of European Law*, VI (The Hague: Kluwer Law International/Martinus Nijhoff Publishers/Academy of European Law, EUI, 1995).
Renders D (ed), *Les subventions* (Brussels: Larcier, 2011).
Ross M, 'Challenging State Aids: the Effect of Recent Developments' (1986) 23 *Common Market Law Review* 867.
—— 'Decentralization, Effectiveness and Modernization: Contradictions in Terms?' in Biondi A, Eeckhout P and Flynn J (eds), *The Law of State Aid in the European Union* (Oxford: Oxford University Press, 2004).
Rubini L, *The Definition of State Aid: WTO and EC Law in Comparative Perspective* (Oxford: Oxford University Press, 2010).
Sánchez-Graells A, 'Digging Itself Out of the Hole? A Critical Assessment of the European Commission's Attempt to Revitalize State Aid Enforcement After the Crisis' (2016) 2 *Journal of Antitrust Enforcement* 157.
Schauer F and Zeckhauser R, 'The Trouble with Cases' in Kessler DP (ed), *Regulation versus Litigation. Perspectives from Economics and Law* (Chicago, IL: University of Chicago Press, 2011).
Schmidt-Assmann E, *La teoría general del Derecho administrativo como sistema. Objeto y fundamentos de la construcción sistémica* (Mariano Bacigalupo et al tr, Madrid: Marcial Pons, 2003).
Schockweiler F, 'La motivation des décisions individuelles en droit communautaire et en droit national' (1989) 25 *Cahiers de Droit Européen* 3.
Schohe G, 'Le statut du plaignant' in Dony M and Smits C (eds), *Aides d'État* (Brussels: Éditions de l'Université de Bruxelles, 2005).
Schwarze J, *European Administrative Law*, rev 1st edn (Luxembourg: Office for Official Publications of the European Communities/Sweet & Maxwell, 2006).
Schweda M, 'Compatibility of State Aid Pursuant to Article 87(3) EC' in Heidenhain M (ed), *European State Aid Law* (Munich: Verlag CH Beck, 2010).
Segura Catalán MJ and Clayton M, 'State Aid Modernisation: Another Reform?' (2013) 14 *ERA Forum* 21.
Shapiro M, 'The Giving Reasons Requirement' (1992) *University of Chicago Legal Forum* 179.
—— 'Two Transformations in Administrative Law: American and European?' in Ladeur KH (ed), *The Europeanisation of Administrative Law: Transforming National Decision-Making Procedures* (Aldershot: Ashgate, 2002).

Simonsson I, 'On the Emerging Obligation for Member State Authorities to Supervise and Enforce EC State Aid Law, and the Resulting Need to Consider Decentralisation' in Wahl N and Cramér P (eds), *Swedish Studies in European Law* (Oxford: Hart Publishing, 2006).

Sinnaeve A, 'Block Exemptions for State Aid: More Scope for State Aid Control by Member States and Competitors' (2001) 38 *Common Market Law Review* 1479.

—— 'Editorial: What to Expect from National Courts in the Fight against Unlawful State Aid?' (2005) 4 *European State Aid Law Quarterly* 1.

—— 'State Aid Procedures: Developments since the Entry into Force of the Procedural Regulation' (2007) 44 *Common Market Law Review* 965.

—— 'Procedures before the Commission, Council Regulation 659/1999' in Heidenhain M (ed), *European State Aid Law* (Munich: Verlag CH Beck, 2010).

—— 'Rights of Interested Parties' in Heidenhain M (ed), *European State Aid Law* (Munich: Verlag CH Beck, 2010).

Sinnaeve A and Slot PJ, 'The New Regulation on State Aid Procedures' (1999) 36 *Common Market Law Review* 1153.

Slot PJ, 'Procedural Aspects of State Aids: The Guardian of Competition Versus the Subsidy Villains?' (1990) 27 *Common Market Law Review* 741.

—— 'Administrative Procedure' in Hancher L, Ottervanger T and Slot PJ (eds), *EU State Aids* (London: Sweet & Maxwell, 2012).

Smith MK, *Centralised Enforcement, Legitimacy and Good Governance* in the EU (London: Routledge, 2010).

Smith MP, 'Integration in Small Steps: The European Commission and Member State Aid to Industry' (1996) 19 *West European Politics* 563.

—— 'Autonomy by the Rules: The European Commission and the Development of State Aid Policy' (1998) 36 *Journal of Common Market Studies* 55.

—— 'How Adaptable is the European Commission? The Case of State Aid Regulation' (2001) 21 *Journal of Public Policy* 219.

Snyder F, 'The Effectiveness of European Community Law: Institutions, Processes, Tools and Techniques' (1993) 56 *The Modern Law Review* 19.

Soltész U, 'Scope of Judicial Review' in Heidenhain M (ed), *European State Aid Law* (Munich: Verlag CH Beck, 2010).

Spector D, 'L'économie politique des aides d'État et le choix du critère d'appréciation' (2006) 2 *Concurrences* 34.

Stein E and Vining GJ, 'Citizen Access to Judicial Review of Administrative Action in a Transnational and Federal Context' (1976) 70 *The American Journal of International Law* 219.

Struys ML, 'Questions choisies de procédure en matière d'aides d'État' (1993) 29 *Revue Trimestrielle de Droit Européen* 17.

Sykes AO, 'The Questionable Case for Subsidies Regulation: A Comparative Perspective' (2010) 2 *Journal of Legal Analysis* 473.

Szyszczak EM, *The Regulation of the State in Competitive Markets in the EU* (Oxford: Hart Publishing, 2007).

Tomkins A, 'Of Institutions and Individuals: The Enforcement of EC Law' in Craig PP and Rawlings R (eds), *Law and Administration in Europe—Essays in Honour of Carol Harlow* (Oxford: Oxford University Press, 2003).

Trebilcock MJ and Howse R, *The Regulation of International Trade*, 3rd edn (London: Routledge, 2005).

Tridimas T, *The General Principles of EU Law*, 2nd edn (Oxford: Oxford University Press, 2006).

—— and Poli S, 'Locus Standi of Individuals under Article 230(4): The Return of Euridice?' in *Continuity and Change in EU Law: Essays in Honour of Sir Francis Jacobs* (Oxford: Oxford University Press, 2008).
Usher JA, 'Direct and Individual Concern: An Effective Remedy or a Conventional Solution?' (2003) 28 *European Law Review* 575.
Van Gerven W, 'Of Rights, Remedies and Procedures' (2000) 37 *Common Market Law Review* 501.
Venit JS, 'Brave New World: The Modernization and Decentralization of Enforcement under Articles 81 and 82 of the EC Treaty' (2003) 40 *Common Market Law Review* 545.
Von Bogdandy A and Bast J, 'The Federal Order of Competences' in Von Bogdandy A and Bast J (eds), *Principles of European Constitutional Law*, 2nd edn (Oxford: Hart Publishing/ Verlag CH Beck, 2009).
Waelbroeck D, 'Private Enforcement: Current Situation and Methods of Improvement' in Lianos I and Kokkoris I (eds), *The Reform of EC Competition Law: New Challenges* (New York: Wolters Kluwer, 2010).
Waelbroeck M, 'State Aids in the Fight among Competitors' in Raffaelli EA (ed), *IV Conference Antitrust between EC Law and National Law* (Brussels: Bruylant/Giuffré Editore, 2000).
Wakefield J, *The Right to Good Administration* (Alphen aan den Rijn: Kluwer Law International, 2007).
Ward A, *Judicial Review and the Rights of Private Parties in EC Law* (Oxford: Oxford University Press, 2000).
—— 'Locus Standi under Article 230(4) of the EC Treaty: Crafting a Coherent Test for a "Wobbly Polity"' (2003) 22 *Yearbook of European Law* 45.
Weiler J, 'The Transformation of Europe' (1991) 100 *Yale Law Journal* 2403.
Weinberg J, 'The Right to be Taken Seriously' (2012) 67 *University of Miami Law Review* 149.
Wils WPJ, 'Should Private Antitrust Enforcement Be Encouraged in Europe?' (2003) 26 *World Competition* 473.
—— 'Discretion and Prioritisation in Public Antitrust Enforcement in Particular EU Antitrust Enforcement' (2011) 34 *World Competition* 353.
Winter JA, 'Supervision of State Aid: Article 93 in the Court of Justice' (1993) 30 *Common Market Law Review* 311.
—— 'The Rights of Complainants in State Aid Cases: Judicial Review of Commission Decisions adopted under Article 88 (ex 93)' (1999) 36 *Common Market Law Review* 521.
Yeung K, *Securing Compliance* (Oxford: Hart Publishing, 2004).
Zemplinerova A, 'The Community State Aid Action Plan and the Challenge of Developing an Optimal Enforcement System' in Lianos I and Kokkoris I (eds), *The Reform of EC Competition Law: New Challenges* (New York: Wolters Kluwer, 2010).
Zinsmeister U, 'The Role of Third Parties in State Aid Cases' in Association Europénne des Avocats (ed), *Un rôle pour la défense dans les procédures communautaires de concurrence: congrès organisé les 25 et 26 novembre 1996—A Role for the Defence in Community Competition Procedures: Congress Organized on 25 and 26 November 1996—Die Rolle der Verteidigung in europäischen Wettbewerbsverfahren* (Brussels: Bruylant, 1997).

INDEX

www.ingramcontent.com/pod-product-compliance
Ingram Content Group UK Ltd.
Pitfield, Milton Keynes, MK11 3LW, UK
UKHW020812290926
15470UKWH00003B/1115

9 781509 906598